The Me I Know:
A Study of Adult Identity

Susan Krauss Whitbourne

The Me I Know:
A Study of Adult Identity

WITHDRAWN

Springer-Verlag
New York Berlin Heidelberg Tokyo

SUSAN KRAUSS WHITBOURNE
Department of Psychology
University of Massachusetts at Amherst
Amherst, MA 01003, U.S.A.

With 1 Figure

Library of Congress Cataloging in Publication Data
Whitbourne, Susan Krauss
  The me I know: A study of adult identity.
  Bibliography: p.
  Includes index.
  1. Identity (Psychology)   2. Adulthood—Psychological
aspects.   I. Title.
BF697.W44   1986   155.6   85-27726

Printed in the United States of America.

9 8 7 6 5 4 3 2 1

ISBN 0-387-96261-1 Springer-Verlag New York Berlin Heidelberg Tokyo
ISBN 3-540-96261-1 Springer-Verlag Berlin Heidelberg New York Tokyo

To my children

Preface

For the last 5 years I have been living with 94 adults. These 94 adults made up the sample of people in a study on adult development that Dale Dannefer and I began in 1980. This book represents my efforts to condense the almost 200 hours of tape-recorded material from the 94 adults into a form that captures at least some of the diversity and also some of the commonalities in their answers to the question "Who am I?" My version of their answers is based on their reflections about themselves as family members, workers, and people with a goal in life. In arriving at the conclusion that adults attempt to see themselves as loved, competent, and good human beings, I believe that I have done justice to these people and their answers to my interview questions.

Arriving at the point of being able to write about these 94 people's identities has not been an easy process. Countless attempts at numerically based rating systems were tried and discarded progressively, until finally I decided to read all the transcripts in sequence, person by person rather than question by question. What I found when I approached them as total individuals was surprising to me. I found a vibrant theme of certainty and self-assuredness in their identities that flew in the face of my previous ideas about developmental change in adulthood.

When Dale Dannefer and I began this study, it was with the conviction that adults do not put on and cast off new personalities at regular, 5- or 10-year timed intervals in adulthood. We believed that developmental change was a more continuous process that did not have clear beginning and end points of vacillations between turmoil and stability. In approaching the identity interview analyses, my area of responsibility in the study, I believed that I would find continuous shifts in identity according to variations in people's experiences. Instead, I have found an amazing constancy to adult identity, both in content across people and in the process through which individuals arrive at and maintain a body of self-knowledge during adulthood. To be an adult means that one has an identity, a sense of purpose, a sense of what is important and what is not. Even if one is not sure of all the answers, to be an adult means that one behaves as if one did. To be sure, change is an ever-present possibility in the adult's means of implementing this identity and even in specific facets of the content of identity. However, the basic tendency in adulthood is toward verifying the belief that one's purpose in life is good.

This conclusion, as pointed out in the opening paragraphs of Chapter 1, probably applies only to the kind of "normal" adults who were in the study's sample. For a group of adults like those in the sample, though, this conclusion about the nature of adult identity helps to explain a variety of kinds of answers to the broad questions used in the interview. Throughout this book, the reader will find examples of transcript excerpts that illustrate in great detail the variety of mechanisms the respondents used in order to preserve their positive image of their identities. There are also examples of adults struggling with the process of trying to forge a new, positive identity out of an experience or revelation that has caused them to plummet downward in their self-estimates of worthiness. Both kinds of examples are consistent with the interpretation that adults strive to have a basic sense of purpose and goodness about themselves. They are also consistent with the interpretation that the route to this goal is not a direct one. On the contrary, it often involves confronting painful truths about the nature of one's identity. Without such confrontations, it is probably impossible for growth of identity to occur in adulthood.

I am extremely grateful for the insightful interviewing conducted by my research assistants at the University of Rochester, Susan Roxin and Gregory Smith. Without their superb rapport-building and probing skills, I would not have had the rich interview material I was so fortunate to have for my analysis. The research skills and theoretical insights of Dale Dannefer, the coinvestigator of the original study, provided me not only with the chance to collect the interviews, but with ideas and encouragement that I will always value. There are also many individuals at the University of Rochester who helped me in writing transcripts and conducting preliminary analyses, including Pat Palmer, Lisa Elliot, Tim Chambers, and the EDH 475, Adult Development, class at the Graduate School of Education and Human Development, Spring 1982. The Spencer Foundation and the University of Rochester have my deepest thanks too for providing Dale and me with the financial support to conduct our study.

The actual writing of this book was conducted with the helpful support of my colleagues and family during the summer of 1985. I am very grateful to the editorial staff at Springer-Verlag for having confidence that I could write the book, and then for having given me so many suggestions about how to do it. My psychology department colleagues at University of Massachusetts at Amherst have also been of great support to me, particularly Seymour Epstein. Finally, it is to my family that I am indebted for their support in my writing of this book. My husband, Richard D. O'Brien, added to his encouragement of my work on this manuscript his insights about many of the transcript excerpts and greatly enhanced my commentaries on them. My children, Stacey Whitbourne and Jennifer O'Brien, deserve credit for putting up so graciously while I sat buried every day under piles of transcripts.

It goes without saying that I am tremendously indebted to the 94 adults whom I have come to know so well. They gave far beyond what they received in consenting to partake in what must have been an extremely demanding task. I have tried as best I can to screen their individual identities in presenting the transcript excerpts in this book, and hope that my efforts have succeeded in protecting the confidentiality I promised them. I hope that their efforts will have proven to be worthwhile.

SUSAN KRAUSS WHITBOURNE

Contents

Part I Adult Identity Processes 1

  1 Who Am I? 3

     The Myth of the Mid-Life Crisis 7
     A Study of Adult Identity 13

  2 A Theory of Adult Identity Processes 17

     Forms of Identity Assimilation and Accommodation 19
     Theoretical Implications 36

Part II Family Identity 37

  3 Love Is Not Enough 39

     The Importance of Closeness, Communication, and Companionship ... 39
     Family Tasks and Responsibility 48
     The Dual Nature of Family Identity 60

  4 Men and Women in the Family 61

     Family Networks 61
     Centrality of the Family Identity 63
     Personal Fulfillment 69

  5 Parents and Children 81

     The Family Life Cycle and Identity Accommodation 86
     Unpredictable Sources of Identity Accommodation in the Family 95

Part III Work Identity 99

     Intrinsic and Extrinsic Work Involvement 99

  6 The Competent Worker 101

     The Importance of Interesting Work 101
     Autonomy 106

Intellectual Nature of the Work 110
Having the Chance to See Results............................. 114
The People-Work Character of a Job........................... 122
The Intrinsic Meaning of Work: Reflections and Qualifications 126

7 A Spoonful of Sugar.. 129

The Monetary Rewards of Work................................ 130
The Conditions of Work: Creature Comforts and Convenience 138
The People Factor 151

8 "Just a Housewife" 161

The Work of the Homemaker 162
The Importance of the Homemaker's Work 167
Finding Alternate Sources of Competence 173
Reflections on the Homemaker's Identity 179

Part IV Integrative Themes 183

9 Family and Work Identities: Conflict or Compatibility?......... 185

Sources of Conflict Between Family and Work Identities 186
Compatibility Between Family and Work Identities 200
The Conflict and Compatibility Models: Implications for Identity 211

10 Purpose in Life 213

Honesty—A Word Often Heard................................. 214
Values in Interpersonal Relationships 226
Values: Summing Up 239

Appendix A Adult Identity Process Interview 241

Appendix B Methodology of the Adult Identity Process Study 247

Appendix C Categories of Interview Statements 255

References 259

Index 263

Part I
Adult Identity Processes

1
Who Am I?

Who am I? Philosophers, psychologists, and sociologists debate endlessly without arriving at an ideal theoretical answer to this question. In fictional and nonfictional accounts of people's lives, adults are depicted as being in turmoil because they do not know the answer to this question. The conclusion of the study reported in this book is quite the opposite. Most normal adults know the answer to this question in the practical context of their everyday lives. Normal adults know that they are loving with their family and competent in their work, and that they follow a code of ethics that gives their life its purpose. They may not be correct about how well they fit these criteria, but they believe that, for the most part, they do. It is this answer that gives adults their sense of identity.

Having as an answer to the question "Who am I?" that "I am loving, competent, and good" may be such a basic feature of psychological adaptation that it makes the difference between whether an adult lives a life that is "normal" or "abnormal." According to one theory of the abnormal personality, it is when adults do not have any answer to this question that they suffer from psychoses such as schizophrenia (Laing, 1960). Without the ability to place one's sense of existence squarely in the middle of one's everyday surroundings and activities, these routine places and events quickly become bizarre and unfamiliar. Moreover, if adults have as their answer "I am unloving, incompetent, and bad," they can fall victim to neurotic ruminations about their entitlement to an existence in their families, workplaces, and communities.

The scope of this book, though, is restricted to the average adult who is living a reasonably average life in relatively average circumstances. Although what is "average" shows a considerable degree of variation, the degree of variation within this range was limited here to exclude severe adjustment problems. This book is a report on an investigation with a sample of 94 of these "average" adults, 24 to 61 years old, who took part in an interview study in which they shared their perspectives on "adult life"—their feelings about their families, work, values, and their own aging. These areas were chosen as the topics to cover in the interviews because of the general importance to adults of issues related to family, work, values, and aging (e.g., Rosenberg, 1980; Smelser & Erikson, 1980).

In particular, the areas of family and work formed the central focus of the analyses in this book. It was found in the course of the study that it is the self-appraisals in these areas that permeate all other areas of identities. Together, the areas of family and work unite into an integrated sense of identity as an individual with a purpose in life; a purpose that is expressed in the everyday activities carried out at home and in the workplace.

The title of this book is based on a rather circuitous and often abstract theoretical debate in the literature of the philosophy and psychology of the self, described in its most well-known form by James (1890) and Mead (1934). It is the difference between the "I" and the "me" that forms the basis for this title and for the core of the theory that holds that adults really do know who they are. The difference between the "I" and the "me" is based on the fact that the self can be the "subject" as well as the "object" of an action; that is, one can refer to oneself in a sentence as both "I" and "me." In the case of "I" it is the one who is doing, and in the case of "me" it is the one to whom the verb of the sentence, the action, is applied. Thus, by the term "subject" ("I") is meant the self as the active agent, the "doer," the originator of actions and thoughts, the perceiver of experiences. Conversely, the self is "object" ("me") when it is the "done to," the one that is thought about, acted upon, or perceived. While the same grammatical distinction can be made in the case of the second and third person pronouns, the debate applies only to the first person singular (and probably plural as well).

The crux of the debate centers on the fact that individuals cannot actually observe themselves as agents of their own actions. Unlike other agents of actions, who can be observed as subject and object, the self can only be observed as the object. The self cannot see itself performing the actions that have known consequences. I can see the words I type in front of me, the "objects" of my actions, but I cannot see myself performing the action of typing. I can see whether the flowers I plant in the garden grow or die, but I cannot see myself on my hands and knees putting them in the soil. I can see the way my family reacts to my face when I know I am smiling at them, but how can I know how I look to them? How, then, can I know myself as an agent of my own actions?

The central thesis of this book is that the adult, the "I," answers the question "Who am I?" in an indirect fashion and takes for granted the fact that he or she can never see the "I" directly in action. Instead, the adult sees the results of these actions in the roles that the "me" carries out in the major life areas. I see that other people read what I write, and, if they react favorably, then I am satisfied that I am a competent author. I see that the flowers I planted last June are spreading to fill their beds and am satisfied that I am a good gardener. I see that my family knows I care about them by the interest I show in them and am satisfied that I am loving. I know myself through the results of my actions in the endeavors that serve my purpose in life. I need no other information in order to formulate an identity. Whether I saw myself with my own eyes or not, it would not matter. I would be a good writer or a good mother regardless of what I could see of my own actions. The main determinant of my identity is the effect of what I do and whether I am loving, competent, and good at doing what I set out to do.

In keeping with the emphasis on the individual's self-evaluation in defining his or her identity, the main focus of the interview analysis was phenomenological.

The answers were examined from what was thought to be the individual respondent's own perspective. The answers to the interview were analyzed by the usual psychological procedures of content analysis and ratings. However, to provide an understanding of the identity of the persons who generated these answers it was necessary to engage in the largely subjective process of becoming totally immersed in the entire interview as a unit. Taking this perspective made it possible to form a hypothesis about what sort of identity the respondent had to have in order to produce the response. Through this kind of analysis, it was possible to observe both the content of the adult's identity and the processes through which that content developed.

This method and the kind of processes it was used to analyze are illustrated here with examples taken from the interviews of three respondents. These respondents diverged greatly in their life circumstances, but, more importantly, they diverged in their perceptions regarding themselves and their experiences. The first respondent's excerpt comes from her identity interview in the area of values[1]:

Q: Could you describe for me your major value?
R: Well, I don't know. I think you have to be happy and content with what you've got and make the most of every day. Whatever God has given you.
Q: How strongly do you feel about this?
R: Very strongly. It's just, I think if you don't feel strongly about those things it's easy to be swayed by not keeping up with the standards and goals you accept for yourself.
Q: How do your values affect the way you feel about yourself?
R: Well, I think if you're very satisfied with yourself and your accomplishments then that means you're living up to your values and standards. So if you have standards and values and don't live up to it, then it's frustrating and upsetting. You don't feel good about yourself. As I said before, you always feel you could do better. But at the same time, you do your best. That's the most you can do . . . I wouldn't want to become unhappy or frustrated because that would be too . . . hard to cope with.

What kind of identity would a person have to have in order to produce these statements? Clearly, it must be an identity as someone who is almost completely fulfilling her personal "standards and values." Her identity as a "good" person is something she reinforces by making sure she does not become "unhappy or frustrated." She maintains this identity by doing her "best" most of the time, and by not thinking too much about the times when she does not. In contrast, an individual who lacks this same conviction about his sense of purpose presents a more fragmented self-description:

R: . . . I have a very weak ego structure, to start out with. A very messed up ego structure. And it's not good, but the only effect it has on me, on me, is slight confusion, is a slight confusion because I'll tend to approach something and then act leery about it. And then look at it, and tend to take parts or reject the whole thing. It doesn't coalesce . . . my life style, as it has been for quite a while, simply cannot continue. I woke up to this and, uh, I've tried to change myself around . . . change is not easy, just not easy.

---

[1]The "Q" refers to "question" and the "R" to response in interview transcripts.

This respondent's disorganization with regard to a purpose in life represents a lack of a consistent identity, one that is the mirror image of the cohesion and conviction of the prior respondent's sense of purpose and goodness. Such an extreme degree of confusion and self-doubt was rarely observed in this sample of relatively well-adjusted individuals. However, there were many other cases of respondents undergoing a more circumscribed examination of their identities in one or more areas of life. This examination was directed at trying to formulate an altered identity, but one that would allow the individual to continue to maintain a basic sense of goodness and competence. In the case of a recently separated woman, for instance, it was her identity as a wife that she was presently questioning in making a transition to an identity as someone who is "independent":

Q: When did you (begin to make this change)?
R: I guess in July the separation came. There have been problems in the past, and I'd say over the last three or four years I've only had to become independent. I could not depend on my husband for financial support and along with that because you're out working and establishing different contacts you're becoming independent in a lot of other ways. And, of course, this may have contributed to the separation too, a different relationship. Sometimes it's sort of scary and frightening because I didn't, you know, plan this to happen. I wanted the more traditional role as a housewife and mother. I didn't want it. And in some ways it hasn't been too lonely because my family is here. But I worry about hanging too much on them for companionship. You know you've got to build a life of your own outside of your family.

Having to arrive at a new identity with regard to her family has not been an easy process for this woman. However, it had its benefits, as can be seen in her answer to a later question:

Q: How do you feel about your situation?
R: It feels good. I mean it feels good to be without my husband's presence here...the peace I enjoy, just not having to deal with somebody's else's frustration, plus my own. I don't know how long it will last! (laughs)

Despite the fact that she felt better about her new independence, there were lingering doubts about her previous behavior as a wife:

R: ...with my marriage...you realize that it takes two people. And you have to accept a certain amount of blame for reasons why it didn't work out.... There was a separation three or four years ago, then we went back together and tried to make it. The only thing I realize now is that I don't think it was a wholehearted effort on my part...

Although her emerging identity as an independent woman is one that "feels good," she must reconcile these new feelings of competence and self-sufficiency with awareness that she failed in her efforts to be a loving wife. When she achieves this reconciliation of the old and new identities, she will be able to establish once again a feeling of contentment with herself. This feeling of contentment will be based in part on being able to see her husband happy and in part on her ability to find other rewarding interests:

Q: Do you foresee any more changes and, if so, in what direction?

R: I guess as far as my husband goes, I would like him to find some contentment and happiness, find what he wants out of life . . . . I guess the same things for . . . myself. What you call happiness, or contentment, or peace.

By seeing her husband happy, the respondent will have vindicated her sense of having done the right thing even though she hurt her husband by leaving him. At the same time, she is seeking ways outside the marital relationship to verify her sense of competence: "Just trying to be a good person, lead a good life, and a valuable life."

The "data" analyzed in this book are the interview transcripts, such as those examined here, which illustrate and elucidate the complicated processes that account for the variations in the way that adults maintain their identities as loving, competent, and good people. These processes include some that facilitate a stable identity and others that promote an evaluation of one's identity within the context of one's experiences. Both of these processes are based on different routes to the same goal of fostering an adult identity that is rooted in the individual's basic sense of worth as a human being. The theory of adult identity processes will be presented briefly in the next chapter and elaborated throughout the book on the basis of information gained from the transcript analyses.

The Myth of the Mid-Life Crisis

The Question of Age-Linked Stages in Adulthood

It is currently popular to characterize the adult personality as being in an ever-changing process of building and rebuilding in a series of renovations that follow a preset schedule. The culminating point of these stages is regarded as the period of transition between early and middle adulthood (e.g., Levinson, Darrow, Klein, Levinson, & McKee, 1978). Alternatively, some researchers believe that the adult personality does not really change at all throughout the years from late adolescence to old age (Costa & McCrae, 1980). The position of this book is that neither extreme accurately characterizes the process of adult development. Adult identity does not undergo regular, predictable shifts in its structure and content according to a timetable set by the individual's chronological age, nor does it remain invariant over the adult years. Instead, it is assumed here that the individual's identity can change in adulthood when there is the right combination of circumstances and readiness or need on the part of the individual. If neither of these conditions are met, the adult's identity may never change. If change is necessary for the individual's sense of well-being *and* the opportunity for change is present, then adult identity may take on a new form at that point. Trying to predict when these conditions will both be fulfilled is regarded as an impossible task and one that does not add to an understanding of the underlying mechanisms of change and stability in adulthood.

In the study described in this book, regularities according to age did not appear in the respondents' reactions to themselves or their life circumstances. Instead, the respondents were concerned with issues related to their identities that transcended particular age demarcation points. One of these issues was the meaning of "age" as a chronological index of the aging process:

Q: How do you feel about your age?

R: Well, it was very traumatic (laughing) as I was hitting 50, it was very traumatic. But now I don't think about it anymore. It doesn't bother me very much.

Q: How long ago did you turn 50?

R: (7 months ago).

Q: So, at that time, it seemed pretty—

R: It bothered me, I didn't like turning the old wheel.

. . .

Q: How does your age affect the way you feel about yourself as a person?

R: I guess it doesn't affect me. Anyway, I never thought of age affecting me.

Q: This sounds like a little bit of contradiction, since before you said that, when you turned 50, that sounded like that age bothered you, but now you adjusted and worked to it.

R: Right, and it doesn't bother me that much. Not sure that it won't bother me again when I hit 60.

Q: So, it's more the sound of the number than it is the age?

R: It's changing into a new series of numbers. I guess another 10 years.

Q: What is it about the numbers that—

R: When you hit 50, it's like all of a sudden you're ten 10 years older. You're in your 50s instead of being in your 40s, which even at 49 you could still say you're in your 40s and it sounds better. Nobody likes getting old.

Q: What is it about getting old that nobody likes?

R: You see your life's end coming closer. I think that's basically it, which I realize doesn't mean a thing because you can still get hit crossing the street when you're 10 and be killed. But you lived half a century, been around for quite a while. It's a funny thing that kind of hits me at this particular time.

It is the "turning the old wheel," like the odometer when the number 9 mile is passed, that seems to have created difficulty for this respondent around the time of her 50th birthday. However, the respondent's concerns in the latter part of this excerpt reveal preoccupation with some very basic issues related to aging. Her concerns were echoed by others in the sample who regarded themselves as being near chronological turning points. Approximately one-half of the sample described as important the fact that they were near, had recently passed, or were glad that they were not at a particular age marker point. Apparently the idea of beginning a "new set of numbers" is one that makes a large impression because it sensitizes the individual to the continuous progression of time as it brings nearer the end of life.

In addition to its meaning as an index of time's passage, age was also important because of its relationship to events in the realms of work and family. Two-thirds of the sample (32 women and 31 men) described features of their work or family life that reflected the influence of age. Those associated with family life were often described in a positive way. Younger persons reported seeing themselves as having become more mature or responsible as a function of reaching the age of starting a family. The older members of the sample, particularly women, were glad to have passed the age of heavy responsibility for taking care of children. Both women and men expressed negative views about having experienced age discrimination in their present jobs or as a discouraging factor hampering their search for different work. Not all of these individuals were "old" in a traditional sense, and some were even quite young (close to 30). It is possible that some of these statements about age discrimination reflected a defensive strategy to protect their sense of competence as workers, particularly when they came from younger persons who would not have been subject to true age discrimination. The other large group of statements concerning the effects of age on work related to retirement, and almost all of these were positive. Either individuals were looking forward to having more leisure time, or they were planning second careers for themselves after retirement.

The general correlation of aging with physical and mental well-being was also of importance to the respondents. Health was seen as a more important influence on an individual than age for a large cluster of respondents (11 women and 11 men). A general "slowing down" or loss of mental and physical energy associated with aging was reported by less than one-third of the sample (10 women and 17 men). All but one of the women in this group were over 40 years of age, but they represented less than one-half of the over-40 women in the sample. The men who reported a general slowing as characteristic of aging ranged from 26 to 54 years. The younger men who made this observation about themselves were some of the more active sports enthusiasts in the sample, a factor that probably made them more sensitive to slight losses of speed or agility. There was another group of respondents, most of them women (7 women and 3 men), who were concerned about having gained excessive weight: The "middle-aged spread."

In addition to the lack of age specificity in any given concern related to age, there was even more powerful evidence contradictory to the mid-life crisis position regarding adult development. No agreement could be found among the sample about what constituted a "good" or a "bad" age relative to the respondent's own age. There was a 50-50 split among the 14 respondents who commented about whether or not they would prefer to be younger than their present ages. Statements about particular ages were grouped for analysis into the categories into which they naturally clustered: 20–23, 25, 30, 35, 40, 50, 55–60, and 70 and over. A very simple classification of these statements as "positive" or "negative" about the given age or age period revealed virtually equal numbers on either side for each age from 25 and over. The only variation in this pattern was that fewer men than women referred to the age of 50 as being significant (8 women and 2 men). There were virtually equal numbers of statements from men and women at ages 30 (8 women and 7 men), 40 (8 women and 8 men), and also 35 (3 women and 3 men).

More important than the number of statements per age marker point was the fact that there were no consistent differences in content among statements associated with the 30-, 40-, or 50-year markers. What did emerge were some revealing statements about the respondents' perceptions of what they thought *should* be important for these marker ages. The following excerpt is from a respondent who firmly believes in the validity of male mid-life crisis:

R: ... You see, you have caught me in a very strange time. Like I'm, uh, let's see, 1981, 11 minus 3 is 7 [sic]. I'll be 37 next month, right? And you know, 40-year-old men flip out, you know, they just go a little bonkers, uh, in this particular case, I'm a slightly early bloomer . . .

This statement came in the midst of the Values Identity interview, in which the respondent described himself as "searching" for a value system. By placing himself within range of 40 years (although he was closer to 35 years old), the respondent could attribute his present state of confusion to a situation over which he had no control rather than to his own poorly defined identity in this area. It was his identity regarding his values, rather than anything intrinsic about his age, that gave special meaning to the 40-year marker point.

To reinforce this point about the relative nature of age-related "crises," consider the following excerpt from a 30-year-old man whose present concerns fit almost every criterion of the full-fledged age-40 crisis as it is typically described:

Q: How do you feel about your age?
R: Traumatic. Turning 30 really made me stop and say "Gee, what have I done with myself up to this point. And what did I think I would be doing, and what should I be doing?" That's sort of an ongoing discussion with myself, if you want to call it that. . . . Up until the last birthday, age was just an anniversary date. And all of a sudden, I don't know what it was, but suddenly, you know, "My God, I'm turning 30!". . . all of a sudden I went into a great deal of introspection. . . . It was very upsetting. It was not your basic Happy Birthday, is what it was.

Included in what he regarded as "traumatic" about turning 30 were the death of a parent, having become one of the "old veterans" instead of a "newcomer" at work, looking at young women as being "too young for me," "rethinking my perception of the aging process," having "reached a plateau in terms of assuming privileges and getting more responsibility," being "less radical" in his opinions, and having become more "aware of expectations of others of me."

It is clear that turning 40 was not the cause of this respondent's wrongly timed "mid-life crisis." The excerpt revealed that the respondent was partly reacting to the death of a parent. Analysis of his family identity transcript also revealed that the respondent was undergoing change in a long-standing pattern of relationships with his father and brother. In the area of work, the respondent was also heavily involved in an identity change process as he evaluated his accomplishments and considered the possibility of a new career direction. The crisis in the area of age, then, was a reflection of changes going on in the respondent's primary areas of identity.

The age of 30 was regarded far more favorably by another respondent, satisfied with her identity as a mother, and at the same time looking forward to the prospect of returning to work on a part-time basis.

Q: Do you think there's possibly a time where you would feel differently because of a certain age?

R: I suppose.

Q: Can you elaborate on that?

R: There's different stages. I'm 31 now, and I used to think "Boy, when I get to be 30." Now I think, "I'm 30, I've had my children, gotten through so far, I do wonder what I'll do at 35 or 40." I know I'll work part-time, as the children get older. I'll work into full-time, I look to those years as doing more of what I want to do, pushing them off to do more on their own.

Q: Why do you think that you will have these kinds of questions, at a later age? Why do you think you will be doing more things for yourself?

R: I think everybody does. I think as everyone gets older, they look at their lives, and wonder why they did this and wonder what they're going to do.

. . .

Q: Things are starting to change now for you because of your age?

R: Yes.

Because her identity in the areas of work and family was so positive, the popular idea of an age-30 "crisis" was totally foreign to this respondent:

R: I find that some of the articles in the magazines are a lot of baloney. I think they can cause a lot of problems. If you read a story about a woman who turns 30 and leaves her husband, they have all these goofy articles in women's magazines, you think "Do I have that problem?" Half the time you don't. It's a waste of time.

Another woman, at the age of 29, was facing the opposite situation in her life. She was in the process of abandoning her successful and rewarding career in order to become a full-time mother. Age 30 was perceived as a major turning point having almost crisis proportions because it meant giving up her secure identity as a competent worker for an uncertain future identity as a mother:

Q: How important is it to you that you're 29?

R: It was important when we made the decision to have a baby. I decided that if I'm having a child, the first one will be before I'm 30, just, I don't know why, but that's how I always felt it would be. That's when it struck home that, well, next year you're gonna be 30, so do something now . . .

. . .

Q: What kinds of things do you focus on when you think of being 29?

R: I guess I think the next stage is 30, I think maybe I'm better off staying 29, I'm not sure . . .

In having decided that she would have a child no later than age 30, the respondent herself was responsible for having given this age marker its special meaning. Her ambivalence about making the transition from work to motherhood was therefore not a function of anything intrinsic about age; her ambivalence was due to a conflict created by her own competing identities in the areas of work and family.

Similar contrasts between positive and negative approaches to a particular age marker could be seen in other respondents who discussed the importance of a particular age (even though their present ages were different). For example, a a 48-year-old woman's claim to have gotten a "better outlook on life" after turning 40 contrasts sharply with the attitudes of a 26-year-old woman:

R: . . . I think when I turn 35, I think that's a tough age. That's how I feel. Because 35, you're starting to get closer to 40. . .

It is not simply the case that having passed a particularly significant age causes the individual to feel, in retrospect, that it was not as dreadful as was feared. Indeed, there were individuals whose attitudes toward their ages in the 40s and 50s confirmed the worst fears of their under-30 counterparts. If age had a uniform meaning, either as a physiological or a social indicator, there would not have been the extreme variation in how particular ages were interpreted by the respondents. Moreover, if age had a consistent psychological impact on the individual, as is claimed by the age-stage and mid-life crisis positions, then there would not be the variation that was observed in the ages at which similar inner phenomena were taking place. Instead, the meaning that was given to a particular age was a function of what that age signified about the individual's identity in major life areas. Similarly, the processes of self-evaluation in which some individuals engaged at particular ages could be attributed to mismatches between identity and expectations that happened to be occurring concurrently with those ages. These mismatches may, of course, arise out of an association made by the individual between that age and a given experience (such as the woman who decided to have a child at age 30).

It is probably impossible to try to attribute cause and effect in such a complicated and convoluted process. However, that is not the point of this analysis. The point has been to show that explanations of adult developmental processes that are based upon age are overly simplistic. These approaches reduce to numbers what are exceptionally intricate relationships between the individual and experiences in the years of adulthood.

THE QUESTION OF SEX DIFFERENCES IN ADULT DEVELOPMENT

A second point of criticism about the generality of the "mid-life crisis" to normal adults is based on the assumption of some writers that men and women undergo different "crises" and for different reasons in the middle years of adulthood. Supposed sex differences in developmental trends throughout adulthood have formed the basis for theories (Gilligan, 1982) and research (Reinke, Holmes, & Harris, 1985) concerning adulthood. It is recognized here that differences in early socialization between males and females are not to be ignored. However, these differences are not regarded as a sufficient basis for a fundamental split between men and women in their orientation to self and life. What the theories of adult development that focus on sex differences are describing are differences in gender identity, and relatively superficial ones at that, involving the performance of social roles and associated thoughts and feelings.

The men studied in this book were concerned about their feelings, their needs for close relationships with other adults, their appearance, and nurturing their children. These are areas that are thought of as reserved for women only by the theories that describe sex differences in adult development. The women are concerned about such "masculine" preoccupations as the need to earn a living and engage productively in work. In short, men and women were concerned about the same desires, life goals, and modes of self-expression. Both men and women valued such principles as honesty, the "Golden Rule," consideration for the feelings of others, hard work, and personal happiness. Men and women were also equally likely to question their identities, engage in self-deception, be emotionally dependent on others, and be insecure about their motives. Some differences occasionally emerged in particular areas of identity. Also, there were variations in attitudes toward work and household roles that followed traditional sex-role lines. However, these differences were of little importance compared to the basic similarities between men and women in how they answered the question "Who am I?"

A Study of Adult Identity

An interview on adult identity, reproduced in Appendix A, was given to a sample of 94 adults living in the metropolitan area of a moderate-size city in Upstate New York. The people in this sample were drawn from a wide range of socioeconomic levels. Their family situations were extremely varied, including single adults, married adults without children, married adults expecting a child, parents in small families, parents in large families, remarried, divorced, and widowed persons, stepparents, and grandparents. Some of their occupations were bartender, life insurance agent, school administrator, scientist, student, homemaker, secretary, hairdresser, machinist, engineer, and construction worker. There was an equal number of men and women. Their educational levels ranged from ninth grade to the Ph.D. level. The demographic characteristics of this sample are presented in tabular form in Appendix B.

The sample was selected at random from telephone directory listings. A telephone call, which followed an initial letter describing the study, was used to make appointments with interested persons who fit the sampling criteria of age, sex, and socioeconomic status. The respondents were paid $20 each for their participation in the 2- to 3-hour interview session. The sample selection and interviewing took place over a 9-month period from late December, 1980 to early September, 1981. One year later, 57 members of the original group responded to a mailed questionnaire sent to all 94 people. This questionnaire provided information on major life changes that had occurred within the past year.

The interviewers were two graduate students in counseling, matched by sex with the respondents they interviewed. The male interviewer was in his early 30s and the female in her late 30s.

The interview itself began by asking the respondent to complete a "pie" diagram showing the "Most Important Areas of My Life." After the pie diagram was completed, the interviewer began asking questions about the largest section of the pie to determine why it was important to the respondent and what about the area was of importance. Originally, it had been intended that so-called content-free questions be asked about identity in the largest area of the pie, which we believed would have a structure comparable to that of the Work section of the interview. It was thought that respondents would include as smaller areas of identity such things as leisure or community involvement, and that family would be just one of many such areas mentioned. However, in 84 of the 97 interviews, the largest area in the pie diagram turned out to be family. Since this became apparent early in the study, the "content-free" questions were transformed permanently into questions regarding family, and appear as such in Appendix A. However, the procedure of asking such questions about family only if it was first in importance was retained throughout the course of the study, and so data from these questions are available only for those 84 persons who regarded it as their major area of identity. Moreover, since there were too few respondents giving "content-free" responses in any one given area, the data from this section of the interview were not analyzed. It is recognized that this procedure resulted in a more limited sample for whom family was the most important area of identity and, for this reason, the results on family identity must be viewed with a certain degree of caution.

The responses to this interview were analyzed from verbatim transcripts taken from audiotape recordings. A content analysis was performed in which the statements taken from individual transcripts were sorted into similar categories within each area of the interview. The model of adult identity was used in a general sense to guide the analysis of identity processes from the transcript material. From this analysis, there emerged the specific subcategories of the identity processes within each identity area. The present method was not, then, biographical; that is, individuals were generally not the focus of the analysis. However, biographical material was used where the interpretation of a response was facilitated by knowledge of a person's background.

Additional ratings of the content categories formed in the areas of family and work were made by graduate students as a check of the reliability of the content analysis method. The agreement of these ratings was sufficiently high (84%) to ensure that this categorization method was sufficiently accurate. Apart from this reliability estimate, though, there remains the question of the validity of the interview responses. There is no way of knowing whether the respondents were giving truthful answers to any of the questions they were asked. This is a problem that is not unique to this study; it pervades all of the social science research that uses survey methods and questionnaires, as well as interviews. The interviewers were alerted to the possibility that respondents might be trying to present themselves in a favorable light. To attempt to overcome this problem, the interviewers were instructed to follow up any responses that seemed suspicious in this regard. These follow-ups involved asking for examples, clarification, or additional responses to the same questions given in a rephrased form.

In analyzing the responses from the transcripts, a similar form of skepticism was applied. The transcripts were scrutinized for contradictions, inconsistencies, apparent exaggerations, and evasion of questions as a basis for suspecting that the respondent was either deliberately or unknowingly engaging in deception. In many cases, when this deception was suspected, it was possible to interpret it in terms of the identity process model. However, because there is no way that all instances can possibly have been found, there remains the need to regard with some doubt the truthfulness of this, and any other, information based entirely on self-report.

The study's findings form the basis for the rest of this book. The next chapter presents the fuller elaboration of the adult identity process theory, along with definitions and examples from transcript segments of the various forms of the identity processes examined. This chapter gives the overall theoretical background against which the respondents' transcripts have been interpreted. The definitions and examples in this chapter are also useful for understanding the basis for identity process ratings and for becoming familiar with some of the kinds of issues that are to follow in each of the chapters on family, work, values, and the integrative relationships among each of the these basic substantive areas of adult identity.

2
A Theory of Adult Identity Processes

The primary definition of adult identity that forms the basis for the theory of adult identity processes comes from Erikson's (1963) use of the term "identity" to mean the individual's answer to the question "Who am I?" Erikson's general answer to this question was that identity is a psychosocial entity: a product of individual factors unique to the individual combined with experiential factors derived from social forces. The issue of establishing a sense of identity was considered by Erikson to be a primary focus of adolescents. However, he also considered identity to be a part of the personality that was essential for the successful resolution of psychosocial issues later in adulthood, and as a part of the personality that could be reexamined at any point after its initial emergence.

The adult identity processes that form the basis for the interaction between the individual and the individual's experiences were derived from Piaget's theory of child development (Piaget & Inhelder, 1969). These processes are assimilation and accommodation. In Piaget's theory, these processes are responsible for the development and maintenance of intelligence, defined as the quality of the individual's adaptation to the environment. Assimilation is the process of taking in new information in such a way that it "fits" in with what the individual already knows or is capable of doing. The toddler who calls every adult man "Daddy" is showing assimilation. She is using this word because it is the only word she has in her limited vocabulary to describe a man. Later in her development of language, she will show accommodation when she uses different words to distinguish her father from the other men she sees. Accommodation, then, is the process of making a change in oneself to take into account new experiences that require the formation of new categories, ideas, or attitudes.

The process of identity assimilation and identity accommodation are hypothesized to operate in precisely the same way with regard to adult identity as assimilation and accommodation do in the development of intelligence. Unlike Piaget's theory, though, there are not hypothesized to be any stages in the individual's tendency to use the identity processes. Instead, the identity processes are regarded as having the potential to be used at any time and in any relevant area of the adult's identity.

The starting point for the theory of adult identity processes is the assumption that the normal adult strives to feel loving, competent, and good. When this identity is achieved, the adult feels a sense of happiness and well-being, and when this identity is thrown into doubt, the adult feels anxious and depressed. The motivation for having a favorable identity is partly hedonic; it feels better to feel happy than to feel sad. However, another part of the motivation for a favorable identity comes from the feelings of mastery that accompany the belief that one has done well at work, in the family, and in life's tasks in general.

Identity assimilation refers to the process through which the adult tries to interpret experiences in a manner that is consistent with an identity as a loving, competent, and good person. This process makes the environment a place that can be understood in terms that reinforce the individual's existing identity instead of in terms that challenge it. In contrast, when the experiences one has are so discordant with an identity as a worthwhile person, it is necessary to examine one's identity through accommodation. Identity accommodation may result in a changed identity that is "sadder but wiser," but still basically favorable. There may be times when the individual uses identity accommodation without being directly provoked, through a quest for challenge or growth in new areas. However, the adult's primary tendency is to try to maintain the present identity through assimilation while being able to make identity accommodations when experiences or personal needs create the demand. It is when this optimal state of balance is achieved that the individual is said to be in equilibrium between identity and experiences. Adults in a state of equilibrium feel that they are loving, competent, and good, but also are aware that they are not perfect and are ready to change themselves if necessary. This optimal state of equilibrium between the identity and experiences is illustrated schematically in Figure 2.1.

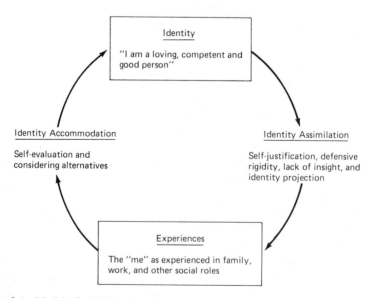

FIGURE 2.1. Model of adult identity processes.

Why is the state of equilibrium regarded as optimal? Piaget's theory does not directly provide suggestions for answers to this question or the related issue of what motivates individuals to seek equilibrium between their identity and their experiences. For this it is necessary to look to other theories that deal more directly with personality and the self-concept. The theories of Rogers (1951) and other humanistically oriented theories of personality are clear in suggesting that the motivation for equilibrium between the individual's identity and the experiences to which he or she is exposed is to reduce anxiety. This anxiety is what the individual would feel if made aware that there was something wrong with his or her identity because it does not fit with the individual's experiences. To avoid anxiety originating from a contradiction or threat to one's identity, the individual has two choices: to change identity if this is what is required, or change the way the experience is interpreted if this is mandated by the situation. If either of these strategies is used, the individual will once again be able to achieve equilibrium between identity and experiences.

There are cases, though, in which individuals resist making changes to their identity when the situation demands it. As the disparity between experiences and identity continues to widen, the individual will be forced to use identity assimilation more and more as a way of keeping from self-awareness the situational demands for change. Conversely, an individual whose identity is not well enough defined to make it possible to make decisions and take action may try to "get by" through overreliance upon identity accommodation. This person will let the situation determine what he or she will do rather than follow a direction for action set by personal preferences and goals. In both cases of disequilibrium, the individuals may feel a short-term sense of well-being. Over the long run, though, the excessive burden being placed upon the dominant identity process will cause a breakdown. At that point, the pendulum may begin to swing in the opposite direction and the converse identity process may begin to take hold.

The interview data gathered in the present study provide some evidence for the mechanisms through which adults move from equilibrium to disequilibrium and back to equilibrium again. However, with only one interview on which to base the assessment of identity processes, this developmental movement can only be inferred rather than directly examined. In addition, since the data are entirely self-reported, it is impossible to know the "objective" nature of the respondents' experiences. In describing the results of analyses of identity processes, these problems will be addressed and attempts made to circumvent them. However, it is recognized that the present data form only a starting point for more complete long-term developmental analyses.

Forms of Identity Assimilation and Accommodation

The broad definitions of identity assimilation and accommodation capture the essence of the identity processes, but, because they are so general, they require considerable refinement. In searching the transcripts for illustrations of these processes, there emerged subgroups of related excerpts that seemed to be based on the same underlying types of processes. These subgroups then became the basis for describing the specific ways in which the identity processes seem to function. In general, the varieties of identity assimilation that were found involved the use of various kinds of defense mechanisms through which the individual denied or distorted the apparent reality of an experience in order to maintain a favorable identity in the relevant area. In many ways, these processes fell into the category of "self-esteem maintenance" strategies (Tesser & Campbell, 1983) or the self-centered and self-preserving actions of the "totalitarian ego" (Greenwald, 1980).

Rather than only being motivated by a desire to feel good about the self, though, the identity processes also are motivated by a desire for the feelings of effectiveness associated with a relatively accurate view of one's experiences. The various forms of identity accommodation are therefore needed as a counterbalancing influence to these processes of identity assimilation, which enhance the individual's identity. The forms of identity accommodation had in common a process of appraisal by the individual of how well his or her identity as a loving, competent, or good person "fit" a particular kind of experience. Some individuals went beyond this appraisal process and actually tried to change their identities as a means of reducing the discrepancies they encountered in their interpretations of their experiences.

In order to provide the most accurate assessment of either identity assimilation or identity accommodation, it would be necessary to have objective evidence on the nature of the "reality" of the individual's experiences. From another perspective, though, information that comes from outside the perspective of the individual is unnecessary. The respondent's view of reality is, after all, what is influencing his or her identity.

The method that was actually used to analyze the identity processes represented a middle ground between these two positions. Part of the reason for adopting this position was practical. With the self-report method, "objective" evidence was obviously not available. However, given the validity of the phenomenological perspective, this lack of outside information does not necessarily represent a serious drawback. In fact, the phenomenological perspective was crucial as a first step in determining the respondent's views of the type of person he or she was in each identity area. It was obligatory to the analysis that the viewpoint of the respondent be accepted noncritically in order to make a hypothesis about the nature of the respondent's identity (the "me").

The next step was to search for probable instances of identity assimilation that would be consistent with the hypothesis concerning the nature of the given individual's identity. The presence of identity assimilation was surmised from two types of evidence, both of which involved looking for inconsistencies between the respondent's identity and experiences. One type was based strictly on the interview responses. This evidence consisted of the presence of apparent exaggerations and contradictions in the interview responses that had the effect of portraying the individual in a manner consistent with the hypothesized identity. The second type of evidence came from discrepancies between the interview responses and the biographical information that the respondent provided in a separate questionnaire format. Identity accommodation usually, but not always, was associated with self-criticisms and introspective ruminations on the part of the respondent. Confirmatory evidence of accommodation also came from the finding of congruities between the interview responses and the respondent's "objective" circumstances as determined by the biographical questionnaire.

Having described the adult identity process theory and the methods used to investigate the theory, it is time now to bring to life the adult identity processes in greater detail and with some examples from transcript excerpts.

IDENTITY ASSIMILATION

Identity assimilation is the process through which the individual imposes his or her identity as a loving, competent, and good person upon the interpretation of experiences. The various forms that identity assimilation can take all involve some degree of distortion and denial of factors that are inconsistent with this identity.

Self-Justification

The first form of identity assimilation to be examined includes statements that appear to represent an attempt on the part of the respondent to justify his or her identity as a loving, competent, and good person. Self-justification is regarded to be a form of assimilation because it involves a process of imposing one's identity onto experiences without simultaneously looking for any weaknesses in the "fit" between the two. There is a defensive quality to the individual's assertions that conveys the message: "I'm right about myself and what I'm doing is right, and that's that." This appears to be the sense of the following excerpt:

Q: How do you feel about being a mother?
R: ...and yes, you know how I feel about myself. I'm the pillar, I'm the pillar in this house. Without me, things just don't go right.

In this brief statement, the respondent is expressing precisely the sentiment that characterizes self-justification when it is directed at enhancing an individual's sense of competence.

Another respondent shows self-justification in regard to his family situation, but in terms of maintaining his identity as a loving husband and father:

Q: How does your family affect the way you see yourself?
R: I see myself as a good parent now...

Part of his identity as a "good parent" includes responsibility for his family:

R: I realized when I got married that I was going to have responsibilities and they remind me...when I come home and see them, I realize it's worth it.

It is to this sense of responsibility that the respondent attributes his need to sacrifice one of his cherished leisure-time activities:

R: . . . I like hiking and canoeing. . . . Now that I've got a family, I just can't see doing that because if I got hurt, then they've got problems. I'm more worried about them than about myself.

Q: So your family takes on greater importance than yourself?

R: Oh yeah, definitely. They're number one.

. . .

Q: How does your family affect what you do in your daily life?

R: As far as leisure activities right now, I have to do something where the wife can come. She enjoys the outdoors too, but right now it's hard with the baby. So, we have to go somewhere other than hiking and canoeing. Anyplace I go I try to get the wife and baby to come along. We're family now. I think we should be together.

Up to this point, there is no reason to doubt that the respondent's love for his family has been directly translated into the action of giving up his favorite sport. The evidence for identity assimilation comes from his next response, in which this interpretation is called into question:

Q: Do you ever question or wonder about your family?

R: Sometimes maybe when we've had a little spat or something like that, and I think there's a reason why people have those spats, and it's more fun to make up and I think back to when I was single . . . and the things I used to do and, okay, some of the things I still do, I still go hiking. I still go canoeing . . .

It is this contradiction in his own statements that suggests that the respondent is using the self-justification form of identity assimilation. It enhances his identity as a loving family member to show how much of a martyr he has been for the sake of his family. That this family identity is not consistent with his behavior is suggested by his inadvertent admission that he in fact has not given up sports.

In the cases of self-justification, the position could be taken that the respondents are being deceitful in purposely trying to portray an overly favorable self-impression. This position would apply particularly to the second respondent, where evidence is presented in one response that casts doubt on another. The first respondent did not make a similar "slip," so there is no way of judging how accurate she was about her family's inability to function without her. It is only through reading into her statement an exaggerated sense of self-importance that the identity assimilation rating is apparent.

What is really at issue is not the veracity of the interview answers, though. Of importance is the fact that these statements reveal how the respondents would *like* their identities to be perceived. This is where the phenomenological perspective becomes critical in order to determine what kind of identity would produce the respondent's statements. Having made this determination, the more skeptical, "reality"-based approach must then be adopted. The search for inconsistencies and possible distortions provides the necessary counterperspective needed to form a basis for rating whether the respondent shows the self-justification form of identity assimilation.

Identity Projection

Another form of identity assimilation is a combination of self-justification and the defensive mechanism of projection. The individual who uses the identity projection form of identity assimilation describes in an extremely negative way the beliefs or practices of "other people" in order to appear, by comparison, as having a favorable identity with regard to the characteristic in question. The self-justification inherent in this form of identity assimilation is the individual's ability to emerge from the comparison as having an identity as someone who is loving, competent, and good. The projection component of this form of identity assimilation is the implication that perhaps the negative qualities that the respondent points to in others are qualities that he or she in fact possesses. To admit to having these qualities would, though, be counter to the individual's identity as a person who is loving, competent, and good. In order to protect this identity, the individual must make a strong case against the merits of these negative qualities.

The first excerpt illustrating identity projection concerns the work identity of a full-time homemaker regarding the possibility of her seeking work outside the home:

Q: How seriously are you considering this?
R: Well, quite seriously. I would like something, especially for the winter.
Q: The reason?
R: When you're in the house all the time, you do get bored, I think. I don't watch a lot of TV like a lot of them do. I like to be busy.

The "them" who watch television are, by implication, other full-time home-makers. The respondent was at a point of having mixed feelings about how fulfilled she was with her work in the house. Her case is presented in greater detail in Chapter 8 because it illustrates the kind of ambivalence shown by other home-makers in the sample. The excerpt presented here shows how it enhanced her identity to think of herself as someone looking for paid employment. By distancing herself from the "typical" homemaker through projection, she could reinforce this identity as a competent worker even further. However, the potential that she would fail in another job was so threatening to her identity that she could not seriously consider it. Instead, she set up so many impossible criteria that a new job would have to meet that there was no risk of her actually finding one.

Another category of projection statements were based on self-attribution of favorable qualities. A particular belief or behavior that was a part of the respondent's identity was claimed to be a view held by many others. By showing that "everybody" feels this way, the respondent can gain an imaginary consensus of supporting opinions. Ordinarily, this positive type of projection took the form of attributions to a generalized large number of people, such as "everybody," but occasionally the respondent claimed to have the assent of a single, higher authority:

R: ... But what you find, and I imagine Reagan finds this too, that no matter what level you are, there continue to be obstacles and frustrations.

The respondent was describing his inability to make progress in his work because of bureaucratic "narrow-mindedness" in his organization. By showing that not only he, but the President, cannot accomplish important goals, the respondent is able to preserve his identity as a competent worker.

The identity projection form of identity assimilation is in some cases difficult to distinguish from self-justification. As will be seen in examples described in subsequent chapters, there are many instances in which self-justification involves criticism of other people. However, the key feature of projection is that the respondents attribute to others the less savory characteristics of their own identities. In the kind of criticism that qualifies as self-justification, individuals severely downgrade the competence or worth of others in order to enjoy the benefits of the comparison. Both cases involve distorted perceptions of other people in regard to the self, and so if used consistently over time can lead to a disequilibrium between identity and experiences.

Defensive Rigidity

The third form of identity assimilation is the inability or unwillingness to consider the possibility that one is not a loving, competent, and good person. Alternatives to the individual's present way of doing things are regarded as threats to this identity and so are ruled out before they are given serious attention. The reason that this form of identity assimilation is called "defensive" is because it represents an attempt to defend the individual's identity from any outside threats. Individuals who use this form of identity assimilation have an identity that is based on such a precarious foundation that it cannot withstand the risks entailed in challenging it. The "rigidity" of this assimilative process is in its autocratic exclusion or discounting of such potentially challenging alternatives. The narrow perspective taken by the adult who uses this form of identity assimilation can be seen in the following excerpt:

Q: How do your values affect the way you feel about yourself?
R: ... These values tell me how I must live and how I must perform at various times, so they have to affect me, but I have just never really thought about me personally and what they are doing for me personally.... I guess it's, you know, if someone told you a rule do not step on the grass, I don't think about whether I'm upset or indifferent or whatever because I can't walk on the grass. The rule is don't do this, and if I'm told a reason for it, for the value, I think values have their own reasons so I don't really question how I feel about it.

The implication of this statement is that values, like rules, are not to be questioned once they have been laid down. Defensive rigidity also appears in statements indicating that the respondent has always wanted this identity and will always feel the same way in the future. A similar kind of rigidity is shown by statements indicating that the respondent's identity is "a way of life," "natural," and "instinctive." These terms imply that the respondent has no choice, that he or she is fulfilling a predetermined destiny, and that little introspection about the desirability of this identity is either required or even healthy.

The respondent whose interview on values was just excerpted continued a discussion of values that illustrated this belief in the invariance over time of one's identity:

Q: Do you ever consider having a different set of values?

R: I don't think so. I think I'm not that flexible of a person in some ways. If these are my values, especially after the way I was brought up after 16 years of a Catholic education, it's really instilled in me and I can't see changing some of these out of a fear, I guess, because that's the value and that's the way it should be, and there's just no way I could change it because it would not be as good of a value if I had tried to change it. It would cease to be a value somewhat if I was trying to change it.

For this respondent, to initiate questions would cast doubt on the wisdom of an identity adopted in youth, and hence might invalidate the purpose of the adult years lived so far. Another related tendency that falls in the category of defensive rigidity is a resistance to social changes that might reflect negatively on an identity taken on by the individual before those social changes took place. This same respondent, whose interview exemplified almost every variant of defensive rigidity, also expressed an aversion to the "values of today":

R: . . . they are not the right values for me. They are not my way of life and how it has been shaped up at this point and I can't accept some of those values and I don't want to then have my children to have those values. I want my children to have my values.

The interviewer then initiated a series of questions based on the incorrect assumption that the respondent was engaged in a self-evaluation process. In the interchange that followed, the content of the particular value being discussed emerges:

Q: You are thinking about these other values and you are having some questions about your own values, it sounds like it makes you re-evaluate your own. What is it that you are thinking about? What kinds of values are you thinking about?
R: . . . A prevalent value right now is of course just living together and getting to know one another during that stage so you know whether or not you want to commit your life to that person and I can't see that as a value at all . . . . The safety of marriage means more to me than the living together . . . it's a prevalent value now because many people live together now and I know many people that do it, and I think "Gee," and I have to stop and think about it, how wrong is it, how right is it, but in my mind it comes out that's a wrong value . . . . I'm not questioning my own values. I am just being presented with another set of values . . . . I'm not going to say "Oh, okay, I'm in favor of that," or because someone else decides to have an abortion, I'm not going to say "That certainly has merit, that's fine." . . . I don't very often change my opinion or my own values. I see someone else's and I think this is what my own is, and I think about mine for a while, and I think about their's for awhile, and maybe discuss it . . . but it comes back to this is my value and this is what I've always believed in and I don't change my values too often.

Having set the record straight that she is not questioning the values of marriage and her antiabortion position, the respondent attempts to show that she is really an open-minded person after all toward "today's values." Underlying her defensive attitude toward these values may be concerns related to the respondent's own sexual attitudes as well as a desire to protect a long-held identity from threats to its validity. To observe younger persons engaging in what is regarded as sexually liberated behavior raises a direct challenge to the respondent's own identity as a "moral" adult.

One category of respondents who stated that they were not considering any alternatives or doubting any feature of their home life gave as their reason the fact that they were satisfied, content, and comfortable with their present identities and the life-style associated with their identities. One respondent used the word "housebroken" to describe this attitude with regard to marriage. Others described things as going "smoothly" and so not requiring scrutiny. A logical question is, why should these people be classified as showing defensive rigidity? Maybe they really are happy. In fact, maybe they are happier and more secure in their identities than people who question their views about themselves. The answer to this question is that happiness does not necessarily exclude awareness of alternatives. The following excerpt is from the interview of a respondent who "enjoyed" being married, but nevertheless admitted to having an occasional doubt:

Q: Do you have any doubts or questions about being married?
R: No. Well, I couldn't say no, but I couldn't put my finger on any either. I think we have questions to a certain degree, just as you go through life.
Q: At this point are you contemplating any changes in any aspects of your marriage, or...?
R: No. Everything's pretty stable right now...

The respondent tries somewhat to avoid admitting to having questions in changing the pronouns out of the first person singular into the second person. Nevertheless, this kind of response signifies that happiness and a flexible attitude toward one's identity are not mutually exclusive. Many cases of identity accommodation, in fact, were noted in people who were quite satisfied with their identities but able to think about possible limitations or areas where there could be some improvement.

Another suggestion of the process of identity assimilation is when the respondent closes questions off prematurely, before they can be resolved in a way that is potentially damaging to his or her identity. The next excerpt illustrates how a respondent can try to minimize the importance of some very disturbing negative feelings about work:

Q: How do you feel about this kind of work?
R: ...There are days when I come home and say "I want another job."
Q: So you might get angry?
R: Yes. Very much so. I come home and talk to my husband about it and so we just talk it over and say "Don't worry, you're doing okay." And then the next day I'll go back and things seem to be a little better.

Were the respondent to follow through on her negative feelings about work, she would risk the uncertainty of searching for new employment. She can maintain her position at her present company by keeping her anger in check instead of letting it develop to its logical conclusion.

Through defensive rigidity of any kind, then, the individual builds a wall of fortification around an identity that does not have the internal strength to withstand occasional self-doubts or challenges from others. In order to maintain this internally weak identity the individual must exert firm control over all incoming information. Any experiences that might reveal the individual to be wrong about this identity are not allowed to penetrate through the barriers. A consistency between identity and experiences can therefore be maintained. The danger in this form of identity assimilation is that the individual's identity becomes more and more fearful of being invalidated the longer it goes without being put to a test. As this happens, the individual restricts the range of new experiences further, and the process becomes self-perpetuating.

Lack of Insight

In this form of identity assimilation, individuals protect their identities from discrepancies with experiences by refusing to examine the implications of their own thoughts or behaviors, which might reflect negatively on an identity as a loving, competent, and good person. The most obvious cases of this form of identity assimilation are the ones in which respondents overtly avoid or have difficulty in reflecting upon their own motivations, needs, and characteristics when asked about how they feel about themselves. These cases included people who greatly hesitated in answering, could not answer, or did not answer questions pertaining to the effects of their family, work, or values on their feelings about themselves. Some respondents replied, in answer to these questions, that it was something they had never thought about—"a question I never ask myself."

The example given below illustrates how this form of identity assimilation appeared in the interview transcripts. It is a series of questions in which the respondent seems to be evading questions about her feelings about herself as a wife and can only focus on her ideas about herself as a mother. This is a lengthy example because the sense of avoidance can only be discerned by following through the interchange between the interviewer and the respondent:

Q: What about being a wife? What is important to you about being a wife?
R: Um, well, I guess just being home. My husband likes it when I'm home. He's got his supper when he comes home. He doesn't want me to go out to work. He wants me to be there.
Q: That sounds like it's important to him about it, but what's important to you about being a wife?
R: About being a wife?
Q: Yeah.
R: Being a mother and taking care of the house. I don't know, I enjoy taking care of the house. I take care of the yard, stuff like that.
Q: Okay. How do you feel about being a mother?
R: I like it a lot. I've always liked children...
Q: How do you feel about being a wife?
R: Didn't you just ask me that?

Q: No.

R: No?

Q: No. I just asked about being a mother.

R: Oh. Oh. I like being a wife! It's okay! (laughs) Everybody has their ups and downs. (laughs) Basically okay.

Q: You say basically okay. Can you elaborate on that at all? Would you like to elaborate?

R: No. I really like being a wife. I guess, you know, my husband's good, so (laugh) there's no problem.

. . .

Q: What effect does being a wife have on the way you feel about yourself as a person?

R: I don't know. (laughs)

Q: It's different, isn't it!

R: Yes!! (laughs) It's a different question! Um, it makes you more mature than you were before you were married. You know, you have a lot of responsibilities.

Q: How about the way you feel about yourself?

R: What, being a wife?

Q: Yes.

R: How does it affect myself?

Q: Uh huh.

R: In what way?

Q: How you feel about yourself; how you think about yourself.

R: No, I feel okay about myself. (laughs) Kind of a funny question. Uh, I feel good. Like I said, I'd like to get a job when I'm, when the kids are in school. Then I'd probably feel better . . .

Q: It sounds like when you talk about being a mother, it's very rewarding, but the wife part of it is a little more difficult to define.

R: Yeah, I can't . . .

Q: You don't know what's more difficult about it.

R: Yeah.

Q: Do you recognize that? Do you see that?

R: Yeah, I know what you're saying. Yeah.

Q: Okay. How does being a wife affect what you do in your everyday life?

R: My everyday life?

Q: Uh huh.

R: Um, I don't know how to answer that. Um, I don't know. (laughs)

Q: Do you think it does affect it? What you do in your everyday life?

R: Does it affect my life?

Q: What you do.

R: No, no.

One interpretation of this interview is that the respondent resents her husband's insistence that she stay home with the children. She stated that she would "feel better" if she could work outside the home, but this identity as a working woman would be inconsistent with her husband's ambitions for her. Were she to contemplate this divergence of views to any great extent, it would lead to open acknowledgment of some unhappy feelings toward her husband, hence her avoidance of the whole topic. An indication that all is not well, in fact, appeared in her indirect statement about "ups and downs."

This long example is one of the best representations of the lack of insight form of identity assimilation as shown by avoidance of questions. In addition, it also shows how the respondent failed to acknowledge what seems, to an outside observer, a direct and large effect of being a wife on her daily life. Although claiming there was "no effect," she had already stated at the outset of the interview the fact that her husband desired her full-time presence in the home. Again, for her to admit this openly in answer to a forthright question seems to be inconsistent with her attempt to preserve her identity as a happy, loving wife.

Another respondent exemplified a different kind of lack of insight, in which he did not avoid questions, but did not realize the implications of his answers. At one point he described himself as cutting down on the amount of time he devoted to work:

Q: So it sounds like your work affects the rest of your life?
R: Definitely, very much so. Right at the present time, though, I'm . . . backing off and taking more time for myself than I used to. I used to work 18 hours a day, no spare time, 7 days a week, but now I've backed off on that especially because I had been sick and I had no choice, but I planned on making time for myself, I'm scheduling time. If I'm gone and something happens, it happens. It can happen while I'm there, too.

However, the respondent's claim that he had "backed off" is challenged by another of his answers:

Q: What about your work is important to you?
R: What about it is important to me?. . . I feel that I can do well in business or I would not be in business. I spend probably 80 to 90% of my time in business, of my hours that I'm awake. Ten percent of my sleep hours, and it's very important. It comes first right now. It has come first and will come first for probably up to another two years before I can see where things will be to a point where I can back off and work maybe an 8-hour day . . .

Why does the respondent contradict himself? There does not seem to be a self-justification motive behind the discrepancy in his two statements. He has no doubts about how hard-working he is, and so does not have to "fake" a high degree of involvement on a daily basis. Instead, it seems more likely that he is a workaholic and does not realize this about himself. He would like to think that he is cutting back and making work less a part of his identity, but he does not carry this desire through to his behavior.

Compared to defensive rigidity, lack of insight may have a greater potential to be overcome and replaced by a more introspective approach to one's identity. This would be particularly true in the case of the latter respondent. He was at least aware that he had let his work become overly intrusive into his personal life. Even though he had not yet made the necessary changes, the respondent's recognition of a need to change may have represented a crucial first step to doing so. With such an acknowledgment, a disequilibrium characterized by a predominance of identity assimilation begins to be balanced by the process of identity accommodation.

IDENTITY ACCOMMODATION

A realistic appraisal of one's identity, one's experiences, and the congruence between the two is what constitutes the process of identity accommodation. Just as with analyzing cases of identity assimilation, it is also desirable and necessary to be able to draw some inferences about the "reality" of the individual's experiences when trying to decide whether and for what purposes identity accommodation is being used. However, as with the analysis of identity assimilation, there is little objective information on which to base such an analysis when the primary method used to obtain information is a self-report interview schedule.

One potential difference between the evidence needed to rate identity assimilation and that needed for identity accommodation is that it is less important to determine exactly what the individuals situation is like in an objective sense in studying accommodation. The critical factor requiring examination is whether the individual is trying to assess the quality of his or her experiences and is allowing the possibility of alternative solutions or a change in identity to be considered, if necessary. The problem from the point of conducting an analysis of the interview material then becomes one of achieving some assurance that the respondent really is going through such a process, rather than just attempting to appear introspective for the purpose of making a good impression. Because of this potential for respondents to exaggerate the degree of questioning or objectivity shown toward their identities and experiences, it is still necessary to approach self-reports of identity accommodation with some skepticism. Where the reported results of an identity accommodation process are positive the responses must be carefully examined to discern any inconsistencies and possible distortions about the respondent's reported use of "honest" appraisal.

Favorable Changes in Identity

One way in which identity accommodation is manifested is as a reported positive change in identity as a result of having had certain experiences. Individuals who use this form of identity accommodation state that they have improved their identities as being loving, competent, and good on the basis of an experience or experiences in a given area. As clear as this definition appears, in practice it is very tricky to implement. Statements in which these claims are made may be the product of an identity assimilation process in which the respondent has distorted the perception of an experience in order to arrive at a positive conclusion about its effect.

The least verifiable cases of identity accommodation were those in which the respondent described generally positive effects of a position in family or work such as "feel good" or "better" without any further elaboration. Also difficult to interpret were those that had a self-serving quality:

Q: How does your family affect the way you see yourself?
R: ...Well, I think it makes me feel better. It makes me feel, um, better that I'm more honest with them. I think they feel, you know, the same way.

It is to the respondent's advantage to regard his family as feeling "the same way" toward him as he does toward himself. Subject to a similar kind of doubt are statements such as "I feel good" because "I have such good kids," or "the boss thinks I'm doing a good job." A rating of identity accommodation is more clearly warranted when the response is more specific, as in the following excerpt from a bakery worker:

Q: How does the work that you do right now affect the way you feel about yourself?
R: Well, I would say that this particular job makes me feel a little better about myself because I went into it not knowing what to do. I just started working in the bakery and the lady left and said "Would you like to do it?" and I said "I have never done it before," I had no idea what to do, and they said "Well, there's the utensils, go to it." And since then, they said their business has tripled. That makes me feel, it makes me feel I can accomplish something myself.

It is not possible to determine whether the respondent really did accomplish something, or whether there were other negative incidents that were not reported. However, the respondent's approach is one that appears to be sensitive to the need to document a favorable statement rather than make a global conclusion whose validity is completely impossible to verify.

Somewhat more indicative of an "objective" attitude on the part of the respondent is a response that leans in a favorable direction but is qualified by statements to the effect that the respondent's perception may not be accurate. In this category of identity accommodation were expressions of "hope" that the individual was effective within the family at fulfilling desired goals. These responses were not necessarily self-critical, but instead seemed to represent attempts to qualify a self-description that might otherwise appear to be overly conceited. Although such qualifications may be made out of false modesty, the individuals who use them are at least sensitive to the dangers of a totally biased and uncritical self-acceptance. Such an attitude is reflected in the following excerpt:

Q: How do your values affect the way that you feel about yourself?
R: . . . I guess this is why I enjoy my work so much, because I'm with people who are very caring and supportive and friendly and you just feel good about being with people like that all day long, and I hope that I am that way myself, that I would be there for other people if they needed someone to talk to, that I would be open to that.

The respondent admits to the possibility of not fulfilling the value of being caring, but still gives the overall impression of having a favorable self-perception in that regard.

Almost neutral in its affective tone is the belief that any favorable effects of identity-confirming experiences can be balanced by unfavorable effects of disconfirming experiences on the identity of the person as loving, competent, and good. The overall flavor of such comments is usually more positive than negative, particularly when viewed in the context of other statements given during the interview. The following excerpt gives an example of such a statement:

Q: Is the way you evaluate yourself, the way you think about yourself as a person, is it influenced by the fact that you're a chemist?

R: Probably the way that I've looked at myself is not so much a chemist but, you know, a scientist, an investigator in general. It sort of became a very broad sort of concept of myself. A scientist versus a factory worker versus an engineer or any other general kind.

Q: Well, a professional. How about, then, being a scientist? Does that affect the way you see yourself, your view of yourself?

R: Yes it does. If I have a good day at work I come home and I feel real good that I get something accomplished and I start looking for the next thing to accomplish. If I had a rotten day at work, I'm a grouchy son of a bitch.

Q: You think that's, let's say, if you were in some other profession, you also felt the sense of accomplishment. Is it different being . . . a scientist?

R: I don't know. If I was a factory worker or if I were inclined to be a factory worker and brought a sense of accomplishment, I imagine I'd feel the same way. But, um, I just feel that that particular choice of profession had to do with the way I wanted to direct my life.

The almost equal balance of the "good day" versus "bad day" statement is tipped toward the favorable end, then, by the final statement in which the respondent provides an implicit affirmation of the benefits of having chosen this particular work identity.

With this almost neutral statement of the effects of the individual's experiences on identity comes the turning point in examining identity accommodation as an effect on self-evaluation. The next group of statements represent either explicit statements regarding the doubts individuals have about themselves or open acknowledgment of negative changes in their identities associated with their experiences in a given area.

Self-Doubts and Unfavorable Changes in Identity

When there is the perception by individuals of discrepancies between their experiences and their identities as loving, competent, and good people, they may engage in an evaluative process of trying to determine whether their own personal shortcomings were the cause. The first step in this process is determining whether there is in fact a discrepancy. The following respondent, unmarried at the age of 30, was trying to set his own priorities in life, as distinct from those set for him by his parents:

Q: What effect does your relationship with your parents have on the way you feel about yourself as a person?

R: It's an important consideration, my reaction.

Q: Does it determine the way you regard yourself? You think of yourself?

R: In a way, yes, in that it gives me sort of a reference point I can sort of, I can look at in what I have accomplished and I can say is this what is expected of me and conversely what have I accomplished with respect to what either one of them has accomplished.

The respondent does not say that there actually is a disparity between what he has accomplished and the goals of his parents. The respondent was comparing his identity as a good son with the quality of his actual experiences up to that point, but had not arrived at a conclusion.

If the individual does conclude that a discrepancy between identity and experiences actually exists, then the next step is for him or her to look for its source. At this point, there may be a period of active self-doubting about whether the individual's self-estimation needs to be downwardly scaled. Such a self-appraisal was evident in the following respondent's self-doubts about her effectiveness as a sister in fulfilling her identity as the protector and supporter of her younger siblings:

Q: How does your family affect the way that you see yourself?
R: Hm. I think that because I am older, that's made me more protective. More willing to be there if I'm needed in case of an emergency.
Q: How has that affected the way that you feel about yourself?
R: Maybe I'm overprotective. Maybe on occasions they feel that I'm being over-curious or doing, asking questions that really aren't, shouldn't be in my department.

Again, although it is not possible to know how close to reality the respondent's self-perceptions were, the important point about this example is the fact that she appeared to be seriously entertaining the possibility that her identity as a good sister and the perceptions of her family were poorly matched.

At its most intense, self-doubting can take the form of an active confrontation between the individual's identity as a loving, competent, and good person and direct knowledge from an experience that proves this identity to be false. This was the case of a parent who lamented having given her child too many experiences at too early an age:

R: . . . And there are things we thought we were doing right that maybe was not exactly right. Maybe it hurt him instead of hindered him [*sic*]. An example I'll give you is we've moved quite a bit. But in moving, you could say we more or less rationalized our moves: "It's not hurting him. Look at the exposure he's getting.". . . To me, I said "That's so unique! For a five-year-old. Look at the exposure he's getting . . . . He's seen so much more than any other child has ever seen. Great! School's got a terrific day camp; the kids had something to do every day: What exposure!" [said ironically] . . . And then the time comes when he had to stay home. "Aren't we going someplace today?" "It's so boring here!" "There's nothing to do." "We're staying home again two days in a row? Wow!" The kid is so used to doing things, extraordinary things, different things, now he's looking for it. And it's not there. And now I can say "Wow, maybe it wasn't so neat to take him everyplace.". . . What we thought we were doing right when he was younger we rationalized I guess to make us feel it was right, but maybe it wasn't such a neat thing to do . . . . Last year was very hard for him. We stayed home most of the time. He was just like a basket case . . .

The respondent was not only questioning her identity as a good mother, she was finding that her present experiences disconfirmed her prior beliefs that she was acting in the best interests of her child.

Having reached the point of seriously challenging one's identity, the next logical step that the individual would need to take in order to regain an equilibrium would be to consider making changes. These changes could either be in the experiences associated with the individual's present situation, or they could

involve assuming an altered identity. These routes toward reducing disequilibrium are examined next.

Looking at Alternatives

If the individual decides on the basis of a self-evaluation that the change needed
to ensure an equilibrium is in the situation and not in his or her identity, then a
process may be initiated in which a search for more congruent experiences is
made. The following respondent described the course of such a process, begun
several years earlier and being implemented at the present time:

Q: Do you ever think about leaving this work behind and trying something else or, uh,
   being involved in some other kind of work?
R: No, but I've already gone through that. Uh, a few years ago. Do you want me to tell
   you about that or, uh?
Q: Sure.
R: Okay. Well, I graduated from high school in 1977 and, well, I was a senior in high
   school, and two years after that I worked in a gas station as a mechanic. I've always
   been involved in sports cars. And, well, it was Memorial Day, 1979, and I was drag
   racing, and I broke my leg. And so I had about six or eight weeks to think and do nothing except lay around and I decided that, uh, working on cars I wasn't making enough
   money, which I guess is important to me. Uh, and I, I guess that I felt that, uh, I wasn't
   going my full potential, working on cars, although I think that it is a respectable trade.
   Uh, so I decided to quit that work and go to school . . . and I've been going to school,
   well, ever since that time . . . I like it so far . . . and I think within the field there is
   enough different work that if I'm not satisfied in one area of it I could go to another.

The respondent's decision to change work "experiences," actually to a new
field altogether, resulted from an evaluation that his previous work was not fulfilling his requirements for an identity as a competent worker. He did not change
his identity, but instead changed his experiences to match his ideas about what
would be economically and emotionally rewarding work. In the next example,
the respondent was changing her identity regarding the strict religious values she
had been raised with:

R: . . . There was no room for questioning, it was just yes and no or black and white. It
   wasn't any room for reasoning. Now that I look back on it at the time, of course, I
   thought well, that was it, and as they say, you never questioned anything, so that I
   don't think it was all that great either, but now they've swung a little bit more the other
   way too much. In my personal opinion, I think they've got to switch back a little more
   to the middle.
Q: Could you share what you feel about questioning is positive, and second of all what you
   feel is negative, because it sounds like you've got some positive and some negative
   feelings.
R: Well, yeah, right, I think it's good, but I also think that some people get carried away
   with analyzing and questioning and everything. I guess it isn't the questioning as much
   as the experimenting and the freedom, and all that they seem to insist on.
Q: You thought that some questioning was good. What did you think was good about it?
R: It opens up your mind, for one thing, it gives you different sides of the story and there

wasn't enough of that in my day, so I think that's great. I really do, and I think the young people today are fortunate.

Although the respondent had not completely changed her values to fit the current generation of young people, she had changed her identity considerably from what it had been. It was now possible, in her mind, for an individual to be a "good" religious person even if he or she did not accept every aspect of the religion's moral code. This change in her identity had come about through exposure to a more liberal social atmosphere in which questioning is regarded as normal and almost expected of young people. Unlike the respondents whose position in this area was firmly entrenched through identity assimilation in the views of the past, this individual was able to remain open to change through identity accommodation.

If examining alternatives leads to a better match between identity and experiences, then the identity accommodation process has led to a satisfactory outcome. However, it is possible for individuals to be overly accommodative. If the process of examining alternatives turns into chronic indecisiveness or lack of a firm identity, then the individual will be in a state of disequilibrium that can be as maladaptive as being overly assimilative. The following excerpt is from a respondent who depicts a painfully unrewarding career in which he never arrived at a clear sense of his identity as a worker:

Q: What do you find attractive about your business?
R: I don't know if there's anything really attractive about it. A job.
Q: Anything attractive?
R: No. Just an everyday job. That's about it.
Q: How important is it?
R: A source of income, that's about all you can say. As far as being real happy, I was never overly enthused about going in. It was just a job.
Q: Any effect on daily life?
R: No.
Q: Just a job to go to? Get a salary?
R: Yes.
Q: Before recent changes were made in your company, did you ever question or consider getting out of it?
R: I thought about it, but like when I come out of the service, I never, I had more education coming, free schooling, I never knew what I wanted to do. All of my life has been the same way. I still don't know what I want to do. Just waiting to retire. I never have really accomplished anything, I never expected to accomplish anything, so what can you expect to gain when you don't have any certain thing in mind?
Q: Did you have any specific alternatives in mind, ever?
R: I worked as a maintenance helper in different factories, used to make bottle parts; before they went out of business I worked in a jewelry company. I've done a little bit of everything.

This individual, because of his continual drifting from job to job, was obviously someone who did *not* have an answer to the question "Who am I?" However, this was true only in the area of work. In his family life and in his values, he had definite views of himself as a loving and good person. His case illustrates the possibility that identity areas can compensate for each other when they are integrated into the total person's overall identity. As will become clear in the last section of this book, integration is a crucial feature of identity in adulthood. Because identity is an integrated entity, the evaluation of a person's identity in any one area must be tempered by the evaluations reached in the others.

Theoretical Implications

Analyses of the identity accommodation process illustrate very dramatically the possibility that the adult's identity as a loving, competent, and good person can change, at any point in adulthood, and in any area. The feelings of well-being that are associated with a positive self-perception reach their peak potential when the individual is in a true state of equilibrium between identity assimilation and accommodation. If the individual's identity as a loving, competent, and good person is achieved at the expense of having to rely upon identity assimilation, the ensuing feelings of well-being will be much more vulnerable because the individual's identity is less resistant to challenges to its validity. As assimilation becomes the primary modality of interaction between the individual and experiences, there is a gradual erosion of the ability of the individual's identity to withstand disconfirmation from experiences.

Proponents of the view that people try to maintain a positive self-image at all costs through self-esteem enhancement strategies have ignored this potential danger to the individual's adaptation. By the same token, those who regard the adult as in constant movement from crisis to crisis in a chronological sequence ignore the tendency that individuals have to retain a favorable and stable identity despite exposure to painful and difficult experiences.

Adults do adjust their identities as loving, competent, and good people to their circumstances in a self-correcting fashion through identity accommodation. While it is more difficult to accommodate to negative information about oneself than to identity-confirming information, this accommodation can and does occur continually throughout adulthood. In the following chapters are revealed the processes through which adults know themselves and through which they change this knowledge when it ceases to be correct or useful for their adaptation.

Part II
Family Identity

An overwhelming majority of the adults in the sample had their involvement in their families as their first and foremost area of identity. Of the 94 members of the sample, 84 of them made "family" the largest sector on their "pie" diagram describing what was most important in their lives. There is no question, then, that the adult's identity as "loving" makes up a major part of the answer to the question "Who am I?"

The potential for family involvement to make up such a large proportion of the individual's identity has generally not been given sufficient attention in the popular and professional literature on adult development. It is true that family researchers regard the "transition to parenthood" to be a major turning point in a person's life. Throughout the family literature, there is a consistent message that one of the more profound of first-time parenthood's effects is upon the individual's sense of identity (Entwistle & Doering, 1981). However, variables relating to identity are rarely given enough attention for this simple conclusion to be elaborated any further. Instead, the major focus is usually upon the effects of parenthood on marital satisfaction. In this context, identity is regarded as a factor of importance to the extent that any changes in identity affect the couple's happiness with each other in their new status as parents (e.g., Cowan, Cowan, Coie, & Coie, 1978). Beyond what is known about the parenthood transition, there is virtually no empirical literature concerning the effects of family involvement on adult identity. The impact on the lives of parents as their children proceed through the "family life cycle" has been extensively described (Aldous, 1978; Duvall, 1977). As yet unexplored, though, are the deeper psychological effects of being a parent on the adult's sense of identity.

The 94 adults in the present study provided many thoughtful and articulate descriptions of how their identity had been molded by the experiences within their own families, as parents, as spouses, as lovers, as children, and as siblings. The categories that emerged from content analysis of the interview materials are shown in Appendix C, Table C.1. Many of these categories have already been described by other researchers in the context of benefits and costs of parenthood (Chilman, 1980; Fawcett, 1978; Hoffman & Manis, 1978; Walster, Walster, & Berscheid, 1978). This correspondence with the established literature helps to reinforce the present study's findings. By looking at these areas of family involvement within the overarching framework of adult identity, some coherence may be made of what is now a widely scattered and uneven area within the psychology and sociology of the family.

The analyses presented in the next three chapters have as their major conclusion the proposition that, for most adults, the family provides a major reference point for identity. Adults wish to regard themselves as loving people. In contemporary Western society, this desire is most often expressed within a network of family relationships centering around the nuclear family group of parents and children. The adults in the present sample not only regarded family as an important area of their lives, but also engaged in complex identity processes that had as their goal the establishment and maintenance of the adults' images of themselves as loving. In addition, many of the adults in the sample went further to define the love and care of their families as their singular purpose in life. Thus, the family was such a magnetic force that it had the power to transform the rest of the individual's life into efforts aimed at the support of this primary source of identity.

3
Love Is Not Enough

Artists, authors, and songwriters regard love as the key feature of adult family life in Western civilization (Swidler, 1980). "Love" was present in the family identity responses as a word that described the feelings of adults for their spouses and children. When the word was used, though, it was never defined further. The respondents took it as a given that love was a definition sufficient unto itself.

However, what was particularly surprising about the use of the word "love" was its relatively infrequent occurrence in the responses. Only 5% of the total statements referring to the family contained the word "love" either alone or as part of a longer statement about the relationship in general. Although the adult's identity was not defined in terms of "love," it was defined in terms that certainly have the same meaning, including the ability to enter into close relationships with family members and to be concerned with the family's emotional well-being. The quality of the emotional relationship was a major theme of family identity, with almost three times the number of responses (14%) as love.

It is perhaps the case that the word "love" is so vague and ill-defined that the respondents preferred to talk about specific factors present within their family relationships that contributed to their identities as good parents, spouses, and children. These specific factors also pertain much more strongly to the quality of day-to-day interactions that form the basis for happiness or unhappiness in the adult's family life (Gilford & Bengston, 1979; Kelley, Berscheid, Christensen, et al., 1983). In exploring the factors that pertained to the quality of the family relationship, a number of consistent groupings emerged that highlight the importance of closeness and good communication. Analysis of these groupings shows how adults refine the answer "I am a loving person" in answer to the question "Who am I?" with a good deal of specificity.

The Importance of Closeness, Communication, and Companionship

CLOSENESS

The participants in a close relationship have frequent interactions that highlight their mutual emotional needs for each other. Closeness, then, implies both reciprocity and strong feelings. Reference to this element of their family relationships was made by some respondents in the sample (4%) as an opening to a more in-depth description of the factors within the relationship that contributed to the adult's identity as a loving person. In some cases, closeness meant marital intimacy, as can be seen in the excerpt of a respondent married for 20 years:

Q: What's important to you about being a wife?
R: Ohhh, sharing my life with someone in a close relationship, having an intimacy that can't be achieved in any other way. There's no comparison in being married to someone.

Being involved in a network of family relationships was the meaning attached to closeness by a number of other respondents. In these cases, closeness referred not so much to the quality of the intimate relationship as to the feeling of interdependence upon a support system of relatives who could be counted on to provide actual help as well as emotional nurturance. This meaning of closeness will be explored in the next chapter in terms of intergenerational family relationships.

COMMUNICATION

Almost but not completely synonymous with "closeness" in an intimate relationship is the quality of communication. In contrast to the fairly superficial descriptions that respondents provided about feelings of love that they had toward family members, the respondents talked at length about what communication meant to their family identities. It was clear from these respondents' statements that the identity of a "loving" person includes the self-perception that one is good at communicating feelings in an open and honest fashion. This appreciation of the value of communication of feelings can be seen in the following examples:

Q: Is there any possibility that at some time in the future you think you might (have any doubts about the relationship)?
R: No, I don't really think so. We've seemed to, in our over the, even in the last, let's say, couple of months, covered all the bases. We agree, I would say, on a good majority of everything and the things that we don't agree on we at least come to minds in being able to discuss and talk it over. You don't always have to agree with somebody. But as far as the relationship, I have no doubts.

* * *

Q: What do you get out of being a wife?
R: Like sitting and talking to him if something's bothering me, or like not having to say anything, just know that he knows that something's bothering me. He'll just come up and just, I don't know, hug you or something. Or just going out and going for a walk together. Just the two of us. Not even talking or anything, just walking...

In both of these examples, the individual was describing communication in the context of the marital relationship. The first respondent described the importance of being able to discuss areas of disagreement and come to some sort of understanding with the spouse. In contrast, the second respondent valued a less verbal form of communication. It was her husband's ability to sense her mood without her saying anything that made her feel as though they were communicating well. In addition, engaging in interactions in which nothing at all is said made her feel that they understood each other so well that they could communicate their feelings silently.

Both of these responses concerning the quality of communication referred to the respondent's ability to express and interpret the feelings of the spouse. In contrast, a more practical version of communication was referred to by the next respondent when asked to describe his family situation:

R: ... when we have to do something we discuss it, then we go out and buy and, uh, I'm not one of these guys that goes out and buys and then comes home and says, uh, I bought something, and she does the same thing, so . . .

This respondent's identity of himself as one who could communicate well with his wife focused on his openness with his wife regarding family expenditures. By discussing things with her instead of acting independently, he was showing himself to be a good communicator. His statement almost verges on a concern for the material that is found in a large group of responses concerning the "instrumental" or "extrinsic" feature of family life described later in the chapter. However, the underlying sentiment of this response concerns not so much the content as the process of mutually sharing viewpoints through open discussion.

It was not only with regard to mates and other romantic partners that the respondents regarded themselves as good communicators. The ability to have open communication with one's children was a critical aspect of family life for respondents who valued their identities as loving parents. In particular, these respondents regarded as an important sign of their effectiveness as parents the fact that their children felt free to come to them with problems:

Q: Please describe your family.
R: Well, I've got three daughters, two of which are in college, one is in high school, and we're very close. Um, I think they confide in me an awful lot, they confide in me and my wife, and they seem to be a lot closer than some of my friends' children.

* * *

Q: Why is your family important to you?
R: ... We are that kind of family. Caring. And that's very important to us, and I'm very happy that I know my kids can come to me or my wife with anything at all and get some attention and sometimes even reasonable solutions to all kinds of problems. . . . If there's a big problem we don't get all that excited about it. We work it out. And no one starts using diatribes or anything like that . . .

The explicit meaning of these statements is that the parents are able to help their children. The implicit message, though, is that these parents regarded their children's willingness to talk to them as concrete evidence of how loving the respondents were in making their children feel comfortable and open with them.

It is interesting that there is one feature about communication notably lacking in both of these statements. The men who provided these answers did not refer at all to communication with their wives as an important part of their identities as loving family members. Working things through with their children and having their children feel free to come to them with problems was a main focus of their family identity. Since their wives were never mentioned in the interview, it is not possible to know whether the husbands were taking for granted a good relationship or trying to avoid talking about an unhappy one. In any event, it would appear that their relationships with their wives were an insignificant aspect of their identities compared to their relationships with their children.

An identity as a person who was capable of engaging in open communication also extended to family members other than spouse and children. The following excerpt describes a respondent's perception of his ability to communicate well in his relationship with his brother:

Q: Do you have any questions or doubts about how you feel being a brother?
R: No, no.
Q: Why not?
R: Well, as I said before, we get along together so well. Some brothers don't get together for 15, 20 years, or every time they see each other is at a death. I see my brother at, on the average of maybe 2, 3 times a week. I feel lucky. If we do have a problem we talk about it with each other. This is the way we settle things. I think it's a good relationship . . .

His brother's interest in getting together with him provides this respondent with direct evidence for his own identity as a loving person. The respondent feels especially "lucky" in this regard because of his perception that most brothers do not have such frequent interactions. Not only does the respondent have the opportunity to interact with his brother and enjoy his company, but it reflects favorably upon his identity as a loving person to have a filial relationship that differs so strikingly from the norm.

All of the statements seen so far have been very favorable in tone and in the qualities of the relationship being described. It is possible that the respondents who produced these statements were biased by identity assimilation in the direction of providing a positive image of themselves. Identity assimilation would, then, be motivated by a desire to maintain one's identity as a loving person. Obviously, it is very reinforcing to one's family identity to see family members as responding to one's own ability to communicate well. However, there was no evidence in the excerpts themselves or in other parts of the interviews to question the accuracy of these respondents. If anything, their statements were quite specific, giving details to support their assertions of good communication with family members.

When it is based on a realistic appraisal of family experiences, the verification of one's lovingness received from interactions with spouses, children, and other relative constitutes identity accommodation. More difficult to accommodate to is the possibility that one might not be a loving person because communication with family members is either lacking or outwardly hostile. To counter the potential damage to identity that honest appraisal of such experiences would cause, the individual may engage in identity assimilation. This is what appears to be happening in the following excerpt from a man in his 30s who complained at great length about problems he was having with his wife. In this excerpt, he laments specifically about their failure to express their feelings toward one another:

Q: How important to you is your home life?
R: Oh, very. I'd like it to be a lot better than it is, you know, but we're working on what we can do. I mean, I can't go in somebody's head and straighten them out. I can't always find out what's bothering me, although I try.
Q: Well, what about it is important to you?
R: About it? That we show each other true love, you know, genuine love. Okay? And I try to do that all the time, and I know she does. But we have our idiosyncracies that both one another. Or a certain idiosyncracy stands in the way. But I don't like to get into arguments with people. I think that's important. You don't have arguments. . . . I like a calm relationship. I know you can't always have one, that's not always healthy, but you know, I think, you know, a loving-caring one, you know, help the other person, show an interest in what they're doing, a genuine interest.

It is important to this individual that he see himself as someone who can communicate in a "calm" way, showing love and care toward his wife. In order to maintain this identity, he engages in self-justification. Even though he admits to having certain "idiosyncracies," he presents himself as being more concerned than his wife about the quality of their communication.

This excerpt is useful in illustrating just how impossible it is to determine what "really" is happening in any one-sided view of the quality of a couple's communication. It is when one partner "blames" the other for shortcomings in the relationship that the potential for identity assimilation to be influencing the response becomes particularly apparent. In her study of married couples, Ebmeyer (1986) reported large differences between married partners who provided answers in separate interviews to a series of questions concerning their marriages to each other. Some of these disparities concerning the events that took place in their daily lives were so large that it was difficult to believe that the couples were really married to each other (Whitbourne & Weinstock, in press). Based on that study, any statements from one partner alone about a family situation must be regarded with great caution. The evidence that can be used to support the rating of self-justification from only one partner in a marriage may be found more in the overall tone of the response rather than in exactly what is said on a word-for-word basis. A series of extreme statements portraying the spouse as the cause of all the problems in the home, lazy, disputatious, and a consistently poor parent provide a basis for suspicion that the respondent is exaggerating.

Given this background, consider now what this same man troubled by lack of good communication with his wife had to say about the source of his marital difficulties:

R: . . . Um, my wife is a neatnick, and I can't put any fingerprints on the chrome. She'll open the door with a towel, right? And I'll go up to the refrigerator and open it, my hands will be clean, you know, maybe a little sweaty, you know, and she'll say "I'll get it." I know why she wants to do it. So I don't get fingerprints on it. Right? Well, that tends to make somebody, you know, instead of relaxed.

. . .

Q: Do you act differently (because of your marriage and home life)?

R: Take my shoes off when I come into the house. (laughs) I never used to. There's just little petty things, actually, nothing substantial. I think right now, other things like that, petty.

Q: Why do you do those things?

R: Oh, because my wife requests it. OK? Or something else. I wouldn't normally if I was living in a home . . . I come home from work on Sunday, I put on some eggs and bacon, alright? I wouldn't do that now. If I come home from work at 12:00 at night, I'm hungry, right. I would not necessarily go downstairs and have something to eat, a couple of sandwiches. A couple of times, my wife's gotten upset about that . . . Well, when someone starts yapping at you for, you know, something like that, you come home at night and want something to eat, she acts a little perturbed because you're getting something to eat. . . . I'm trying to overlook that. I'm trying to say to myself, "Well, I ate two good meals today." You know, put it on myself to overlook it.

Q: Do you ever question or doubt your marriage and home life as it is now?

R: . . . Yeah. You probably, you're in psychology, right? When you study neatness. She is a perfectionist. Neatnick, you know, right down the line!

Q: That's uncomfortable for you.

R: Yes, and then she calls me sloppy if I leave a book on the coffee table, right? I believe in being neat. You got to be, you can't be sloppy, the house has to be clean. But when you get to the point where you open the refrigerator door with the towel so you don't get fingerprints on the chrome, which you can't see because when you close the door, it would be a strip about that wide, you kind of wonder. . . . But like I say, I try to reason around it. You see, I'm the kind of person that doesn't want a rift.

This respondent then goes on to complain about his wife's neatness in areas of the home outside the kitchen (his desk, his workbench). While acknowledging his love for his wife, he clearly sees her as the source of his marital problems (and himself as the innocent victim). Although it is entirely plausible that his wife really is an obsessively neat woman, the respondent's attitude of professed innocence and understanding suggests that his perception of the situation is distorted in favor of his attempt to justify his identity as a "calm person" and a "loving" husband.

A more tempered form of identity assimilation appears in the following excerpt from a 29-year-old woman:

Q: Do you think a lot about it? (questions concerning relationship with husband)

R: No, I really don't. I just think there are times when you get angry, when I would get angry at my husband, and I think "Well, why do I stay here, anyhow? I could go and do this." But then, half an hour later you forget that you even thought that, and everything's all gone, and it's nothing permanent or eating at me that eventually will cause me problems.

Q: What in your situation keeps you from doing something else, having these doubts be larger?

R: I think it's probably 90% of the time I'm very happy. . . . It's not important enough and even when it does, it's not a serious consideration. Just a fleeting thing.

This respondent verges on using identity accommodation as a means of resolving her difficulties in communicating with her husband in admitting that there are problems at times. She is not portraying an overly rosy picture of their marriage in order to maintain her identity as a loving person. When she admits to getting angry, she is recognizing that there are flaws in her own behavior. It is when she dismisses the seriousness of the problem that she shows what appears to be the process of identity assimilation. By minimizing the extent of the unhappiness she is feeling, she is able to preserve her identity as a loving wife who is contented with and committed to her marital relationship. It would be too threatening to this identity to think seriously about the implications of her dissatisfaction with the relationship.

In contrast, a more intense scrutiny of the quality of her marriage was shown in the excerpt of an interview with a woman who was questioning how happy she was as a wife:

Q: You mentioned some questions about your relationship with your husband. Could you share those with me?

R: Well, uh, I don't know always if we, my husband and I, are happy or healthy in our relationship as we could be if we were in another situation. I sometimes wonder if we're a bit of a weight or problem in each other's life. I don't feel as close to him as I'd like to, um, but I think very highly of him as a person. . . . I feel very bad about the fact that I feel critical of him and the fact that I have recurrent bad dreams and I'm sure it must bother me a lot. I've talked sometimes to friends about this and I've talked in a negative or critical way, and when I've come home or he comes home and I'm very happy to see him. . .

Q: When you have questions about your relationship what do you tend to focus on?

R: Hm, well, I first try to determine if the current circumstances, what their part in my feelings are. I'm always examining myself and my own thoughts and motives, and I find that my pro and con feelings on most subjects change from day to day.

This respondent is clearly involved in an intense process of examining her relationship with her husband, her identity as a wife, and the seriousness of their problems, and is far from any kind of resolution. She is aware of problems in the quality of communication with her husband, and she shows no tendency to attribute all the fault to him. In fact, she acknowledges that he is not really a bad person by her statement that she is happy to see him. Moreover, rather than minimizing the extent of her dissatisfaction, she appears to be deeply involved in considering her ability to retain an identity as a loving person within the context of the relationship.

COMPANIONSHIP

Another feature of a relationship that is closely aligned with communication is companionship. Associated with companionship is the perception that family members are so close emotionally that they would continue to interact even if they were not legally bound to each other. The most extreme form of this sentiment is shown when the respondent actually states that the position in the family is not a "role" but that family interactions are voluntarily initiated. There was a cluster of statements (7% of all family responses) concerning the importance to family identity of the qualities of companionship and friendship, and almost three-quarters of these (72%) were in regard to the spouse. For the individuals who expressed this sentiment, then, their identity as a loving person also meant that they were a "liking" person who could be friendly with the important people in their lives.

Most of the responses within this category of statements had in them specific mention of and examples of the concepts of companionship and friendship. A typical statement in this category was "we are companions." Some of the respondents whose statements fell within this category in addition appeared to be attempting to go beyond traditional role definitions in their conceptions of themselves as family members, as revealed in the next three excerpts:

Q: How do you see yourself in the family, as a mother and a wife?
R: Yeah, I guess so.
Q: Well, is that how you picture yourself in the family, or how do you picture yourself as...?
R: Um, well, I guess it's as a mother and wife type of thing. Um, I guess we have a very, we have a very different relationship from, um, my husband and I are best friends first. Then I guess we get into the husband and wife business...
Q: How do you feel as a wife? How do you feel about being a wife?
R: Um, I guess, I don't know. I guess "wife"'s a kind of funny name. It should be more like a mate. Because "wife" I think incurs a feeling of duty and I don't feel that way. I feel like just a pair.

* * *

Q: Could you start off by telling me something about your marriage and its importance to you?
R: One of the big things I guess is the companionship of being with someone that you love, and sharing things with that person. Being a friend...
Q: ...Do you see your role in the marriage being a companion to your husband or do you think of yourself as a wife or how do you think of yourself within that relationship?
R: I think of myself as, I guess, his wife as well as closest friend. And I feel that I should, that I can talk with him about most things that I would not talk with anyone else. And I think, I don't think of it as a role, just fixing his meals, that type of thing. I think that's a very minor part of it and it's not the important area.

* * *

Q: What's important to you about being a father?
R: Well, I don't go along with a typical macho-type thing. I think it's, uh, the father should be participating in the household, belong in the house, cleaning out something. That it's someone they can relate to, that they don't have to be afraid of, can talk to. Be open, kind of loving. It's not some kind of dominant figure that you have to be afraid to go to, can talk with.

Being a "friend" to family members meant, to these respondents, that they were not bound by traditional role expectations of what a "wife" or a "father" was "supposed" to do. By seeing themselves in this manner, they could have the double benefit of living up to their own ideas of what a good and loving family member should be, and also have their identities as loving persons reinforced through reciprocation of their friendly attitudes. As with the positively toned statements regarding communication in family relationships, there is no way of knowing whether the respondents here were using identity assimilation to portray themselves in a favorable light. While there is no particular reason to doubt their veracity, the possibility must remain open that the respondents were leaving out evidence that would disconfirm their identities. Whether accurate or not, these respondents had, at least in their own minds, good reason to think that they were being successful in implementing their identities as "companions" to those they loved. The respondents felt good about themselves because they were at a point of equilibrium between their identities and their experiences within the family.

It is not only as a "friend" that an individual can define his or her identity as a loving family member. There also were respondents whose identity in the family was as a person who follows the guidelines for attitudes and behaviors dictated by a more conventional adoption of family roles. For these respondents, companionship and camaraderie were regarded as unimportant and perhaps detrimental to the quality of interactions in the family. They deliberately and resoundingly rejected any idea that they should relate to their families in any but the traditionally role-prescribed formats. Three men in particular took precisely the opposite position of the non-"macho" father quoted above, as exemplified in the following excerpt:

Q: What about your family is important to you?
R: Just that they are mine and I'm the king of them. It's one thing about my family; I'm the boss. What I say goes. If my wife doesn't agree with it then she will say "What about this?" and if I think that she has the better idea then I'll say "Okay, let's do it this way." I've got the last say in this family. What the kids want, they will come to me and ask for and if I think "Okay, let's give it to them," they'll get it. If I think it's a little bit out of hand I'll say "No."

It is doubtful that this man's wife or children regard him as a companion, given his assumption of the traditional male "head of the house" role. At the same time, he seems unconcerned about his family's interest in him as a friend because his identity as a loving family member is as one who dominates everyone else. As will be seen later, many women also expressed very traditional role-bound attitudes toward their family relationships, and both men and women often dwelt upon the theme of "responsibility." What is important about the above excerpt is that the individual's stereotyped definition of the male role actually precluded any thoughts of interacting as a friend or companion to his family members, but it did not detract from his identity as a father. His statement illustrates the importance of interpreting statements regarding identity from the perspective of each individual. Rather than impose a value judgment and label his statement as "old-fashioned," the statement must be examined from the standpoint of what kind of identity could have produced it. Despite what seems to the observer to be an overly narrow interpretation of the "father" role, to this respondent it is precisely this definition that enables him to derive an identity of himself as a loving family member.

Family Tasks and Responsibility

The statements by the adults in the sample about their families reflected the fact that more than love or even good relationships are needed in order to maintain an identity as a loving person. In addition, a loving family member must be able to run a household and provide an income to keep the family sheltered, fed, and clothed. The separation of role functions in the home from feelings toward family members implied by this distinction is a classic one in the family literature, going back to the writings of the sociologist Talcott Parsons (Parsons & Bales, 1956). More recently the dichotomy between intrinsic and extrinsic motivation for involvement in the family has been added (LaRossa & LaRossa, 1981). When an individual wants to engage in an activity because of intrinsic motivation, it is because he or she is interested in the activity itself and not in the rewards that may ensue. In contrast, extrinsic motivation is directed at seeking results because of the rewards that these results will bring.

As applied specifically to the family, intrinsic motivation is expressed as concern for the feelings of family members and a desire to maintain good relationships. Closeness, communication, and companionship may all be regarded as intrinsically motivating facets of family life. In order to be intrinsic, furthermore, the motivation must apply specifically to family members as individual people with their own unique qualities. Involvement in the practical affairs of family life is, in contrast, an extrinsic factor of family identity. Extrinsic motivation is not directed at family members as people. Instead, the family members are regarded as occupants of given positions within the family such as "mother," "husband," and "child." In addition, when extrinsic motivation is primary, the individual is preoccupied with considerations of equity; that is, "getting something" in return for the contributions and sacrifices made on behalf of family members (Walster et al., 1978).

The intrinsic-extrinsic distinction is useful not only as a basis for categorizing statements about the family, but also as a basis for understanding family identity. An adult whose identity in the family is determined by the ability to meet intrinsic needs may be thought of as more psychologically involved than an adult who is trying to fulfill extrinsic needs only. The intrinsic qualities of family life have the potential to negate or confirm the adult's identity as a person who is "loving" in the sense of being able to communicate and share close feelings. In addition, when family members are regarded as important for the intrinsic reason that they are loved as individuals, their rejection or acceptance cannot be readily exchanged for the reactions of others.

On the other hand, if the adult's involvement in the family is based on the extrinsic motivation to provide for the material comfort of family members, an identity as a loving person can be obtained by "buying" their outward affection. There is little of the emotional intensity of a relationship based on feelings. Even more important, from the standpoint of identity, an extrinsically based relationship holds little potential threat to the individual's basic sense of self-worth. If the person's identity is defined as one who can fulfill the material needs of the family, then the affection of family members can be won regardless of how loving or unloving the person really is. There will be no reason for the individual to ponder his or her fundamental sense of worth as a person with a particular psychological makeup. Similarly, if one's family members have little significance as individuals, their role can be filled by someone else should the relationship not work out satisfactorily. The individual does not run the risk of having his or her identity as a loving person contradicted by the experience of rejection.

Although it is a useful way of thinking about family identity, the intrinsic-extrinsic distinction often became blurred in the analysis of actual statements made by the respondents in the present sample. Many respondents appeared to be intrinsically motivated to perform their "extrinsic" duties within the home and family. Rather than regarding household duties and responsibilities simply as necessary evils, selfless and loving attention was lavished on the tasks involved in cooking, cleaning, providing financial support, and attending to the needs of children. These tasks therefore became an additional way that the individual could verify that he or she was a loving person.

HOUSEHOLD TASKS

A number of respondents described in a matter-of-fact way their need to fulfill their family roles by managing their house and home life. The household tasks these respondents mentioned included the predictable ones of cleaning, laundering, cooking, grocery shopping, and home maintenance. To the extent that these statements are focused on fulfilling a range of duties and obligations they may be regarded as purely based on extrinsic motivation. The respondents who offered these descriptions of what was important to them about their families were clearly focused on carrying out family roles rather than on the quality of emotional relationships with family members. However, almost half of the statements, using a conservative estimate, were not so clearly extrinsic. The following examples illustrate some of these mixed intrinsic and extrinsic statements:

Q: Perhaps you could tell me something about your family and home.
R: ... (describes family)... I like my little old house; it isn't fantastic, but I like it. It's very important to me. This backyard, all the flowers and the garden; that's important to me.
Q: Do you put family and home together?
R: I think I do.

This respondent then goes on to answer questions concerning the importance of being a mother and a wife, and in both cases includes her feelings about the house itself as a physical entity. These answers show that, for her, performing family functions is an expression of her identity as a loving wife:

Q: What is important about being a wife?
R: ...I have my two lovely kids, and my husband of course, whom I love very much, and I like cooking and ironing his clothes and keeping the house nice and neat.

The respondent who provided this statement is not a full-time homemaker. Unlike the full-time homemakers in the sample, her responses would not seem to be a simple function of her need to feel competent as a worker (see Chapter 8). Instead, this respondent appears to derive satisfaction from performing her tasks in the home because they are a way of showing how much she loves her family and the house in which they share a family life. A similar blending of role performance and feelings was also found among men:

Q: Do you think your involvement with your family affects the things that you do in your everyday life?
R: Sure does. Definitely.
Q: Could you give me some examples?
R: ...I maintain a house, and work around the house to keep a good place for a family to develop.

The performance of household chores may, then, carry with it emotional connotations involving intrinsic motivation. By maintaining a well-run and well-equipped home, the adult can feel that he or she is carrying through on obligations that involve both emotional and practical components. It is not enough for an adult to feel loving toward the family; it is also important to the adult to feel that the family's needs to have shelter, food, and clothing are being met. As will become more and more evident throughout the analyses to follow, the normal adult has gone beyond the romantic notion of what the adolescent thinks "love" is about. Love involves feelings, but it also involves accepting responsibility for loved ones.

MONEY

In the field of occupational psychology, the desire to work for money is regarded as one of the most clear-cut forms of extrinsic motivation that exists. In the context of family life, though, the role of money and related financial factors can have a much more ambiguous character. Having adequate income has been found to relate favorably to marital satisfaction in general (Renne, 1970) and more specifically to the traditional wife's happiness with her husband (Scanzoni, 1970). Although not a particularly large category of responses, statements concerning money were found, in the present group of adults, to share many of the intrinsically oriented qualities of household tasks. In addition, there was a sex difference, with more statements from men (11) than women (5) in which money was described as an important component of family identity.

There were several undercurrents running through the statements concerning money that, with such a small total number, may have been totally idiosyncratic to the sample. Nevertheless, they provide useful material with which to demonstrate the intertwining of intrinsic and extrinsic factors within family identity. One cluster of responses expressed satisfaction with the financial state of the family. The fact that there was no economic "strain" seemed to contribute to the enjoyment of family relationships. A good example of this type of response is the following:

Q: Do you ever have any questions or wonder about this kind of relationship? Is it the best one to have, or,?

R: I don't know. I've never given it any thought. I guess it's comfortable. You know, when things are comfortable, you don't worry about them, you don't wonder about them and say "Hey, you know, is that the best kind of relationship?"... And my kids never dunned me for money they didn't need. There were times when my son was in college and he was working full-time as a salesman and I'd say to him "Do you need any money for books?" And he'd say "No, I've got money in my account." And I'd say "Well, how about tuition?" "Gee, I think I can cover this next semester." So, you know, we never got sucked in, and my kids never became dependent on us in terms of support, financial support. Yeah, they still feel, hey, they can call on the old man and ask for a little bit of advice, you know, that kind of thing, um, so I've never felt that I've had any kind of reason to feel that this is not a good relationship because my two kids never have taken advantage of me. My daughter was the same way . . .

Apart from the fact that this respondent's son and daughter sound like the ideal kind of adolescent children to have, it is clear that his freedom from financial strain contributed to this man's good feelings about his relationship with them. In addition, his children's ability to support themselves independently seemed to verify this respondent's identity as a loving father who raised his children well.

In contrast, respondents who felt financially pressured reported either less positive feelings toward family members or appeared to be in varying states of personal or marital distress. Three respondents who were not as lucky as the man in the previous example were faced with economic burdens in trying to support their children through college. Two others described the marital problems that stemmed from their perceived financial pressures, as can be seen from this excerpt:

Q: Do you have a questions or doubts about your family situation, about being a father or a husband?

R: Uh, well, the only thing I worry about, I'll tell you the truth is financial, that is about the only thing. I mean, every month you're scraping trying to pay the bills and if you get sick you gotta come up with this or that, then there's always a bill you don't know about. That's about the only thing that gets me ticked off, about being married, 'cause there's only one income . . .

Q: Does that, or anything else, lead you to question whether or not you want to remain married, or, uh, change the marriage in any significant way?

R: Yeah, uh, sometimes when we were, yeah, I've had my, my, uh, blowups and I've gotten mad but like I've said, it's mostly economical. It's not that I, you know, don't love her or whatever. It's just the natural thing. It's the economic, it's the pressure of not having the money to . . . Not, not that you don't have the money to pay the bills. You pay your bills, but then you can't do anything. You don't have the money to go out or do this or do that and you just stay home, you know, and after a while it's a grind, 'cause you know you're home all night long.

Perhaps less serious in some ways but obviously a source of unhappiness was the following respondent's frustration over his inability to buy a new car for himself:

Q: Please start by describing your family.

R: . . . I probably would've had more children but financially the way things are now and so on and so forth, there's only one income in the house. That's mine. . . . I couldn't support more than 5 people. . . . We're getting along, as I say, paying my bills, and so on and so forth. You know, we don't have a lot of money in our pocket to spend every week, you know, but as I say, we're getting by. I don't buy new automobiles. I'm 38 years old, I haven't owned a new car in my life! Most people my age have had 5, 6, or 8 new cars. I've always had used cars. Those two cars out there right now are, um, uh, combined age of about 24 years old. . . . As I say, maybe that's, a lot of people do tie money up in snowmobiles, boats, a lot of people own a lot of camping equipment, you know. I don't. Maybe this is the reason I can just have one income in this house and have ends meet, you know.

These statements exemplify the "life cycle squeeze" (Oppenheimer, 1981) of men whose children are making heavy financial demands upon them at the same time that their careers are providing insufficient income to keep pace with these demands. Both of these respondents had, in some ways, placed themselves in their present predicament, because they preferred not to have their wives work when there were small children in the home. This desire was expressed by several other men, also with a good deal of ambivalence because the consequence was recognized to be an increase in pressure upon the husband to support the family.

The statements of these respondents can be interpreted as indicating the strength of their family identities as traditional male breadwinners. In order to regard themselves as loving husbands and fathers, it was necessary for them to be the sole wage earner in the house. Their use of self-justification to maintain this identity was evident in their description of what they had to sacrifice for the sake of their family. It may have been necessary for them to use identity assimilation because an honest appraisal of their situations might have forced an unwanted change from their present identities. To admit that they were incapable of supporting their families would have threatened to destroy the very basis for their identities as loving husbands and fathers.

CARING FOR CHILDREN

In Chapter 5 it will be shown that a large share of the adult's identity as a loving person is determined by his or her ability to provide for the support of children's physical and psychological well-being. As described in this way, caring for children is a largely intrinsically oriented realm of family identity. A more extrinsic form of motivation regarding the care of children is that they should be well-disciplined at home and not engage in behavior outside the home that reflects badly on the parents. In this sense, the adult's identity as a loving parent is focused less on the emotional relationships with children and more on the outcome of having raised them properly. In addition, when the adult's identity as a loving parent is determined by how well-disciplined the children are perceived to be, the children are encouraged to suppress rather than express their own particular personalities. However, as with family tasks and money, discipline is not an entirely extrinsic proposition.

There were a substantial number (6%) of statements concerning discipline, with a larger representation of woman (16) than men (7). Of these statements, there was a cluster expressing the respondent's desire that the children should "grow up right." The word "right" was rarely defined in any detail in this context. However, many respondents provided explanations of what they believed to be the "right" behavior to teach children in the Values section of the interview (see Chapter 10). If it is assumed that the respondents were concerned with keeping their children out of "trouble" and with maintaining proper codes of behavior for the sake of social acceptance, then the statements concerning discipline may be regarded as extrinsically motivated. However, the respondents often expressed more complicated concerns than these. Scattered through the responses in this category, though, were words and phrases that had strongly intrinsic connotations:

Q: How does your family affect the way you feel about yourself?
R: I feel that I'm here for them. . . . Especially with the children, trying to guide them right just through my own experiences as growing up as a child and what I have experienced and hoping that some of the good things will happen to them that happened to me, hoping the bad things that did happen to me won't happen to them, so I try to guide them that way.

The feeling of caring evident in this response is implied in the respondent's hope that the children do not make mistakes. The respondent's identity as a loving parent in this case includes the desire that the children be happy. In addition, the key word "right" in this statement does imply that it is also important to this respondent's identity that the children measure up to an external standard of behavior. In this regard, the statement is also extrinsically focused.

Interpreting statements made about the outcomes of a parent's attempts to raise children is an extremely complicated endeavor. Obviously, it is in the best interest of the parent to describe the result of disciplinary efforts in a positive light because this will reflect favorably on the parent's identity. It is natural, then, for parents to be biased toward regarding their children as having, in fact, turned out "right" regardless of how this is defined. A more reflective self-evaluation would also include some hints that the current product of one's disciplinary efforts may have some flaws. Identity assimilation may, then, be used in order to protect the individual's identity as a loving parent from this revelation. The general defensive tone and lack of specificity in the following excerpt suggest that the respondent is attempting to maintain her identity as a loving parent through such a process of identity assimilation:

Q: Do you have any questions or doubts about yourself as a mother or about the importance of that to you?
R: No, I don't think so. I think I'm doing what I'm supposed to do.
Q: And you yourself? How do you feel about it?
R: I feel like I'm doing a good job.

Who is to know whether the respondent is in fact doing a "good job"? The respondent provides no details that would support her assertion. In addition, her rigid approach to her identity as someone who is doing what she is "supposed" to do suggests that she has not stopped to evaluate whether or not she has been able to implement her identity successfully.

Added to a sense of having been successful within the family may be an enhanced feeling of self-importance, as the one who makes the difference in having the lives of the other family members come out well:

Q: What is it about staying home that's important to you?
R: It just makes me feel like I'm doing something, you know, important to me. It's more important to stay home and take care of the kids.

* * *

Q: How does your family affect the way that you feel about yourself?
R: Oh, very much so. I know they think the absolute world of me from absolute crazy to "I know that Mom will come through" or "Mom will do this." "Oh gee, I need my pants ironed today." From the very little things all the way up. They would be very upset if something happened in this family and I no longer was here for one reason or another. When you know your family thinks you're the greatest, well, you feel terrific, you always feel terrific. And this is from outside all the way in, too.

It is possible that these respondents are reporting accurately on situations within the family, and that their families really do regard them as important. The second respondent in particular reports some details, in fact, that would support her assertion of self-importance. To the extent that these statements are consistent with the "reality" of their experiences in the family, they would be regarded as evidence for identity accommodation. However, both statements verge on the egocentric. The first respondent seems to regard her feelings of importance as more crucial than the well-being of her children. The second statement represents a perspective in which the respondent's point of view is used to make inferences about how other people feel. For these reasons, the statements appear to represent identity assimilation in which the respondent is attempting to present and preserve an identity that is biased toward a favorable self-representation.

Statements concerning discipline may also reflect an identity assimilation process when they reflect a lack of flexibility or willingness to consider any other way of raising children. The following example is a good illustration of defensive rigidity in the area of discipline:

Q: Are there other areas of your family life that you question or wonder about?

R: Um, not really. I feel comfortable with the aspects of bringing up the kids, answering their questions and providing guidance. I never really felt very strongly about being their "pal" kind of thing. I always felt that I took the more authoritative approach. I'm the leader of the family at least from the male side of the house and I felt comfortable with that.

Q: Do you think there may be a time when you'd consider an alternative way of looking at it?

R: No, not actually.

Q: Do you think there's anything that might keep you from considering an alternative?

R: No. Never had the need to consider an alternative. But I don't just offhand think of any reason that would prevent me.

Q: Do you think there is anything that might cause you to look at things differently?

R: No. You only go through this thing, although we probably went through it more with seven children than people with one or two. Because each child coming along is going to go through the same basic things. So, we've been through it, you might say, seven times, on the average. I think we did things about the same each time and, uh, I don't expect to have the opportunity again to bring up children at my age [early 50s], so I haven't really thought much about doing it differently.

This man regarded himself as the "leader" in the family, and did not allow his authoritative identity to be challenged by the individual needs of any of his seven children. Such an unusual degree of resistance to change could only have been accomplished by an identity dominated by the extrinsic motivation to have children conform to an ideal of exemplary behavior rather than by sensitivity to the intrinsic qualities of parent-child relationships.

Other respondents showed a different form of defensive rigidity, resolving whatever doubts they did have about their effectiveness by "closing off the debate":

Q: Do you have any doubts or questions about being a mother?

R: Oh, don't we all at one time or another?

Q: Would you share some of those with me?

R: Oh, I don't know. When the kids do something that you don't think should be done, you wonder, what did you do wrong? But then you have to stop and think that they're another person, and you're not the end of it all. Know what I mean?

This respondent was able to circumvent an identity accommodation process of evaluating her identity as a loving parent by telling herself that she was not to blame for their transgressions. Another respondent reached the same conclusion about her approach to parenting and attitudes toward what is "right," but after a very different series of events had transpired:

Q: How do you feel about being a mother?

R: I have mixed feelings about that. Right now I feel better about it than I have at other times. My oldest daughter, because she has, um, a lot of problems, you always wonder as a parent how much did you contribute to it or what could you have done about your children's life. But I have gotten over some of that because I've even in the past talked to counselors and things and one thing I did find out was that you can't spend the rest of your life blaming yourself for it and maybe you couldn't have done anything about it anyhow. So, right now in a lot of ways I feel good about it just because the way both girls and I are getting along. We seem to be able to talk, there are some problems, but we still seem to be able to communicate, and work things out.

Q: It sounds like you've been able to get past some rough spots.

R: Yeah, well, life is different now today. Things that I was brought up to believe children don't necessarily believe. You're beating your head against the wall if you keep resisting and say "No, you can't do that because I don't think it's right."

Not only was the conflict with her daughter resolved through a process of identity accommodation (with the help of a counselor), but this respondent continues to make an honest evaluation of her identity as a parent. It is this accommodation process that allows her to admit there are problems and to be willing to listen to, if not accept, a new set of beliefs.

Another situation that involved the individual's evaluation of his identity as a parent occurred with a man who was coping with the delinquent behavior of his 16-year-old stepdaughter:

Q: I'd like to ask you to describe your family for me.

R: Um, I have a wife. I've been married 20 years as of this Tuesday, got married at 31 years old, um, my wife was married before, we have a child who will be 16 years old on Friday. It's her child. We have had an inordinate amount of trouble and problems with her. She has been in foster homes, she has been through a special program at the hospital which is the assistance in essence for teenage pregnancy type situations, she has been in jail, she had some problems early in her life with drugs. Eleven, twelve years old, for almost the last 4 years of our life it has been almost constant chaos. A lot of problems . . . We had thrown the child out of the house originally, she was 13, we have a child of our own who will be 7 in July, June. . . . My honest opinion is that I'm a very good father, pretty easy going guy normally. I seem to get along with people very well, after all the soul searching, visiting psychologists, psychiatrists, chief assholes like Dr. Barney Solomon at the hospital, we realized that we were fairly healthy and that the obvious reasons for the child's problems were certainly possibly divorce, but the guilt trip wasn't there as we saw it. It wasn't as bad as we thought, what we originally accused ourselves of, I've had the child since she was 3, 4, um, we as a family are now operating, um, full foursome, Merilee who is my oldest daughter has been home with us for a year now and we really get along pretty well.

Part of this respondent's description of his family problems (where he describes what a "good guy" he is) may involve identity assimilation. On the other hand, if he really did undergo serious family therapy it is possible that he reached this conclusion through identity accommodation, as was true for the respondent in the previous example.

Frank admission of doubt regarding identity as a good parent was apparent in statements by other respondents whose questioning was not stimulated by such drastic events. The apparent candor with which they examined their effectiveness as parents suggests the use of identity accommodation, as can be seen in the following excerpt:

Q: How does having a family affect the way you feel about yourself?

R: Well, through them I see, I see a lot of myself. I see, um, I see how they pick up things that I do that I don't like. They are almost like a mirror. You know, whether it would be they'll say things verbally that they may have heard me say and come back and say it and make me stop in my tracks. I'll say "Whoa," you know, "somehow I'm leading them the wrong way." You know, at this stage of the game. They do help me back up and regroup. I do use them as, I do use them as a mirror. You know, I can see, I can see a lot of my mannerisms coming out through them that I may not like. You know, and I'll try to stand back and watch them and see which way it's heading. And see how I'm affecting them.

For this woman, questions regarding her effectiveness as a parent led to a piercing examination of the foundations of her identity not only as a parent but more generally as a good person. Another respondent, similarly questioning his effectiveness as a parent, stressed that occasional examination of his identity as a father was beneficial to himself and also to his children:

Q: Do you ever have any doubts about your marriage and family?

R: Yes, um hmm. I do sometimes wonder, I'd only be kidding myself if I thought everything was perfect, because it isn't. I'm human. I make mistakes. The same thing, children, they don't always agree with what I may say or do, we kind of doubt our relationship sometimes. But it's like everything else. You have to question things to be sure that everything is operating smoothly.

This sentiment contrasts sharply with that of other respondents, whose identity was not as open to examination as long as there were no obvious problems: "When things are comfortable, you don't worry about them, you don't wonder about them." Even without an overt crisis involving the misbehavior of one's children, it is still possible for identity accommodation to lead to a critical examination of one's ability to fulfill the identity of a loving parent.

RESPONSIBILITY

As noted earlier, words regarding the family that were frequently mentioned but rarely defined were "love," and bringing the children up "right." Another words used in the same way was "responsibility." Of the 7 women and 13 men who used this word in describing an aspect of their family identities, only 7 elaborated further with a brief phrase. One of these was a fairly ironic remark concerning responsibility found in the following interview of a mother with two school-age children:

R: . . . you know, you're, parenting is not easy. You know, and I tell my husband, you say it's going to be for the rest of your life. Nobody ever said that. This bundle of joy is going to be for the rest of your life . . .

A more commonplace version of this same idea was expressed by another woman: "Once that first child comes, once a mother, always a mother." The idea that one's life is permanently altered by the responsibility associated with becoming a parent is one that will be treated at great length in Chapter 5, because it is such a basic feature of parenthood. For the present purposes, it is useful to consider the meaning that "responsibility" has in relation to the adult's identity as a loving person. Like the other categories of "extrinsic" motivations in family relationships, it can also have an intrinsic meaning.

Responsibility to one's family represents a significant investment of time, energy, and money. To take on the responsibility of having a family means that one's own needs and interests often must take second place to the needs and interests of others. One way that adults manage to maintain this exacting obligation over time is through the way that they redefine responsibility as an expression of their feelings toward the family. Being able to fulfill one's responsibility to the family therefore becomes not an obligation but a way to show caring. To the closeness of one's emotional relationships in the family as a source of one's identity as a loving person therefore is added the extent of one's ability to take on the responsibility of a family. Another way that responsibility can take on a more intrinsic quality is if it is seen as a way to foster relationships with people in the family who are valued as individuals:

Q: What is important to you about being a mother?
R: Well, I guess the word is responsibility. A lot of people say it's my responsibility. I have to. I don't feel that way. I mean, it's my responsibility, I want to. You know, there's a different feeling about it. I took on the role of a mother gladly. I wanted to, I was excited about the whole idea of bringing kids up and could I do it . . . as time went on it became less of an ego trip and more of "Hey, this is really fun. I'm enjoying these people that my husb—they're people and I'm really enjoying helping them . . .

The description of the change in her attitude toward responsibility from regarding it as an "ego trip" to regarding it as an enjoyable experience suggests that the respondent went through a process of identity accommodation with respect to this aspect of her family identity. By frankly admitting that she enjoyed carrying out her responsibility, she also avoided the tendency to use self-justification as a means of elevating the importance of her position in the family. In contrast, others raised the importance of commitment to the family to such a high position that it became their entire mission in life. The woman in the following excerpt shows this extreme form of commitment:

Q: Do you think that being a mother has any effect on the way you see yourself?
R: I'd say you get so used to thinking about others, I can't say I stop and consider too much my feelings on things.
Q: Would that be true, then, in terms of being a wife?
R: Yeah, I would say.

It is very likely that an individual who goes to such an extreme in her sense of responsibility to the family is using defensive rigidity to avoid engaging in introspection regarding her feelings about her identity. By not thinking too deeply about herself, she can protect her identity from threats that would result from discovering through self-evaluation any weaknesses or flaws.

In another case, a judgment that identity assimilation is being used comes from the respondent's description of what appears to be a misplaced sense of obligation. This was the case of a woman whose youngest child was 18, but who stated as her reason for not working outside the home her family's need for her to be "available whenever needed." It is doubtful that her 18-year-old son or any of the other children, all in their 20s, were in need of her constant availability. Subsequent responses made during the interview reinforce the rating of self-justification:

Q: Is there anything that would cause you to question or doubt your commitment to and sense of responsibility toward your children?
R: If anything, I'm more convinced than ever that I did the right thing.

This respondent's strong sense of conviction may be a shield protecting her from self-doubts regarding her decision to maintain a traditional feminine identity as a wife and mother. Another respondent used a somewhat different approach to rationalize her own recent decision to quit her job after becoming a first-time mother. Her own identity as a loving mother was given support by her negative portrayal of the situations facing the children of women who are employed outside the home:

Q: You're not considering going back to work (after the baby is born)?
R: No. I come from a huge family and I have nieces and nephews that are like six months to two years younger than me . . . I've watched them being raised every possible way from the people that go to work two weeks right after the baby, to I have a sister who didn't want anything else after she was married than to have children. And I'm really convinced that for the first years, at least until my kids go to school, that I would like one of us, and that turns out to be me, that's the best alternative, to be with them. I don't want someone else to raise our children . . .

It is likely that this respondent's sense of responsibility for the raising of her children is what causes her to view the children of her relatives in a negatively biased fashion. Although the biased interpretation of the behaviors of others is found in cases of identity projection, the woman in this excerpt does not appear to be using this form of identity assimilation. It is not so much that she wishes to be doing what working women are doing as that she is seeking to justify her own decision to fulfill her identity as a loving mother by taking on the full-time responsibility for her child's care.

A woman in precisely the opposite set of circumstances, in contrast, was questioning her prior identity as a loving parent who allowed her sense of responsibility to dominate her identity. This woman was in the process of having her children "launched" from the home. As a result of this experience, the respondent was undergoing a process of identity accommodation regarding her identity as a mother:

Q: How do you feel about being a mother?
R: It's a big job. I really have to be honest and say that it was all-consuming for me. And I don't know if that's good. I really don't. I don't think it's good, because when it's all

said and done, maybe I wouldn't be having the hard time I'm having today if I wasn't consumed with it. Maybe the girls today are right. They've got the job and the children. I think it must be awfully hard for them because I had the five boys. I don't how I could have held a job down too.

This respondent was also questioning her present responsibility to her husband as a feature of her family identity:

R: At times I feel like I would like to be alone and not have to do for anybody, not even my husband. Not to have to cook for my husband. We're married 31 years in September. That was everything. My whole life. I don't begrudge it. That's basically the type of person that I am; I was. But now sometimes I think I would just like to be by myself. Take care of me. Be able to support myself. Just be my own "man," which I haven't been.

The change in identity that was currently taking place, or at least being contemplated, was reflected in her correction of the statement "I am" to "I was." Whether or not she actually were to make a change, the main feature within her response that suggests the use of identity accommodation is the seriousness with which she is evaluating her identity as a loving mother and considering alternative ways to balance responsibility toward herself with her responsibility to her family.

The Dual Nature of Family Identity

The analyses in this chapter of statements concerning relationships and responsibilities within the family have shown that the adult's identity as a "loving" person goes far beyond the conventional meaning of the word "love." The adult's identity as a loving person is a mixture of the intrinsic qualities involving closeness, communication, and companionship with the set of extrinsic functions through which adults provide for the material and social needs of their families. While these two sets of qualities have a certain degree of independence, they are very much interwoven in reports by adults of the nature of their family involvements. In addition, because both sets of qualities evoke the processes of assimilation and accommodation they each have the power to define and transform a significant share of the adult's identity.

4
Men and Women in the Family

It is assumed by many workers in adult development and related fields that emotional relationships in the family have greater significance to women than to men (e.g., Rubin, 1983). In particular, it is argued that the greater biological and social role involvement of women in parenthood leads to greater psychological investment in the raising and nurturing of children (Rossi, 1984). This investment is presumed to originate during pregnancy and remain high for the duration of the woman's life. A very different picture of men as fathers is emerging, though, as part of the outpouring of research on sex roles that began in the late 1970s. These studies portray men as being keenly affected by their interactions with their children (e.g., Cath, Gurwitt, & Ross, 1982). In part, the studies on fathering may be reflecting changes in society as a whole associated with the feminist movement. Men are being given greater encouragement and freedom to develop as parents through vehicles such as paternity leaves and the awarding of joint custody in divorce cases.

Rather than assume that interest in fathering is a recent phenomenon, it seems equally likely that the importance of fathering to the man's identity as a loving person really did exist but was largely neglected by social scientists. As is evident from the responses to the Adult Identity Interview, men throughout the entire adult age range studied were at least as deeply involved as women in the family domain. The responses of men and women were no different in terms of the importance or the meaning of parenthood to their identities. There were variations between sexes in the subtler delineations of some of the categories of responses, but these were differences in shades of meaning rather than the degree of significance of the family to adult identity.

Family Networks

Although closeness is generally thought of as a feature of a romantic relationship, the more common use of the term closeness among members of the present sample was in the context of a network of family relationships extending to children, parents, siblings, and in-laws. Closeness as used in this sense meant "close-knit," or being bound by strong interdependencies that often served to benefit the individual:

Q: Could you describe your family for me?

R: My wife and child are the most important to me . . . The rest of my family, brothers and sisters, try to stay as close knit as we can. You're going to need somebody's help at one time or another and it's nice to have somebody close enough so you can ask without feeling bad about it or something like that.

Q: It's basically your wife, your son, brothers and sisters.

R: Also her and my parents and sisters and brothers. I think we should stay as close-knit as possible.

Several other respondents also described close relationships with extended family members that seemed to be as important for the benefits they provided as for the feelings that the respondents had toward these people as individuals:

Q: Why is your family important to you?

R: This takes everybody in, too. Joe's mother and his family in (name of nearby town) my mother and sisters and brother, the whole bit, it's kind of the small town idea. Everybody knowing everybody and supporting everybody whether you're right or wrong, whether you have problems or whether you don't have any problems. Just knowing that other people really care about what you do. And how you treat your children and how your children are coming and how your husband treats you and how you treat your husband, without interfering, but just to know that support is always there. Gee, I think it's schmaltzy, but just plain old love, you know? It's there from the whole family out. You're not just this inner circle, you're everybody, and that's the most important.

* * *

Q: Could you describe your family situation?

R: . . . We live next to my in-laws. They do baby-sitting. We see them on a daily basis. They eat supper here, so it's a frequent relationship. We do a lot of things together. We try to spend as much time as we can. We try not to get overly involved with other activities, without taking away from them.

Q: What is important to you about that?

R: Well, they're a real resource. We can get a lot of information, opinions, they're willing to give their opinions, they'll accept our decisions, even if it isn't what they thought we should do. Our boys have really been able to spend a lot of time with them. It's extra attention that probably most children don't get, not being next to their in-laws.

Q: Does your relationship with your in-laws affect the way you see yourself?

R: Yeah, they give some food for thought. It kind of gives you a different perspective, because they've been there. They're sort of looking at it from the other part of the hill. You reflect on something a little bit differently.

What these examples illustrate is that adults in middle life can be considerably aided by closeness to and the availability of family members from the older generation. This observation stands in direct contrast to the more commonly accepted belief that adults in the "middle" generation between children and grandparents are overwhelmed by their dual responsibilities (e.g., Alpert & Richardson, 1980). However, in the following case, the relationship with in-laws was at times too close for comfort:

Q: Does the relationship affect your everyday life? You mentioned they come over.

R: There's some scheduling, and they're in and out at any time, so you might have to be a little wary that someone can walk in at any time. My folks do walk in at any time. We're kind of a very loose and open house, it's like living in the Waltons. (laughs)

Close relationships with extended family members were not only seen in relation to how they could benefit the individual. The next respondent emphasized the sense of responsibility he felt toward his mother-in-law, without alluding to any practical advantages for himself:

Q: How do you feel about being a son-in-law?
R: Well, very good. She's an invalid. She's been in a wheelchair about 25 years now and she's been living with me for about 20 and, uh, I feel it's my responsibility to take care of her. She's part of the family.
Q: How does that make you feel about yourself?
R: Very good, I think I'm doing something. I mean, uh, to me somebody has to take care of, uh, older people, and I feel just great, you know. Not that it's my burden or anything; it's my responsibility. It's just something I think that I should do. It's sort of right, too.

Even without any tangible rewards, the sense of responsibility toward the older family generation was a source of gratification rather than strain for this man. This sense of responsibility seemed to be a direct outgrowth of the respondent's feelings that a family should be close and depend on each other.

The general thesis of this chapter, that men are at least involved in their families as are women, received strong support in this area of extended intergenerational family networks. If anything, the findings supported the opposite conclusion; that men were more likely than women to define their identities in terms of extended family relationships. Many more men (14) than women (5) mentioned a family member other than a spouse or a child as being important to them and they did so in great depth. It is possible that relationships with parents and in-laws were taken for granted by the women in the sample whereas the men were adapting more to their relationships with their wives' parents. Another possibility is that for the women in the sample, their relationships with their husbands and children were so all-encompassing that relationships with parents and others paled in significance. In either event, the finding that the closeness of the family network was of greater centrality to the family identity of men than women is a direct challenge to the usual conclusions found in the research literature that is based on survey statistics. It is possible that the present results are a function of the intensive interview technique used. A more in-depth exploration of men's feelings about their families may be needed to detect the importance to their identities as loving people of their extended family relationships.

Centrality of the Family Identity

Quite apart from the intensity of feelings that the individual has toward family members is the extent to which the family dominates the adult's total identity as a person. An individual might feel very strongly about his or her children but segment them off in importance from other areas of life, with other issues being more central to his or her total identity. A category of statements specifically concerning centrality was found in the interview responses that encompasses the extent to which respondents define their identities in terms of their relationships with family members. This was a relatively prevalent category, including 17% of the total responses. Consistent with the thesis of this chapter, it was also a theme expressed almost frequently by men and women.

IMPORTANCE

The most obvious indicator of centrality is the respondent's overt statement that his or her identity is dominated by the position within the family. The response "I'm a family person" and "I'm a father first" concisely expressed this sentiment. In other cases, the importance of family to identity was indicated by statements expressing the belief that family is the main purpose in life: "my whole existence," "I live for my family," "my sole goal," and "my whole life is circled around him (son)." The reverse of this sentiment was also found—that the respondent would be "empty" or "missing something" without the family. Importance was also expressed by respondents whose family dominated their thought processes, as shown in the following excerpts:

Q: How does being a mother affect what you do in your everyday life?
R: Well, I'm conscious that whatever I do I'm a mother first and anything else comes secondary.

* * *

Q: How do you feel about being a father?
R: ...I'm more worried about them than about myself.
Q: So, your family takes on greater importance than yourself?
R: Oh yeah. Definitely. They're number one.

As can be seen from these responses, family identity was more than just one aspect of identity to many of the adults in the sample; their identities were primarily defined in family terms. The tendency to view oneself as a loving spouse, parent, or both was as common in men as in women.

ACTIVITIES

Even more telling, perhaps, than what the respondents said about the centrality of family to their identities was their reported involvement in activities related to the family. For the women in the sample, this involvement in family activities often translated into the main focus of their work being homemaking or limiting their work outside the home to part-time:

Q: What is important to you about being a mother?
R: ...I like to teach them as much as I can. That's why I don't work. Not for now, anyhow.

* * *

Q: How do you feel about your role (in the family)?

R: . . . I would rather have a certain number of hours to look after these things than to spend all my time outside the house at work.

Some of the more complicated issues that arose regarding the juxtaposition of family and work identities in the homemakers in the sample will be addressed in Chapter 8. At this point, it is worth noting that devotion to performance of family functions was for at least 8 women in the sample a major component of their identity as loving wives and mothers. Their behavior in carrying through this devotion was an indication of the importance of family to their identities.

Other respondents expressed the centrality of family to their identities by claiming that they do "everything together" and spend as much of their free time together as possible. These respondents included men and working women who did not have the opportunity or desire to devote all of their daily activities to caring for the family at home:

Q: What kinds of things do you focus on (with son)?
R: Spending time with him. Sharing things with him. Doing things together with him. Making my time available without overbearing myself. He's 8 years old right now and his mind is really starting to grasp. Sharing, doing things with him, being interested in his school, what he's interested in.

Not all of the respondents were as strongly oriented toward their family life as the father in the above excerpt, though. The next case was a man whose hobby took up a great deal of his time, and he regretted his children's lack of interest in it:

Q: Could you describe your family to me?
R: . . . Uh, we've not all had the same interests which at some times disturbed me. You know, other things. I have an interest in model trains. None of the kids seem to have much of an interest in that, which was a little bit of a disappointment I think, more than anything else.

A diversity of interests was seen as an advantage, though, to this woman:

Q: Could you just tell me about your family?
R: . . . my husband and I have been married for 18 years in September, and generally it's just more whatever you do together. Speaking of together, I find one thing very important. My husband has a hobby, which is extremely good, I think. I think in every family one person or another should have a hobby so you're not so dependent on each other. I go my way and he goes his way. He has his friends who are also people I know and I am included whenever I want to go. He's into hunting, which is not my thing . . . it's time for me to unwind and be alone and the same for him. To be with his own friends and have a good time. That's just a general synopsis of what I think is basic, anyway.

Another respondent, similarly, wanted time to himself for recreation. He seemed to express pleasure that his wife did not have any outward objections:

Q: Does the relationship affect the way you spend your free time?
R: No, I don't think so. If I want to go out for an evening and play cards or golf, she wouldn't object to that.

Of the 35 different individuals who described spending time in activities with family, only these four saw their family involvement as less than all-encompassing. The remaining group, amounting to just under one-third of the sample, and over 40% of the men, regarded their daily activities as an expression of the importance of family to their identities. Whether or not their self-reports were accurate is another question, one that needs to be examined in terms of identity assimilation.

The first example of the use of identity assimilation is one that involves self-justification. It comes from the interview of a man who, when asked to describe his family, painted a picture of the perfect devoted father who spends all of his time with his children:

R: . . . We have a unique family situation. Of course, I'm the father. I like to spend as much time as I can with, um, them. I feel you can never have enough time with your family. I work 40 hours a week, um, I'm a volunteer fireman in the town of (name of town) that takes a certain amount of time, um, but, uh, I try to spend all the time I do have. You know, I don't have a lot of outside interests like some people have. Oh, I know some people have a lot of outside interests, which I don't. I really enjoy just being home with the kids at night. Playing on the floor with them out there . . .

The first clue to this respondent's tendency to use self-justification is his mentioning of his second job as a volunteer fireman. This type of activity, by definition, is one that involves considerable time and availability commitment and is not compatible with a life of "being home with the kids." By coincidence, this was exactly the complaint of a woman in the sample who was currently separated from her husband, the chief of a volunteer fire department in another metropolitan township:

Q: Do you have any doubts about your family? (referring to children)
R: I wouldn't say so, no.
Q: Maybe this would be a good place to share something about your separation. This is kind of what the question is getting at, uncertainties about the family. Would you share this?
R: Yeah, I'd be glad to. . . . My husband is employed through the day and is a fire chief at night in his spare time. And I believe that it had been an obsession with him because he loved this work so much that his family was put aside. And it was always myself with the children. And it just got to the point where he was gone most of the time with his involvement. . . . I felt we were being a little bit neglected. Because once you get to be a chief there's a lot of time spent away from home. And I think that after a while it got to me because I was tired of being alone . . .

It sounds almost as if this woman could have been married to the respondent in question, although the respondent himself was not a chief. Stronger evidence for a disparity between the self-perception of the volunteer fireman and his behavior was provided by the informal notes made by the interviewer after the visit. Although there was ample evidence in the home of the respondent's family orientation (children's toys and games in the living room), "one interesting discrepancy, however, has to do with R's involvements outside of his family. In arranging for the interview on the telephone, he mentioned that it would be difficult to arrange a time because of his busy outside schedule. In fact, the interview had to end by 8:40 PM so that R could leave for a 9:00 PM meeting. His involvement in the volunteer fire department was also evidenced by his emergency radio which was playing when I arrived as well as a volunteer fire department sweatshirt that he wore during the interview. All of the above leads me to wonder how much this is disruptive of his family life."

Another apparent case of self-justification is that of a man in whose interview there was the potential for a disparity between his identity as an involved family man and the reasons for his actions with the family:

Q: How does your involvement with your family affect the way you spend your time?
R: When we, in the past, it was always a family vacation. The boys, both my sons, are Eagle Scouts. I was involved in scouting. When they were little, and were Indian Guides, I was chief of the tribe and chief of the nation. When they were in Little League, I was manager of the team...
Q: So, it sounds like your outside activities, many of them are related to the family, the scouting, baseball, and so on.
R: Scouts, when the boys left scouting, I went on for a couple of years. Just me.

This man had a lifetime pattern of being a high achiever, and his rise to leadership positions in the organizations to which his sons belonged was consistent with this pattern. The use of self-justification is inferred from his claim that he engaged in these activities because of his identity as an involved family man, when it appeared that the chance to verify his identity as a competent person through exerting his leadership provided much of the motivation. His continuing involvement in Scouts after his children were no longer participating is a key indicator of the discrepancy between his identity and his behavior.

Self-justification also appeared to be present in the rationalization that was provided by the father of a 20-year-old son when giving the reasons for not having spent more time with his son when his son was a little boy:

Q: How does your relationship with your son affect how things go in your everyday life... the amount of time you spend with him?
R: ... I spend more time with him now than I did between one and five.
Q: You mean when he was between one and five?
R: In those years. Those years were important. To me, anyway. But like I said, I... couldn't be home and run a business at the same time. Today I got help, it's different. In those days, I didn't have no help, I was all by myself. You know, in other words, I wasn't home but I used to call him on the phone, you know, and 99 times he was sleeping. I have guilt, but no regrets. If you understand what I'm trying to say.
Q: Maybe you could explain it to me.
R: In other words, I feel bad, with guilt that I wasn't there. Those growing years. But in other words, I wasn't doing anything for myself. In a sense it was for myself. In other words, either if I was working at Delco, or any other company, I'd probably have to put in overtime, I would have anyway.
Q: So, you weren't being selfish, you just—
R: Right.

Q: You wish you could have been there but circumstances prevented it.
R: Right.
Q: Sort of out of your control?
R: That's right.

Although he admitted to being less than the perfect father, the respondent ended up concurring with the interviewer's clarification that his lack of involvement with his son was not his fault, after all. While this evidence of self-justification may be biased because it emerged from the interviewer rather than the respondent, the way the excerpt ends is consistent with the respondent's expression of "guilt" but not "regret."

It was not only men who used identity assimilation to present a view of themselves consistent with an identity as a loving family member. The next example from a young married woman introduces the topic of having "second thoughts" about one's spouse and possibly considering alternatives. Rather than take these seriously, though, this respondent dismisses their importance because to admit to having them would contradict her identity as a loving wife:

Q: Do you ever question or wonder about the life you have with your husband?
R: Oh, sometimes I think, you wonder, if I weren't married, I could have done this or if I married somebody else we'd have more money (laughs) but I think that's normal. It's just part of living, I guess.
Q: Is this a serious concern for you?
R: Not really, it doesn't occur to me very often. (laughs) Only if someone brings it up, as a matter of fact.

In her last statement, the respondent added a comment that further strengthens the case of identity assimilation, denying that she herself is the origin of her traitorous thoughts about her husband.

Another variant of identity assimilation involving self-justification is when "other people" are used to make a point about one's own identity. The next case involves a potential challenge to the centrality of the respondent's family identity. The perception of others seems to have been distorted in a way that reveals something important about the individual's own unacceptable desires. This excerpt is one of the best examples in all of the transcript material of identity projection:

Q: Do you feel any particular way because you are a husband?
R: . . . Well, if I wasn't married and wasn't a husband, I don't, I'd probably be doing what everybody else is doing today. Go out and have a good time, whatever, but, uh, that's if I wasn't a husband. But since I am it wouldn't even come to my mind. So . . .

Identity projection is being used in this case as a defense against the anxiety that would result if the respondent were to admit to his own desire to behave in ways that would be inconsistent with his identity as a faithful and loving husband. As support of this interpretation is a remark the respondent made earlier in the interview. A factor important to his identity as a loving husband was that "I'm true to her and I want her to be true to me."

There were only three other persons in the sample, all of them men, who reported having had thoughts of infidelity. In all three cases, the respondents claimed to be working hard to prevent going astray from their wives. They were willing to admit that they had these adulterous thoughts, but were using the defensive rigidity form of identity assimilation to keep these thoughts remotely removed from their identities as loving husbands. For instance, a husband who was unsure about whether he wished to remain faithful or attached to his wife was using firm control over this thoughts about alternatives in order to avoid facing a threat to his identity as a loving husband. The following excerpt was taken from the Values portion of the interview of a man with an expectant wife, regarding his belief in "moral values":

Q: You mentioned moral values. Could you describe a particular moral value?
R: Adultery. That would be number one. That's sad. To me it's sad. Then again, it's so easy to do. I don't know if it scares me or not, but it might scare me if I think about it.

Although men were more likely than women to describe thoughts about adultery, those who were willing to talk about it were clearly upset enough about the whole topic to try to avoid letting it become a serious threat to their family identities. This finding reinforces the idea that the family identity of men has the potential to assume a high degree of centrality.

Personal Fulfillment

Another area of common ground between men and women regarding the importance of family identity was the extent to which both sexes claimed to be experiencing a sense of personal fulfillment from their families. This man's statement expresses this sentiment very clearly:

Q: How would you feel about yourself if you did not have your marriage and family?
R: I think that I would feel very empty; I think that I would feel very self-centered; I think I would feel that I was missing a very big part of my life. I have a lot of friends who do not have children, number one, and some friends not married, and they just seem quite empty.

The category of statements indicating personal fulfillment as a feature of family identity includes excerpts such as this one, explicitly oriented toward personal satisfaction and pleasure as a by-product of family involvement or as a separate motivational force in its own right. There are three subcategories of personal fulfillment: personal happiness, pride, and appreciation of the qualities of family members as individuals. These subcategories overlap to the extent that they all revolve around ways in which the individual derives benefits other than an identity as a loving person from family interactions. In categorizing the statements into these three subcategories the somewhat arbitrary nature of the distinctions cannot be ignored, but the distinctions nevertheless seem worthwhile. In each case, moreover, the feelings are ones equally shared by men and women.

PERSONAL HAPPINESS

This subcategory included statements that were overt expressions of specific ways in which family involvement either increased or decreased the individual's sense of well-being. Because of the large number of statements that fell into this cluster, expressions that shared a common meaning were grouped into smaller groupings.

Enjoyment

The largest grouping of responses (40%) was either simple declarations of feelings of happiness and enjoyment or of unhappiness and discomfort. Almost one-half of these statements included the word "enjoyment" or "feel good" to refer to the emotional state experienced while with children or the spouse. The experience of being a parent was described as "great" and one that has no equal: there is "nothing like it" and "I wouldn't have missed it for the world." Six responses included the word "challenge" to describe the experience of parenting, and the respondents who used this word attested that they meant it in a positive sense. This preponderance of favorable statements about the happiness associated with being a parent contrasts sharply with the emphasis in the family literature on the tribulations of being a parent inferred from studies on parenthood and marital satisfaction (e.g., Glenn & McLanahan, 1982). However, the "joys of parenting" have been amply documented in other sources where respondents were specifically asked about the costs and rewards of having children (Chilman, 1980; Hoffman & Manis, 1978; Miller & Sollie, 1980).

The number of negative statements in this cluster was very small, with only two respondents expressing predominantly unhappy feelings about their family situations. One of these has already been described: the man who was so frustrated with his inability to get along well with his wife (the "neatnick"). The other unhappy respondent was a single woman who had just ended a long-term romantic relationship and saw no prospects ahead of future intimate involvements. Her statement of unhappiness revolved not so much around this situation, though, as around the social embarrassment she felt at being single.

Q: How does (this situation) make you feel?
R: You're under so much pressure of being in the "single swing." You're always under pressure to explain yourself. People are always asking questions. They are always trying to put you or peg you in a certain hole. It seems like you are forever explaining yourself. I find it very trying.

This sense of embarrassment expressed by this woman also brings out the importance of security, another grouping of personal fulfillment statements that was of particular importance to woman.

A questioning of the degree of personal fulfillment he was receiving was evident in the response of this man:

Q: Can you describe any effect your relationship with your spouse may have on the way you feel about yourself as a person?
R: Well, it would by and large be a very positive effect in the sense that it makes me feel wanted and needed by one person which is gratifying to me. And then, on the other hand, there is a negative aspect to it that I get too heavily dependent on one person so that doesn't make me feel too good about myself. So, I feel that I should be less depen-

dent on my spouse for moral support or something. I should be more dependent on myself for stability. That would be the only negative part...

Rather than being a direct expression of unhappiness, this man's ruminations concerning his overdependence on his spouse seem to reflect a process of identity accommodation. He is studying his family identity, examining it carefully for any mismatch between his identity as a loving husband and his experiences with his wife. The negative feature of this questioning process is that he feels the situation does not reflect favorably upon how he would like to regard himself in his marital relationship.

Security

Involvement in a set of family relationships as a source of security was an important aspect of family identity for 22 people, 14 of whom were women. The kind of security provided by the family included support and nurturance, convenience, a basis for the future, safety, and protection from loneliness. Several of the respondents described the security they were feeling in terms that, at first glance, appear to be similar to the centrality category:

Q: Why is he (your husband) important to you?
R: Why is he important to me? Um, he's important to me because, (pause) what can I say? He's my best friend and he's my lover, and he's my confidant, uh, and without this, uh, I think there would be a large void in my life.

The difference between this type of response and one that involves centrality is that respondents who mention security are referring to having a gap or "void" that is "filled" by the family. A family identity that is based on the centrality of the family to the self is one that is defined in terms of its strengths rather than its weaknesses. For clarification of this point, two examples of centrality (versus security) are presented here:

Q: How important is your family?
R: It's my whole existence.
Q: What about it is important to you?
R: It's my whole reason for being: working to help the wife and kids. Everything I do is in regard to how it affects the family.

* * *

Q: You indicated that it's most important in your life. What about it is particularly important to you?
R: Oh, I don't know. I, I feel that there's a lot of need to, um, I don't find a whole lot of meaning to my life but that's, that's the one area where, see, uh, where I have a strong sense of uh, mission or purpose.

A need for security as a means of providing happiness may be contrasted with statements concerning centrality in another way. The valuing of security needs can be regarded as an extrinsic form of motivation, since the rewards that are provided are external to the family relationships itself. An individual can have security needs met in a number of ways, possibly even outside the family, and by a number of different people. An intrinsic family need is one that involves factors inherent in the unique qualities of particular family relationships; it could not be met by other people or through other activities. When the individual describes a family identity as one that is central to his or her identity as a whole, this is a statement that reflects an intrinsic motivation to be regarded as a loving person within the family and nowhere else.

Role Fulfillment

In this cluster of statements there was a distinct effect of sex. The respondents whose statements fell into this cluster were all women. They used almost identical wording to describe their feelings: "I've always wanted a family," "it's fulfilled my ambitions," "I've always wanted to be a mother," "I've always wanted this." There is a certain inflexibility or rigidity about statements such as these that approaches identity assimilation. The women who expressed a sense of personal fulfillment were reflecting on ambitions they had held onto since their youth, and had never allowed themselves to question their identities in this regard.

Another feature of these statements regarding personal fulfillment is that they stem from an extrinsic orientation to the family. An individual can occupy a family role regardless of who is inserted into the slots to be filled by a spouse and children. When an individual speaks of role fulfillment, then, he or she is downgrading the importance of the specific people who occupy these positions within his or her real family. Use of the term "always" is another key to understanding this explanation, assuming that "always" refers back to some point in childhood. It would be impossible for the person to know, as a child, who will make up the family when adulthood is reached. Therefore, anyone could be substituted into the positions within the family and the individual would have found the identity as a loving person that he or she was seeking.

It might be though that, because of its extrinsic basis, role fulfillment is diminished in importance as an aspect of family identity. On the contrary, though, a sense of role fulfillment may be extremely gratifying, since it represents the accomplishment of a childhood dream: the little girl wearing her mother's apron, "vacuuming" and "ironing" with her toys, caring for her "baby" dolls, and playing house with other little girls. Indeed, the feeling of fulfillment may be a powerful force that makes tolerable some of the other frustrations of family life:

Q: How do you feel about being a mother?
R: That's such a general question. Um, I don't really want to say I enjoy, yes, I guess I have to say I enjoy being a mother. I'm very glad, I'm proud to be a mother. It's what I always wanted to do. Um, it's certainly very challenging, certainly very frustrating, but as the children are getting older it's becoming more even more of a challenge, it's becoming more interesting, it's becoming more frustrating, it's becoming more enjoyable! I enjoy being a mother. I prefer being a wife and mother to any other occupation that I have had. And I don't want to give up, you know, any portion of it.

It is unclear from the interview material why there were no men whose responses fell into this category, or even came close to it. One possibility is that, like the women, the men were unaware of or insensitive to the influence of sex-role socialization in childhood. There was no evidence that men engaged in introspection regarding the effect of early influences on the adoption of roles in adulthood; yet, men are generally not as well-prepared as women to assume adult family role obligations as fathers and husbands. The men probably did not have as clear a role ideal for performance of the functions of husband and father, and were not even aware of what had been lacking in their early experiences.

Watching Children Grow

The expression "watching my child(ren) grow" emerged clearly in the statements of 3 women and 8 men as a distinctly enjoyable feature of parenting. This pleasure of experiencing the development of one's own child was described by a father in the following excerpt:

Q: What is important to you about your family?
R: My personal fulfillment is being able to have the experience of seeing babies begin to grow and to, in this case, young girls, but when they grow into young women, being able to see them start from nothing, an egg to a child, and watching the child grow . . . being able to see the child grow and develop.

This statement suggests that part of the enjoyment of watching a child grow is being able to observe the process of human development, a satisfaction that may be related to Kagan's (1978) observation: "Each parent is a scientist testing a personal theory of human development with each child" (p. 34). Although Kagan believed that the eagerness of parents to test their "effectiveness as sculptor of new life" (p. 34) was more apparent in women, the men in the present sample were at least as involved, if not more so, in this aspect of parenting as were the women.

In addition to the simple unmitigated pleasure of watching a child grow, there were some more complex issues apparent in the statements concerning children's development. One is the feeling of having gotten through the trying period of diapers, teething, and tantrums of early childhood, the obligations of the school years, and the rebelliousness of adolescence, and into a time when the children can be enjoyed as people:

Q: Why do you think (family) is so important?
R: . . . I guess probably part of that is just pleasure at seeing the kids grow up and become adults and be able to talk with them about things that they have developed as they have grown up. It's not that I didn't enjoy the kids when they were infants and so on, but that was not the fun part as far as I was concerned, after the kids got into high school. I went through the Boy Scouts and Girl Scouts and all that, but that was kind of a drain, at least a strain, you know, it was something you did. And other things that small kids do. But when they grew up and started coming home with their own ideas and experiences they had, which is what they're doing now, of course, I've really enjoyed that. I think that's probably one of the things that makes me consider family important.

It's rewards that I'm getting for going through the trouble of having children, rearing them and all that. And I think the rewards are great. And you can't find that kind of thing anyplace else.

In this respondent's statement are elements of the changes associated with the family life cycle described in Chapter 5. There it will be seen that, in addition to being a source of exhilaration, seeing the development of children can also be a stimulus for development of the parent's identity.

Another set of more complex ideas regarding the development of children could be observed among the respondents who spoke of comparing their children with themselves when they were children. Others stated that watching their children made them wonder whether their children would turn out to be like them. These forms of self-comparison are shown in the following excerpts:

Q: Could you describe your family for me?
R: My wife and child are the most important to me. Watching him grow up, wondering what he'll be like when he gets to adulthood. Will he follow in my footsteps as far as liking the same things I do?

* * *

Q: What about being a father makes you happiest?
R: It's neat to watch a kid grow up. Makes you wonder a little bit what it was like when you were growing up. . . .

Parents who engage in these forms of self-comparison with their children have moved beyond a simple expression of joy and personal satisfaction. Their introspection begins to border on the identity accommodation process when the results of self-comparison with children lead to a new understanding of one's own identity as a person and a more articulated identity as a loving family member.

Life Experiences

To a small group of respondents (3 women, 5 men), family involvement was a source of happiness because of its "fit" in the individual's life scheme. Three remarried individuals reflected upon their present happiness in comparison with a previously unhappy marriage that ended in divorce. The other 5 expressed happiness with their family situations because they had started their families relatively late, as shown in this excerpt:

Q: Is there something special about being a father and husband you couldn't really get outside of that role?
R: Well, as I say, another thing—I didn't get married, um, I was single for a long time. A lot of guys get married, 19, 20, 21, uh, we're married just approximately 7, 8 years. I was 28 years old before I got married. And even back then, that was a little beyond the age, not *beyond* the age, most guys were getting married 22, 23, 24, you know. And I was single for 10 years after high school, and so on and so forth, I had my good times, you know . . . and maybe this has, maybe I did everything I wanted to do. Maybe this has got me so I'm content to be a husband and father and wage earner.

Rather than being disturbed about being "off-time" (Neugarten, 1970) in their development, the individuals who described themselves as having waited to start a family seemed pleased by their decision. This observation corresponds to Russell's (1974) report that the parenting transition was less of a "crisis" for men in their late 30s and 40s than it was for men in their late teen years and early 20s. A man in the present sample who became a father relatively late in life showed some concern in the Age Identity portion of the interview about whether he would be able to keep up with his son in the coming years (his son was a preschooler at the time of the interview). However, his overwhelming reaction to his "late" marriage and fatherhood was extremely positive:

Q: What about your family situation is important to you right now?
R: I think the, our son, more or less is, he's starting to grow up. This is an addition. Started to jell everything. Not that it really had to because I was married later in life and we both had enjoyed things that, as a single person and I just think it made for a better marriage.
. . .
Q: Why do you suppose you're so content?
R: I think because of something I mentioned before. I think both of us were single for so long and then marrying later in life. I'm 19 years older than she is and, I don't know, I guess marrying later in life with the maturity that you gain kind of helps you in a family situation. Tends to keep you a little bit more relaxed and, uh, less, and there's less of a need to get up and get out and do things. You've been satisfied and I think you're content to do the things you want to do here instead of outside.
Q: Things within the family?
R: That's right.

This respondent's perception of having gained a more relaxed and mature attitude as a function of his age is a view that was shared by many other respondents when asked about age in the Age Identity portion of the interview. Starting a family late in life was also seen as an advantage in that it made it easier to tolerate the many restrictions of individual freedom that come with having a family, a view consistent with the findings of Wylie's (1979) research. Rather than seeing himself as having become too old to change his lifestyle, this respondent regarded his prior freedom from restrictions as a form of preparation for the burdens of parenthood. His response provides one of the many examples of the possibility for change and flexibility in adulthood found in the present study.

PRIDE

The second subcategory of personal fulfillment statements shared the quality of directly or indirectly involving feelings of pride as a component of family identity. The 12 statements in this category were, with one exception, centered around children, and there were an almost equal number of statements made by men (5) as women (7). Although this subcategory is close in meaning to the other two within the overall category of personal fulfillment, the quality of pride has been recognized as a distinct feature of parenting (Fawcett, 1978). For the respondents in the present sample, statements reflecting pride also differed in subtle ways from the other subcategories concerning personal fulfillment.

One word of caution must be inserted before defining the subcategory of pride any further. This stems from the fact that it is not possible to know the extent to which reports of admirable behavior in children were exaggerated. What appear to be overly extreme cases of pride would, when detected, have to be regarded as falling within the realm of identity assimilation. It is a reflection on the parent's identity as a person who expresses lovingness through guidance if the children are successful in what they do.

As a subcategory separate and distinct from personal happiness, pride implies less of a feeling of gratification than one of admiration for the accomplishments of one's offspring. Examples of pride included statements describing children as "good," not having gotten in "trouble," or having done well in school. Pride differs from the simple appreciation or enjoyment of family members' qualities, the third subcategory of personal fulfillment, because it implies respect as well as appreciation. The fulfillment that was associated with pride in their children appeared to emerge from an identification of the adult with the child whose behavior was being praised.

One concern that was expressed by several respondents was over their children's actual or potential involvement in drug abuse. In the context of this concern over illegal and destructive behavior by children, having children who did not use drugs was specifically a source of pride for a parent with this concern:

Q: Why don't you have any doubts (about your children)?
R: Because our kids have been so good, I think. They never have given us any grief and they have been super kids. I don't know if I could still feel the same if they had a lot of problems or if they got into drugs. They've just always walked the straight and narrow.

This statement probably describes a reasonably accurate perception of the respondent's children, since it is based on a set of definite criteria that are at least somewhat objective. It is clear that, for this respondent, the lack of a negative "accomplishment" has stimulated accommodation of her identity to the knowledge that she has successfully raised her children. Had her children failed to live up to these criteria, the respondent might have engaged in a more difficult process of attempting to incorporate this knowledge about her own parenting ability into her identity.

Another way in which identity accommodation is manifest is a change in identity as a result of certain experiences within the family that improve the individual's feelings of pride about his or her own performance as a family member. A number of respondents in the sample believed that they had bettered themselves through their interactions in the family. The proportion of respondents who claimed that their involvement in the family improved their attitudes toward themselves to those who did not was, roughly, 3 to 2. For the majority of respondents who reported specific effects on self-esteem, then, family identity was regarded as an area of strength. While some of the respondents did not elaborate beyond the statement that the family made them "feel good" about themselves, a number of others described specific ways in which their self-confidence had been improved as a result of their family situations, such as the father in this excerpt:

Q: Well, I was wondering if having the role of father has changed the way that you look at yourself, your self-concept, the way that you feel about yourself?
R: (Pause) Well, it's bound to have some improvements, uh, I've, I'm a fairly critical person, I judge myself on rather high standards, or I try to be somewhat objective. I feel I have strengths and weaknesses and I, I think that this, um, is probably one of my areas of strength rather then, um, (laughs) one which is weak.
Q: Uh huh.
R: Perhaps, perhaps, you know knowing that, maybe that's one of the reasons why I would tend to try to put more emphasis on the, my life. It's, uh, there are other areas where I'm not as successful. I don't know, I think you tend to, to want to, uh, to want to think of yourself well and to get into something that is, uh, is, uh, to feel good about.

It is not possible to know if the respondent really is an "objective person" with "high standards," but his willingness to admit to flaws in himself is a hint that he may be giving a relatively honest assessment of the effect on his identity of fatherhood.

A desire to portray the self in a certain light may also affect reports of the opposite effect on self-esteem of family involvement; that is, a lowering of self-confidence. However, this is a much less likely probability since the biases that people tend to show in describing themselves are toward favorable self-representations (Tesser & Campbell, 1983). The kinds of negative effects on self-esteem found in the area of family identity included feelings of inferiority, insecurity, regret, and ineffectiveness. Most (82%) of the statements describing a loss of self-esteem associated with family identity were from women. Of these, one-third referred specifically to the homemaker role and feelings of lack of fulfillment within it. One respondent was particularly unhappy about the kind of identity as a wife and mother that she had chosen for herself and was on the threshold of deciding to seek employment outside the home:

Q: What effect does having this sort of challenge (getting a job) have for you right now? How does that affect the way you feel about yourself?
R: Very inferior. That says it all. You get a job and I've had jobs, but I always feel I'm not doing what I should. The best. You just feel, you know, with training and schooling comes that feeling of you've got something behind you. Where, you see, I don't have anything. Just mothering.

The respondent in this example was describing her role as a worker as much as she was referring to her identity within the family. For the full-time homemakers in the sample, these two identities were very much tied in together. To the extent that the homemaker identity was regarded as inadequate or unfulfilling, a woman's gratification from her identity as a loving family member became commensurately reduced.

SPECIAL QUALITIES

Descriptions of family members by the respondents were, in 13 cases, couched in terms that emphasized their special, enjoyable, and noteworthy qualities. Rather than being accompanied by feelings of admiration or respect, these statements were simple descriptions of "facts," as perceived through the respondent's eyes. This description of the family member's special qualities, as applied to children, was one of the categories in Porter's (1954) definition of parental acceptance and it would seem to extend in a direct way to the spouse or any other family member as well.

To the extent that the descriptions of special qualities related properties of the family member's ability to carry out role functions in the home, they could be regarded as extrinsically oriented, as for example in the following case:

Q: Could you tell me something about your husband?
R: We've been married for 7 years. He's good with the kids and he works hard for a living. He's fun to be with. That's about it.

The husband in this excerpt is described in such general terms ("good", "hardworking" and "fun") that the wife's satisfaction with him could, from her statement alone, be derived from almost any individual who lived up to these standards of performance in the home.

When the special qualities referred to could not be found in anyone other than the family member being described, the statement reflects more of an intrinsic orientation:

Q: How do you feel about being a mother?
R: I enjoy it very much . . . She's a nice little girl. She's got a sense of humor, she gets along well with people, she loves people, she isn't afraid of anybody. She waves at everybody. She's just a very pleasurable child. Very easy to get along with. She's always been easy. Even as an infant.

* * *

Q: Why do you feel this relationship is so important?
R: Well, she just seems to be the type that can do anything. She handles all the finances and she's good at bookkeeping, and she's just an all-around buddy. If I want to go hunting and fishing, she'll go with me, and she's just an all-around wife. . . . She's always in the mood or willing to do something for somebody else. She never can seem to do enough for anybody . . . she works for (name of town) Ambulance, driver and medic, and she just does everything for everybody, that's all. She's an outstanding person.

The individuals described in these two statements also sound like pleasant people who are "fun" to be with. The degree of detail provided in the responses suggests, in addition, that the respondents would have difficulty finding a substitute for this family member.

As with statements concerning pride, it is difficult to draw a line between accurate versus exaggerated descriptions of the special qualities of family members. Indeed, several of what seem to be the best examples of identity assimilation are descriptions of family members that have a false ring because they are so extremely negative (the "neatnick" in Chapter 3). Similarly, some of the pleasure derived from interacting with family members whose qualities are positively evaluated borders on the form of identity accommodation in which a favorable change in identity results from a particular experience or experiences.

The present analysis cannot provide definitive answers regarding the identity processes because of lack of confirmatory evidence concerning the people and relationships described by the respondents. However, because it describes a widespread phenomenological experience within the family, the category of personal fulfillment with its three variations appears to be an extremely crucial component of family identity. Confirming once again the thesis of this chapter, personal fulfillment is as potent an experience within the family for men as it is for women. This feeling of personal fulfillment is a result of the optimal adaptation that can be achieved when the adult perceives that there is a relative equilibrium between his or her identity as a loving person and the circumstances in which that identity is implemented.

5
Parents and Children

Erik Erikson (1963) proposed a theory of psychosocial development that has come to be known as one of the few personality theories adequately addressing the question of how adults change after passing through adolescence. The primary issues described by Erikson for adults to grapple with are identity, intimacy, generativity, and ego integrity. As one of these four primary issues, generativity remains one of the most intriguing and resistant to rigorous study. Generativity, simply defined, refers to productivity in the realms of family and work and a sense of caring for future generations (Erikson & Erikson, 1981). There are huge bodies of literature in the social sciences within both of these realms that should have the potential to answer questions concerning the development of generativity in adulthood. However, because generativity is such a broad concept, it has not lent itself well to the kinds of test materials that would be acceptable in most empirical investigations. The closest approximation to the study of generativity has been made by George Vaillant, who saw this issue as crucial to psychological adaptation in middle adulthood (Vaillant, 1977; Vaillant & Milofsky, 1981). Vaillant's results concerning the adaptive value of achieving the state of generativity in middle life lend support to Erikson's theory.

Given this background, it came as no surprise to find a cluster (12%) of statements in the present group of family interviews referring to the relationships between parents and children in generativity-related concepts. These were all statements pertaining to the desire to secure the well-being of family members through the individual's unselfish efforts to please them, provide for them, keep them healthy, influence them in a positive way, and be a person on whom the family can depend. It was evident that these statements not only referred to the sense of generativity, but also were expressions of significant features of adult identity.

The intrinsic-extrinsic dimension proved to be a most fruitful way of understanding how generativity was related to identity. In the intrinsically oriented statements, the respondent described a desire to provide for the health of family members. A sense of deep concern and caring is what emerges from such descriptions of the parent's efforts to support the physical and psychological well-being of children. This concern suggests a very fundamental incorporation of the individual's identity as a loving parent into the adult's total sense of self-worth. The following excerpt suggests this intrinsic form of generativity:

Q: You indicated the largest part of the circle as "Personal and Physical Welfare of My Immediate Family and Myself." Could you tell me something about what that means to you?

R: ...Um, I think it's just the general understanding anyone ever gives, you know, your most thoughts and affections go towards your husband and children, you know, those are the ones you are concerned that things in life go well for them and that they are, um, well affected by them, or able to deal with them, have good self-esteem about themselves and the things around them and you're concerned that all of life goes well, you know, and that nothing bad befalls them, be it any emotional occurrence or something physical that could happen. Just a general well-being.

Into the extrinsically oriented statements concerning generativity fall those descriptions of concern for the material needs of family members. These material needs include housing, money, food, clothing, and education. The extrinsic nature of this form of generativity was emphasized in the following excerpt:

Q: Overall, how would you say being a father makes you feel about yourself as a person?

R: I don't know. I don't think feeling has anything to do with it. The way I think, I mean, not everybody agrees with me...My wife and I say that we're going to have kids, okay? Now we both, not me alone, took a responsibility, okay? Right or wrong, you should stick with it. I'm not saying that my wife and I had the greatest marriage on earth, we have differing opinions. We don't think alike. But when it came to taking care of the kids, we did the same thing. Blended discipline, "You ain't going out, you're staying home," a kick in the ass, they got it. As far as material things, which society is dominated by that, they got them too. They got good clothes. They always got the best clothes. They ate well. They had the best medical care. That's not feeling. Feeling's got nothing to do with that. That's a responsibility. As far as I see it. Responsibility that you brought them in this world. That's a responsibility until they get old enough for you not to take care of them.

This respondent, in addition to describing generativity in totally extrinsic terms not involving any feelings, also mentioned responsibility as a component of his attitude toward his children. As discussed in Chapter 4, responsibility was mentioned by other respondents in the context of taking care of the material needs of family members. This respondent's statement expressed well the idea that generativity may be present without the underlying psychological process of self-actualization described by Erikson.

In the next example of generativity, extrinsic motivation was also apparent in the respondent's emphasis upon providing for the material needs of children. In addition, a new element was added:

Q: Do you ever question or wonder about how things are in your family?

R: Yes, I do.

Q: Your role as a father.

R: Well, my role as a father, I feel as though I should provide for them, you know, food, clothing, and shelter, education in the future. Hopefully, they'll be interested in going to college, uh, I see at work every day. College. It means so much. I mean, uh, especially Tom, he's 7, when he gets to be 10 years from now, if he doesn't get a college education he's not going to be able to get a decent good job so he can do the same thing for his family in the future, hopefully, that I'm trying to do now. Um, uh, I'd like to see him go on to school. And the same with the younger children. Even Jennifer, being a girl, I'd still like to see her get a good education. I'm saving money right now. Hopefully, I can provide them with an education if they can't get scholarships. I don't know what will be, um, available when they get to be that age, you know, so I'm saving some money. . . . I'm a strong believer in education. I, uh, uh, had a high school education and a year of college, at a community college myself, and I do wish that I had graduated from the 2-year school and went on to a 4-year school, but I didn't. You know? But I do regret it to a certain extent at work. I think maybe if I had a little more education, I might have a little better position than I have, maybe I wouldn't. You know.

The new element added to the concept of generativity was the respondent's desire to see his children have a better life than he did. This mixed expression of regret and concern was apparent in several other respondents' statements about their desire for their children to have a good life, as shown in the following excerpt:

Q: Why is your family important to you?
R: . . . They are important to me in that way if I can try to show them how, oh maybe the mistakes I've made to try to help them so they don't make the same ones and at the same time let them make the same ones.

This respondent expressed the additional qualification on her statement that it may be a good idea to let her children make some of the same mistakes she made in her life to benefit their growth.

It is possible that generativity can go "too far." If an individual allows his or her identity to be totally dominated by the need to be a loving parent, there can be an obliteration of the individual's sense of self. Some of the statements regarding centrality and security described in Chapter 3 border on this extreme form of involvement in parenting. The most clear-cut and concise example of this phenomenon as it applied to generativity was contained in the following excerpt:

Q: What is important about being a mother?
R: . . . I'm like any other parent, you live through your kids.

That this state of self-obliteration was essentially unhealthy for psychological development was evident in the statements of full-time homemakers who were trying to extricate themselves from a perceived sense of oppression due to overinvolvement in parenting. One of these, described in Chapter 3, was seen to be doubting whether the "all-consuming" nature of her parental identity was "good." At 48, she was just beginning to define her own identity as a person independently from her identity as a wife and mother. Another respondent presented a similar view of her situation as she accommodated to the changes necessitated by the maturation of her children:

R: It's right now, at my time of life, it's like I've just gotten to the point where you have to cut the cord. That's not easy to do, really. So you have to find your place at this time with them. And that's hard because I've been very close with them. I didn't work. I felt that I should be with them. . . . They were my whole life, really.

Q: So it's a major change for you?

R: It's very hard. It's from one extreme to the other. And it's an adjustment and I'm going through that right now.

Q: How are you doing that? How are you making the adjustment?

R: Well, you just can't get that involved with them anymore like you were. You can't, they can't be your whole life because they're not and that's the way you want it. You really do. You want them to go off and be happy and do what they want to do, but at the same time, if you were a mother of the 50s and 60s, this is an adjustment. . . So I have to make a life for myself.

For this woman, an identity as a loving parent had totally pervaded her identity as a person. Her attempt to redefine her identity did not include abandoning her children altogether, but rather an effort to establish a more equitable balance.

Also included in the category of generativity were three statements, all made by men, in which the expressed concern for children was so high that it precluded their considering the possibility of seeking a divorce from the children's mothers. This aspect of the generativity theme can be seen in the following excerpt:

Q: Do you ever feel as though you are actively deciding between staying in your marriage and an alternative?

R: No, it never gets that far. I would bet if there were no children, if I didn't have the youngest child, that would make the choice a hell of a lot easier.

Q: Do you feel like the youngest child is a constraint on considering alternatives?

R: I wouldn't say constraint, the word constraint sounds a little strong, it sounds like I'm ready to do it, um, um, if it weren't for my youngest child, Margaret, in the times that I've been pissed or that I would think of walking, I would do it.

. . .

Q: Okay. Do you think there might be a time when you will consider alternatives more seriously, do you foresee that in the future?

R: No, well, if I didn't get along, continued on a basis where I didn't get along for years or months or whatever, and there were no young children at home, the choice would be very easy for me, because then if she and I couldn't get along and I'm not affecting anyone else's life by leaving.

The concern over the welfare of children as a deterrent to divorce evident in this response concurs with a frequently made observation in research on the effects of children on marital satisfaction. This observation is invoked to explain the U-shaped relationship between stage of the family life cycle and satisfaction with marriage (Spanier, Lewis, & Cole, 1975). The explanation is that there are many unhappily married couples with children living at home who stay together for the sake of the children. When the children leave the home to start their own independent lives, the parents then no longer feel constrained from seeking a divorce. The score on marital satisfaction in the latter stages of the family life cycle (after children have been "launched") are artificially high because the only people remaining are the ones who were not unhappy earlier. At the same time, the average satisfaction scores of married couples with children are lowered because of the presence of unhappily married but constrained people in the samples during these stages. Statements like those cited here are anecdotal evidence that reinforces this empirical observation and in addition, suggests a subtle way in which generativity might be expressed.

Generativity was not only expressed toward children, it was also referred to in the context of discussing marital relationships or the family as a whole. This phenomenon is rarely if at all mentioned in the family literature, yet it seems to hold some important implications. Generativity as directed toward the spouse indicates an altruistic desire for the spouse's happiness and good health, as well as personal growth. The respondent sees himself or herself as a loving person to the extent that he or she can help the spouse achieve this state of well-being or at least watch from the sidelines as the process unfolds:

Q: What about, in terms of personal fulfillment, what is important to you about your family?

R: ...The same thing with my wife, being able to watch her grow. She was a student in college, now she's going back to try to pursue a career and finish up. She's quite heavily involved with singing, opera, things like this, and I enjoy watching her experience with that.

Although this respondent derives pleasure from observing his wife's personal growth, the main focus of his interest appears to be an unselfish concern for her well-being.

In general, the statements representing generativity toward family members appeared to be descriptions of a positive and rewarding situation that reinforced the individual's identity as a loving parent or spouse. However, there were also some statements that indicated a failure to have achieved generativity. These are statements that at first glance represent the respondent's belief in a "generation gap." Closer inspection suggests that, instead, they are indicative of the state of "stagnation": the polar opposite of the sense of generativity. Stagnation is represented by a lack of interest in the young and abandonment of any hope that the next generation will ever amount to anything worthwhile. In the present set of interviews, stagnation seemed to be the process underlying statements disparaging the merits of young persons "today." These statements occurred within the broad context of remarks that had a strongly assimilative character of defensive rigidity.

In the first example of stagnation, the respondent was discussing her attempts to come to grips with her changing family situation as her children were being "launched" from the home:

Q: What are you trying to do to work this out for yourself?

R: It finally dawns on you that you're not the most important thing to them. You see it in different ways. You think that's right; it's the way it should be. But I think kids today are different than they were years ago. I think there is less of an attachment there than there was years ago. They don't feel responsibility that years ago kids felt toward their parents. I really don't...

This respondent appears to be resentful of her children's diminished attachment to her as they become older. She resolved this unpleasant feeling by generalizing to "kids today" rather than accepting her reduced importance in her children's eyes as a natural process of growth. Although the next respondent appears to be more desirous of his son's moving toward independence, his criticism of "your teen-agers" seems to indicate not only stagnation, but his reluctance to give up his identity as a protective father:

Q: Do you think the relationship (with your son) will change in the future?
R: ...I'd rather see him to become independent. In other words, self-independent. Not because I don't love him, no, but because I don't want him home, no, that isn't it. But having his own life that has to be on it's own. Be self-independent. Like most of your teen-agers. They want it, and when they get it, they don't know how to handle it. They have no idea what to do with it.

These examples are suggestive of a link between stagnation and a regressive identity in which assimilation is used as a means to stave off doubts and uncertainties about the individual's self-worth. Indeed, Erikson's theory would suggest that problems in achieving generativity can be traced to problems in the individual's identity.

The analysis so far of statements expressing generativity-related concepts has been strictly limited to a glimpse of the respondents' identities at one point in time. However, both an identity as a loving parent and the achievement of generativity are, by their very nature, ever-changing along with the vicissitudes over time in the relationships between parents and children. Although the respondents in this sample were only studied at one point in time, arranging their statements in a cross-section according to the ages of their children yields an approximation to the understanding of family identity as something approaching a developmental process.

The Family Life Cycle and Identity Accommodation

Identity accommodation would appear to be a natural outgrowth of family life, given that the family situation is rarely stable for very long. The term "family life cycle" was coined by sociologists to describe the regular changes that occur in the family as children are born, grow, and move out of the house (Aldous, 1978; Duvall, 1977). In addition to the changes in relationships between parents and children, the adult's own parents and other relatives become older, sometimes infirmed, move away, and die. Marital partners themselves continually change their own individual identities and their own patterns of interaction with each other over the course of their association with each other. The domination of family life by transitions, then, means that family identity should be particularly susceptible to evaluation, reevaluation, and change. Working against the inevitability of transitions, though, are the desires of parents, children, and married partners to maintain as stable and happy a homelife as they possibly can. These desires can stimulate identity assimilation and in so doing interfere with the unfolding of new features of identity in individual family members throughout the life cycle of the family.

The potential for continuous conflict between identity assimilation and identity accommodation adds a strong dynamic force to family life and may contribute to tensions within individuals, within generations, and between generations. In outlining the processes of growth in the life cycle of the family, an attempt was made to capture some of this dynamic tension within the family as it stimulates changes, doubts, and questioning within the adult's identity as a loving parent and spouse.

The starting point for this description is in the stage prior to the entry into marriage. The response of an engaged man gives his perception of the beginning of a series of changes in his life associated with his impending marriage, changes to which his identity was already beginning to accommodate:

R: ...Um, when I first met her, I was just getting out of a really rebellious stage. I was partying a lot. I met her and I totally, almost completely, quit partying except for a very limited extent, and, uh, she's totally changed my life....right now I want a family life, I want a home, I don't want to be going out with different people all the time. She's settled me down a whole lot.
Q: Uh huh. And that's reflected in your behavior?
R: Oh yes. It's made me very conservative.
Q: Uh huh.
R: Reflected in my actions.

This respondent noted changes in his personality that were associated with his changes in behavior and, in fact, the two sets of changes were almost indistinguishable in quality. His report that he was feeling "calmer" was entirely consistent with his self-description of having become more settled and conservative.

In the first stage of the family life cycle, these projected changes being anticipated by the engaged man were by now a fact of life for newlyweds. One individual reported that having to be more thoughtful about her husband's needs caused her to become more reflective about her own wishes:

Q: How does being a "partner" affect what you do in your everyday life?
R: Can't be very selfishly motivated to do anything. You really have to think twice about what impact the things that you're going to be doing have on the other person.

Associated with such a change in behavior are reports by other respondents of having become more "mature" and "mellower" since becoming a husband or wife. The respondent quoted above was also planning to start a family, and projected the following effect of having a child on her identity:

Q: Why or in what ways will that be a change?
R: I think it's going to be a huge change for me, and I don't think it's going to be a very big change for Stuart. It's going to be a big change for me because I love my work.

I love being exposed to people. I guess what I love most is that I'm constantly learning. I love my field. And for me to be detached from that is going to be a big deal.

An expectant father described how he thought his life would change after the birth of his child in similar terms, but as applied to his identity in the area of recreational interests:

Q: So, are you right now planning and preparing for how things will change when the baby comes along?
R: Yeah. I'm trying to, anyway.
Q: Could you give me an example?
R: Well, I play in my company's sports leagues. I play softball three nights a week, and I won't be able to do that next year. And I also want to join the golf team so I'll have to cut it to one night of softball, and that's taking away from something I really like to do, so it's definitely an adjustment I'm going to have to try and prepare for.

The new parents in the sample echoed the preparatory concerns of those who were planning to start their families. These persons in the "transition to parenthood" stage of the family life cycle enumerated the many ways in which having a baby really did create many constraints on their daily life:

Q: How does your family, and your relationships with your family, affect the way that you spend your time?
R: (Laughs) Oh, a lot! It really does! I just never had any idea that a baby took so much time. Demanded so much attention. You always have to arrange your life around, it used to be that I would arrange my life around my husband, you know, and now it's like, um, we both have to arrange our lives around the baby. It's made a lot of difference. Um, it's caused some more arranging, um, and I guess I don't spend as much time sewing, or whatever, but it's worth it.

Counterbalancing the greater time commitments of new parents were some personality changes that were perceived positively: "it gives you a new insight into life, into things in general"; "I find myself trying to be more aware . . . grasp more around me so I can teach my child." The perception of these favorable changes may have helped new parents cope with the many stresses of their change in family status.

This type of response was exemplified in the excerpt taken from the interview of a new mother whose identity was clearly enhanced by becoming a mother:

Q: How does being involved with your family affect the way that you see yourself?
R: (Pause) As a more capable person. Um, since I've had a family of my own, I feel better about myself. I feel more competent, more confident, I feel like I accomplish more, organize my time a little better now.

This experience of a change in self-esteem after the birth of a child was not a uniquely feminine reaction, as shown by the interview with the father of a toddler:

Q: Does being a father and a husband affect the way you view yourself as a person?
R: Yeah, I think so. I think that the challenge that it gives you and the success that you see coming in that challenge probably, I'm sure, makes you a better person. At least

gives you that feeling of accomplishment. That you've seen something happen and something seems to be going right, as opposed to a normal individual not being married and just going on living and not seeing a lot.

The favorable self-image that these respondents described could be a camouflage for feelings of inadequacy or stress associated with caring for a small child, effects that are uncompromisingly dealt with in the family literature (Glenn & McLanahan, 1982). In that case, identity assimilation would be the underlying process producing the responses. The responses would be distorted to be consistent with the individual's attempt to salvage a favorable identity out of a difficult situation in which he or she does not always feel loving toward the new life that has been created. It is, of course, possible that both processes are operating simultaneously and that identity assimilation acts to preserve a sense of stability and routine while identity accommodation allows the individual to cope bit by bit with the massive changes taking place in every part of the new parent's life and identity as a family member.

By the time an adult has children in the toddler and preschool stages, the invasion of children into one's personal life becomes almost complete:

Q: Could you please describe your family situation?
R: . . . I've fallen into the father role more than I'd ever imagined. And right now this is basically setting them up, making sure we've taken care of that business so that then the other projects, you know, so that . . . I'm not too selfish. I have a tendency to be that, because you know, I'm into so many different things and there's only 24 hours in a day. I guess I've fallen into that more than I ever thought I would.

* * *

Q: How does having a family being important to you affect the way that you feel about yourself?
R: . . . My current preoccupation with them almost is not the way that I planned the rest of my life. I think right now it is taking over most aspects of my life . . .

* * *

Q: How does being a mother affect the things you do in your everyday life?
R: Affect what I do? As far as how it affects? I take care of the boys. That's the only thing it would really affect. Just constantly taking care of the boys all day. If I didn't have them, I wouldn't do it.

All three of these respondents describe a daily routine that is dominated by the need to take care of their young children. There is also the sense that they were caught unprepared for such a demanding set of expectations at this point in their children's development. If parents receive little advance preparation for the transition to parenthood stage, they receive even less for the preschool stage. Childbirth education classes and other childbirth literature give only minimal attention to the demands of the newborn, but at least there is some. In contrast, the preschool stage is rarely discussed in terms of its impact on the parent's life. It is no surprise, then, that the respondents in this stage were so caught unaware by the changes in their family obligations and, in turn, their identities as parents.

A finding described in Chapter 4 was that individuals who are older when they start their families feel less hampered by the restrictions on their daily life. The oldest respondent with young children commented quite a bit more favorably than the younger parents about the effects on his daily life of having a toddler in the home:

> Q: There are few things that we don't do together, in fact, we even do the shopping together. I guess I enjoy it more than she does, which is probably unusual, um, when we go out together, we take our child with us for the most part. It's rare that we leave him home with the baby sitter. But there are times when we like to go out alone, and we may go to a concert or a ball game. That's it, just a very comfortable situation.

The effect of this man's child on his daily life signified much of the same intensity of activities as was described by other respondents, but was viewed in terms of a different identity as a father. Because his own identity was more well established outside the realm of parenting, he may have felt less invaded by the intrusion of an active toddler into his home life. In addition, having had a longer term marital relationship that preceded the birth of his child, his identity as a loving husband may have been less threatened by the interruptions of a child into husband-wife interactions.

Respondents with children in the school-age stage referred to numerous effects of a different quality on their everyday life, centering around the need to provide experiences for their children that would foster their intellectual and spiritual growth. While not as total an experience as with preschool children in terms of number of hours of involvement during the day, this kind of change in everyday life also involved significant reordering of priorities. This developmental change was insightfully described at some length and in great detail in the following excerpt:

> Q: Do you think that you do anything especially because of the fact that you have a family?
> R: Oh yeah. Definitely. There are a lot of things, um, right in today, I wouldn't be participating in a lot of functions if it wasn't for the family.
> Q: Could you give me a couple of examples?
> R: Oh, alright. There's a difference when the children are small as when they're, my daughter is 10. We had her for 5 years before we had our son. And the way I categorize it, we really got away with a lot when she was little. We really didn't have to do, um, a lot of responsible things. Now that she's 10 years old, and she also can input information and school comes into it, activities, uh, questioning, how come you don't do this, you know, it makes you step back and say "Oh" you know, "I've gotta reevaluate my priorities." At a point when she was little there was, we felt, no need, really, to go to church. You know, you're not going to take some 2-year-old to church. You're opening yourself up for either embarrassment, or trouble from the lady in the pew next to you, or whatever. So, we were really, you know, kind of blasé about religion at that point. But now, when she's in school, the teaching has to start coming. Because she's starting to pick up from other children, um, school itself, information and she starts questioning and she now says "How come we aren't doing?" "How come we don't do?" You know, "How come Lisa down the street does this and we don't do this?" And it has

made me have to stop and start, I don't want to say become a responsible adult, because I don't feel we were irresponsible when she was small. Just changing the stream. To a lake. You know, now she's in school, we put her in a Catholic school. There are more pressures on us as a family now. You know, because they want to make you responsible for her. "Participate in this." "We need your help." If she was still little, you know, I wouldn't be participating. You know, I would find other things for myself to do. Whether it would just be laying down on the couch reading the paper for 3 hours on Sunday. Having to get up and see that she's involved in the church, or if there's a spaghetti dinner after that, I volunteer to do my part.

Q: What might you do differently if you did not have a family?

R: I probably would be more career orientated. If I didn't have a family there would be more money in my life probably. I would probably concentrate it more to myself. And just getting more education or participating in, like, seminars that I might see that I want to go to that I can't go to because it costs $50. Fifty dollars is a big deal with a family. Fifty dollars may not be such a big deal if I didn't have one. So, I've gotta say I would probably have more time for myself.

Given what the parents of infants and toddlers related about their lives, it was interesting that this respondent regarded her present involvement with her 10-year-old daughter as relatively much more consuming than what she remembered about her involvement with her daughter when she was a toddler. Her metaphor of a "lake" from a "stream" aptly captures this sentiment. However, her observations of the relative difficulty of having school-age versus toddler children were quite consistent with what was reported in one study on fathers at different points in the family life cycle (Harry, 1976). In addition, the respondent's comments about school have also been documented in the literature on parenting. A stressful feature of having a child enter the school system is the accompanying exposure of the parents to judgments by other parents and teachers about the quality of parenting the child has been receiving at home (Klein & Ross, 1958).

The needs to ensure the religious training of children, to become involved in their school activities, and to spend time with them in general in extracurricular activities were examples of identity accommodation also mentioned by other parents in this stage. These examples suggest that it is in this stage of the family life cycle that the adult's identity as a parent is transformed from one whose lovingness is expressed mainly in a nurturant and supportive way to one whose lovingness is mixed with discipline.

There were very few parents of teenage children who spoke of restraints on their own daily lives of having to meet the needs of their sons and daughters. The only two respondents who did speak of effects on daily life focused on the need to set proper standards for the children's behavior:

Q: How does being a mother affect what you do in your everyday life?

R: Well, different things, different standards that I think the children should attain. I feel that I always have to give them an example. I feel independent that I can go ahead and be carefree and do different things and yet, I never want them to think two standards that I would say, that I would act one way and expect them to do another. So, it kind of guides you in the things that you're doing and the way you participate.

This respondent indicated that her maternal role was becoming less burdensome than it was previously, as indicated by the phrase "I feel independent." Her desire to follow certain standards did not appear to be overly burdensome either. In contrast, the following excerpt is from a man who recently became a widower and is now having to assume a more responsible identity as a father than he had previously. This respondent frequently expressed displeasure over the fact that he has had to become a disciplinarian in the absence of his wife, who formerly held that unenviable position in the home:

Q: Is there anything you're doing that shows you're more stern?
R: (Pause) Well, when the kids used to go out, my wife used to ask "Where are you going?" "What time are you coming home?" I'd just sit back and be quiet because she always did this. It was always her part in saying this but now it's my part and if I don't say "be home by a certain time," I mean, they can be out all hours of the night time.

Had he not moved from an identity as a lenient father to one who was actively involved in his children's upbringing, it is doubtful that the effects on his behavior of having teenage children would have been particularly noticeable. His statement shows that he is resisting the incorporation into his identity as a loving father the need to be a disciplining father as well. Other parents, who had already made this transition years earlier, were no longer aware of the potential discrepancies between the two identities as a parent. In fact, those parents saw the two identities as being very compatible, with the identity as a disciplinarian providing a concrete way to implement the identity as a loving parent.

For parents whose children were becoming adults and moving out of the home, the reported effects of being parents on identity were less evident than at any earlier point in the family life cycle:

Q: How does being a mother affect what you do in your everyday life?
R: Oh, it doesn't affect it really at all, I don't think now. With them all out of town.

Although, as in this case, the immediate pressures on daily life that were so important to parents of younger children were gone, many parents were involved with their adult children on a frequent basis:

Q: Does your relationship with your family affect the way you spend your free time?
R: Yeah, well, to a certain extent, yes. We try to get together on family occasions. . . . We still think nothing of calling my daughter, even though she's married, and saying "Hey," you know, "Bob is working late tonight, do you want to go out to dinner with us tonight?" You know? It's that kind of thing. And sometimes she'll say, "Gee, I'm busy." Sometimes she'll say "Gee, that's great. I will." Or "Come on over." This Sunday morning, my daughter and son-in-law are going to come over for breakfast. We got to chatting, so we decided, "Hey, invite them over." My wife invited them. My daughter called back and said Bob doesn't have anything on then. So, fine. It's that kind of a thing. . . . I don't consider the relationship a burden and apparently my kids don't either, or my son wouldn't call from St. Thomas. He'd say "What the hell? Why should I spend my money?" kind of thing. And my daughter wouldn't stop by just to say "Hello" or call on the phone . . .

Although not a "burden," this man's grown children are very much a part of his life, if not on an everyday basis then on a frequent one. The predominant theme, though, of parents involved in the "launching" stage of the family life cycle was sensitivity to the need to change their approach to raising children as the children approached adulthood. There were 11 women and 8 men who were contemplating this process. Not all of these parents were actually in the launching stage. Those who were anticipating it were expressing their thoughts about what might happen when they reached that point.

In general, most respondents expressed the belief that it was necessary to allow children increasing independence as they grew through the teenage years and beyond. Although one respondent noted that the "responsibility doesn't end when they grow up," most concurred in the need to exit gracefully from children's lives. For some respondents, the main concern in this launching process was ensuring that the children remained out of trouble, as shown in this excerpt:

Q: How strongly do you feel about your family?
R: . . . I could stay with them all the time, but they are starting to grow up now where they want to go and they have their own friends. I worry about them, I want to know where they are all the time. Sometimes that's not possible.

However, concern over the well-being of children as they became older and more independent was also shown:

Q: How do you see yourself in the family? Do you see yourself as mainly, think of yourself as a mother, a wife, how do you conceive of yourself?
R: Well, I guess after they have left the nest and are on their own, I can't really influence them any more, you know. My job is pretty much done as far as that goes because there's only one that's under 18. So that I just, at this point, more or less, am a bystander and it would affect me tremendously if they made a wrong choice and were unhappy.

Apart from the desire to ensure the well-being of children once they have left the parental home, there did not seem to be much evidence of trauma among the respondents concerning the transition "out of" parenthood. The parents were, at this point, perhaps relieved to be able to relinquish the identity as both a loving and disciplining parent for the single identity as a loving parent. When change was mentioned as a function of this process, it was not described as a significantly upsetting experience, but as a stimulus for identity change that was either favorable or, at the worst, affectively neutral.

After having spent 18, 20, or more years involved in parenting, one of the critical issues in next stage, the postparental stage, became adjusting to the new freedom and independence associated with not having children in the home. This was especially true, as noted earlier in the chapter, for women who had been so involved as homemakers that they had no identity outside the family. However, once the transition was made, the change in identity could be regarded as having had favorable effects in the long run:

Q: Did you have questions or doubts about being a wife and mother and that's why you went to work?

R: Well, it started out when my two daughters were ready for college. And I was very content to be at home and just take care of them. Then when I started working, I began to enjoy it more than I thought I would, and now I can't envision anything but working! (laughs)

The disparity between the conflict reported by the women going through the transition to the postparental period and the expressed enjoyment of the women who had completed the transition is striking. It is consistent in a general sense with empirical findings on the postparental transition that show it to be a benign or positive event after it has occurred both for women (e.g., McCubbin, Joy, Cauble, Comeau, Patterson, & Needle, 1980; Menaghan, 1983) and for men (Lewis, Freneau, & Roberts, 1979).

Adults in the postparental stage also regarded themselves as in the process of changing their identities as spouses:

Q: What is important about being a wife?
R: I guess as we get older, my husband and I, now that we have everyone through school, are concentrating on ourselves at home. He has about 10 more years of work before he retires. But we have to pay attention more to our house as we kind of let things go. And I think pay more attention to each other. Do more things, maybe take trips.
Q: What about this is important to you?
R: It is important because the years slip by and I think you see so many of your friends lose their husbands. Makes your own a little more important. (crying)

The change in this woman's focus from a loving parent to a loving spouse was given added intensity by what she observed happening with her friends. The possibility of widowhood is one that emerges for the first time to a serious extent in the later years of the marriage: "There's always that possibility at our age right now of becoming a widow." Another difference between the pre- and postparental identities as a spouse was alluded to in the following excerpt:

Q: When I asked you what's important about being a wife, I imagine that has had some adjustment with the children being primary for such a long time?
R: Yes. You see how it will go. The other way, like it was in the beginning. And that you can't go back to what you were before the children. So that's an adjustment too, for both my husband and myself.

Although this respondent did not specify what prevents her from going "back to what you were," her statement is consistent with the literature on postparental couples. In the traditional family, it is often difficult for wives and husbands to find a common basis for sharing and communication if their separate involvements in work and family spheres of activity have drawn them apart. Now on their own with these involvements greatly minimized, the factors within the relationship that either enhance or detract from intimacy will become more apparent to both partners (Aldous, 1978). This respondent was not certain whether she would in fact be able to return completely to her prior identity as a loving wife.

This analysis of identity processes throughout the family life cycle fleshes out, from the point of view of adult identity, the effects of family transitions on parents. This analysis, like other descriptions of the family life cycle, has focused mostly on normative cases; people whose lives follow the socially prescribed patterns of becoming engaged, getting married, and having children, in a series of invariant stages. It would be erroneous to conclude, though, that this series of stages is inevitable, fixed, and universal (Feldman & Feldman, 1975; Hill & Mattesich, 1979).

The conclusion that seems more appropriate from this analysis is that there are widespread and substantial effects of the development of children on the individual's identity as a loving parent and spouse. Ultimately, these effects translate into effects on the individual's overall identity as a person. To some extent, these effects are linked with the ages of children, since children have different developmental needs at different ages. By examining the identity accommodation that takes place along with the ages of children and stage of marriage, the influence of changing daily routines and obligations on the adult's identity as a loving family member can be seen. This description also revealed the large amount of anticipation and planning that occurred when the respondent was in one stage toward what would happen in the next stage. It seems reasonable to conclude that because of the pervasiveness of real and potential change throughout the family life cycle, the possibility for identity accommodation to occur is ever-present, even for the man or woman with the most staunchly assimilative identity.

Unpredictable Sources of Identity Accommodation in the Family

The transitions during the family life cycle described in the previous section revealed many stimuli for identity accommodation due to the changes in family patterns as children move through stages of dependence and independence. The area of family identity is unique in the sense that developmental changes in children are inevitable and roughly predictable (Clausen, 1972). Adults can therefore take advantage of this predictability to prepare themselves for subsequent changes in their family situations that might influence their identities as family members. Anticipatory identity accommodation can then be used as a means of adaptation as each new stage is approached. This predictability of family life cycle changes may serve as somewhat of a buffer protecting the individual from some of the stress associated with the demands for new behaviors and changes in responsibilities that are part of family life. Even with the predictability of the family life cycle stages, there were still surprises in store when the actual transition from one stage to another took place, as in the preschool stage. However, these surprises were relatively minor compared to the completely unexpected nature of idiosyncratic self- or situation-induced stimuli for exploration of alternatives.

In contrast, the cases presented in this section were not associated with any particular age or stage, yet had similar characteristics in that they stimulated a close scrutiny of the "fit" between the individual's family identity and the experiences that he or she was having within the family.

The first case example of exploration of alternatives was a brief description of how a woman resolved the decision to have a child out of wedlock when she was a teenager:

R: When I was pregnant with Michelle I thought "Should I do it, keep her? I'm not married. What should I do? What will people think? Will I be able to work? How am I going to support her?" But I just said, I supposed things could be worse. It gave me a real incentive. . . . And I did . . . It gave me a lot of drive. Because I was able to work, to pay my bills back. And I said this is what I want . . .

For this respondent, becoming pregnant before she was married violated her family identity as a "good girl," as suggested in her question "What will people think?" By "showing" those people that she could successfully overcome the odds against her, the respondent was able to salvage what she regarded as her damaged identity in their eyes. She was also able to salvage her own sense of self-respect by taking this course of action.

The next respondent, who is divorced, explains a similar kind of situation in his attempts to establish a permanent relationship with his married girlfriend:

Q: You said before that the relationship might change. Can you talk about that?
R: Well, ideally, sure, I would like to see it, and this is just my thoughts, I'd like to see her and I in close proximity and in a marital status, and that you know, if, yes. And, uh, to where we could, you know, spend more time together, and not on the telephone, or you know, just spend more actual time together . . .
Q: Are you seriously considering this as an alternative?
R: Uh, I am. Yes. I am. But I cannot, I can't pursue with all seriousness, I cannot just, I can't do it. . . . That's not me. That's not characteristic of me. Nor is it of her, either. Uh, to leave. . . . So I think we're both . . . accepting what we have.

Although he claims to be accepting his situation, this acceptance is not a static one. Given the opportunity, he would, in his words, "do it"; that is, get married. Either alternative he chose would have an influence on his identity. If he were to marry her he would continue to "mature in the relationship" as he has already. At the same time, he would be violating his own moral code of "disrupting" her marriage. For him not to pursue the relationship, though, would mean that he could not have the close relationship he so earnestly desires to fulfill his identity as a loving, intimate partner:

R: I have discovered this in the few years that, no man can live alone . . . You've got to have another person to relate to. . . . A person that you can go to and say "You know, uh, this is a very deeply rooted problem that's on my mind," and discuss it with this person. In other words, everybody needs somebody. And this is what I've come to realize. We cannot close people out. We cannot close out life.

It seems likely that the conflict that this respondent is undergoing will continue into the future.

Another group of individuals were evaluating alternatives that they thought they might implement at some point in the future. In the case excerpted below, the respondent was contemplating a change in how much emphasis he places on his family identity as compared to his identity as a worker:

Q: Are there any major changes in the next 2, 3, 4 years that you yourself would be initiating...?

R: ...There's some areas I'd like to develop a little bit more than I have done in the past. I'd like to, uh, I'd like to make more, uh, I'm a, I would say I have a fairly, uh, good career position. In a way I'm still, I'm very effective at what I do, but, um, I haven't left, there's no big monumental task, I haven't been working toward any large goals in that area. I've just been kind of, uh, doing things from day to day...(instead of) thinking in terms of your big accomplishments. In a sense I'm kind of, kind of groping a little bit for what that might be. So that, if there, if there was a change, uh, there might be some opportunities for my career that could come up just, that might influence my roles as father...

While not as dramatic a change in identity as the others described in this section, the diminution of his involvement in the family through increased work activity would have major implications for this respondent's identity as a loving father.

These situations in which individuals were evaluating alternatives to their present identities in the family show how identity accommodation may occur in ways totally unrelated to the family life cycle. In addition, the types of concerns shown by individuals considering alternatives were not specific to either sex, since both men and women were evaluating their identities as spouses or romantic partners, parents, and workers.

Respondents whose marriages were coming apart, whose children were in trouble, or who were examining their degree of involvement in the family were experiencing events and inner changes that could not possibly have been predicted years, or perhaps even months, before they occurred. Consequently, they were less prepared when these changes took place than they were for the normative changes of the family life cycle. There are also fewer guidelines from relatives, friends, and society in general regarding what to expect or what possible solutions to follow when the type of change is specific to the individual's particular situation. All of these factors mean that when the identity accommodation process is set in motion by a unique personal event or a new understanding of self, the individual may experience more distress and confusion until a new family identity can be found. Although the family presents a constant source of challenge to the adult's identity, then, its rhythmic patterning of change may serve as a reassuringly stabilizing influence.

Part III
Work Identity

While the emotional life of many adults is dominated by their family relationships, the productive energies of adults are usually oriented toward their work. However, the distinction between these two realms of life is often not this clearcut. Both men's and women's work lives can involve strong emotional attachments. Their family lives, in turn, can be drastically affected by their work commitments. For the present purposes, though, it is worthwhile to regard work and family as encompassing different spheres of the adult's identity. Both areas contribute to the adult's identity, but in different ways.

The 94 adults in this study had a great deal to say about how their identities were tied to their work. Their attitudes toward work ranged from enthusiastic to indifferent to angry and embittered. The kinds of factors about work that were regarded as important ranged from the fact that it made one's fingernails get dirty to the opportunity it gave to earn a decent salary to the chance to use one's creative powers of intellect. There were full- and part-time homemakers who reflected varying attitudes toward housework ranging from enjoyment of keeping the house neat and preparing meals to dislike of making beds and vacuuming to feeling unfulfilled and ready to seek outside employment as soon as their children were in school. Although some adults in the sample held similar kinds of occupations, each reflected their own particular concerns about work, concerns that were as much a function of their individual identities as a function of the experiences they had in their employment situations.

In this part of the book, the work concerns of the respondents are described in terms of two basic categories, each of which has several subcategories. The distributions of statements within the subcategories are shown in Table C.2 of Appendix C. The identity processes of assimilation and accommodation are illustrated in each chapter to show how individuals approach these topical concerns about their work and relate them to their identities as competent people.

Intrinsic and Extrinsic Work Involvement

The major point of division that cuts through the work identity statements was between intrinsic and extrinsic work involvement. This division point reflects the well-documented distinction in the occupational psychology literature (e.g.,

Herzberg, Mausner, & Snyderman, 1959; Kalleberg, 1977) between work that is performed because of its inherent interest and meaning (intrinsic) and work that is regarded by the person performing it as a means to an end (extrinsic). Beyond this simple line of division are a set of more elaborated factors within each of the two major orientations. By exploring these factors in detail and with case examples, it is possible to gain an understanding of what motivates adults on a day-to-day basis in carrying out their productive activities.

The distinction between intrinsic and extrinsic work motivation is important not only for describing work identity, but also because of the implications that it has for adjustment and satisfaction. Occupational psychologists are interested in demonstrating the factors that lead to satisfaction with work because they are interested in finding ways to increase the worker's productivity. The straightforward assumption of the occupational psychologist, which seems to have held up in research on work productivity (Lawler, 1982), is that "the happy worker is the productive worker." If the workers are productive, this means, in turn, that the company they work for makes a larger profit.

From the standpoint of adult identity, there is a different reason for being interested in the difference between intrinsic and extrinsic work motivation. Work that is performed because the worker is basically interested in it is work that will more directly involve the worker's identity (Katz & Kahn, 1978). The worker's ability to do the job well will be seen by the worker as a direct reflection of his or her competence (Hackman & Oldham, 1975). The more intrinsically involved the worker is in work, the more central will be this evaluation of competence to his or her overall identity as a person (Lodahl & Kejner, 1965; Wood, 1974). Greater work satisfaction and productivity might ensue from this positive effect on identity, but productivity is not the primary concern from the standpoint of the worker's identity. Conversely, it follows that a worker who has reason to believe that he or she is not competent at work will suffer damaging effects to identity, particularly if the work is high in intrinsic value.

Based on the work of occupational psychologists it would be logical to hypothesize that workers who are involved in their work for the extrinsic benefits it provides (money, status, benefits) would be less likely to have their identities affected to any significant degree by their work experiences. However, if work is valued for extrinsic reasons because it makes possible the fulfillment of other important goals the individual has, then success or failure will have important carry-over effects to the individual's identity as a competent worker. Short of this type of extrinsic work motivation, though, workers who regard their work "as a job" may be expected to have little involvement of identity in their work lives. A worker may compensate for a job that has little intrinsic value by focusing instead on its extrinsic rewards. Even though this worker may be "satisfied" with work, it is unlikely that his or her sense of competence will be challenged to an extent that it influences the individual's identity.

With this prelude to the intrinsic-extrinsic work distinction, the work identities of the adults in the study are now examined in detail.

6
The Competent Worker

When work has the potential to motivate the work intrinsically, success or failure on the job can have a dramatic impact on the individual's feelings of competence. These feelings of competence are basic to the adult's sense of identity because they help to define him or her as a productive human being. Competence at work also has the potential to provide the individual with a sense of self-reliance. The adults in the sample who were working outside the home described in detail the perceived impact of their work on their sense of competence. The terms that they used to describe their work formed a set of related variations around the theme of work's intrinsic meaning. These variations captured different facets of the work itself, including interest value, autonomy, and a number of characteristics of work tasks. From the respondents' statements, it was apparent that the intrinsicalness of work is a dynamic, ever-present, and central feature of the concrete reality of working.

The tasks involved in performing a job are essentially the most basic intrinsic qualities of work. What the individual does on a daily basis in completing work activities is regarded as so important to defining work that the U.S. government devised an entire work classification system based on the degree to which jobs involve working with "data," "people," or "things" (U.S. Department of Labor, 1977). The degree of complexity of these intrinsic qualities of work has been shown, moreover, to have a measurable impact over a period of years on the adult's abilities to deal with demanding intellectual problems (Kohn & Schooler, 1983). At the same time, though, the workers in the sample were anything but insensitive to the monetary features of their jobs. The economic reward function of work can therefore not be ignored as a factor entering into the worker's identity. Economic and other extrinsic factors as contributors to work identity will be discussed at length in Chapter 7. Their existence should, however, be kept in mind throughout the reading of the present chapter.

The Importance of Interesting Work

Whether work is regarded as inherently interesting and stimulating or as boring and repetitive plays a major role in determining whether the work day goes quickly or drags on seemingly forever. In their statements about this factor, some respondents went no further than to say their work was either "boring" or "stimulating." Others described in more depth what it meant to have work that was of inherent interest compared to work that was dull and repetitious. Some felt that the work had lost its interest or "zip" over time; the original feeling of enthusiasm eroded as the job activities became easier and less and less novel. For others, the work had never had much variety or stimulating value at all.

Work involving assembly or production where the tasks were the same hour after hour and workers were required to be "turning in a certain quota every day" seemed especially likely to be regarded as monotonous. Other kinds of work that respondents found inherently boring included clerical work, as can be seen in the following statement:

R: . . . About all I'm doing is taking information from other people and rewriting it into different formats and rewriting job procedures. Rather meaningless, repetitious. . . I just feel that what I do could be handled much better with someone with a lot less qualifications than I got. Definitely doesn't tax you at all. I can do my job 2 hours a day standing on my head.

However, even what would seem to be more intellectually exciting work that demands high-level skills could potentially be regarded as boring, as indicated by this research scientist:

Q: What do you particularly dislike about it?
R: Sometimes the work is incredibly monotonous. Necessary, but monotonous. And that is something that I have found that I really don't have as much patience for as I thought I'd have. You have to do the same thing over 50 times or 100 times, and that gets to me.

In contrast to the dulling effect that monotony has on the worker, work that is perceived as varied and interesting can have an invigorating effect. This effect may prove to be a powerful component of the worker's reason for remaining in a particular job, as shown in the following statement from a research associate:

Q: What is important to you about your work as a research associate?
R: I guess the type of work I do there, which is varied and interesting. If it weren't for that, I probably wouldn't work there . . .
Q: How do you feel about this kind of work?
R: How do I feel about it? Well, as I said before I like it very much because it is varied. Often we go out on interviews and I see the study from helping to organize it from the beginning right to the end, actually doing a lot of the programming of it, and seeing the final results.

As she elaborated upon her initial statement, this respondent also mentioned another intrinsic factor that is covered later: the ability to see the results of her work. For this respondent, seeing a finished product coming from her efforts made her feel that she was directly participating in the research process, as well as having the chance to use many different skills.

Not all workers agreed that work needed to be varied in order to be enjoyed. A woman who performed a clerical task involving mainly proofreading found a certain comfort in knowing her job well and being able to use the same skills over and over again:

Q: The work that you do, then, is that particularly important to you?

R: It is because I've done it for so long and I know it's no big chore for me. I'm content in that particular job because everything again is very familiar. If I had had to get a full-time job elsewhere I may not have been as happy.

This respondent's preference for the routine and familiar may, by virtue of its static quality, represent a form of identity assimilation. Because she did not venture into new territory with her work tasks, she could be guaranteed of experiencing only success. This would reinforce her sense of competence as a worker. Were she to take on new tasks, she might expose herself to the risk of failure.

What is interesting about work may be the work tasks itself, as in the above example, or it may be another feature of the job. One feature that emerged in the interviews of two men was the opportunity to interact with many different people. For the first man, this opportunity was provided by his job as a food service worker in a cafeteria. In this capacity, he not only cooked, but also engaged in a great deal of direct contact with other people (it is also helpful to know that this is the volunteer fireman described in Chapter 4):

Q: What do you find attractive about your job?

R: What do I find attractive? Oh, I would say, I'd have to say, number 1 would be people . . . I see different people, not the people I work with, but in the course of a day I see so many people.

Q: People that you serve.

R: People that I serve. The ones I talk to. The telephone rings 100 times a day, well, 20 times a day, at least a dozen. Okay? Just talking to people. How everyone is a little bit different, the way they think about, you know, their opinions on things, my opinions on things. . . . People never cease to amaze me. No matter, you've seen thousands, but the next one's always different. I mean, everybody's different. It's like a fire. Every fire is different, you know? Every person is different. That's very attractive to me. Just people . . .

Another respondent described what factors had made his previous work interesting. It appeared that the variety of work tasks was the critical feature that he enjoyed. However, it was really the opportunity to interact with his friends at work that gave the job its variety:

Q: What in particular did you enjoy about it?

R: It wasn't, uh, I worked on production, you know, where . . . . it was, uh, tedious, nerve racking. Running a forklift, uh, you were doing something different all day long. You were never, and of course, you're driving the fork life, which is the same thing all day long but you're doing different things throughout the day, uh, one minute you'd be at one end of the factory and you'd be saying "Well, hey Joe, how are you?" and the next minute you'd be at the other end saying hello to Sam or something, so you know, there was a little variety.

This man was able to compensate for what was essentially a fairly routine job by finding variety in the people with whom he interacted. This example suggests that extrinsic rewards can serve to balance a lack of intrinsic interest in work, although they cannot give meaning to work. As the respondent in the above example stated "It didn't have much meaning, it was just a job."

The potential for a job to be interesting and stimulating may depend on the extent to which it matches or provides a "fit" with the needs and skills of the worker (French & Kahn, 1962; Holland, 1973). Regardless of the actual nature of the tasks, then, a worker may be very satisfied with work that is seen as tailor-made to his or her individual talents. The identity process involved in such a perception is assimilation, because the worker is imposing his or her own identity onto the work experiences rather than having experiences determine the nature of identity. Secondarily, the perception that one's work is congruent with one's own interest and aptitudes may arise from a desire to "make do" with a situation that is less than optimal. It may be easier to change one's perception of one's job rather than one's job itself in order to achieve a feeling of satisfaction.

There were two kinds of identity assimilation processes apparent in responses concerning the fit between worker and job. Several respondents used the phrase "I always wanted to be a(n) _____" to describe the reason for their satisfaction with work. That this phrase represents assimilation follows from reasoning similar to that in the case of role fulfillment in the family. If a job is perceived favorably because the worker "always" wanted to have this job it means that he or she is not examining specific features of the job as it is being experienced. Instead, it is the job as it was and is imagined to be that is determining the perception of satisfaction. In the following excerpt, the respondent's vacillation around the question of whether she would ever seek alternate employment reinforces the judgment that her "always" wanting to be a teacher represents an assimilation process:

Q: In the future would you consider an alternative to what you're doing?
R: Um hmm. Except that I still anticipate that I would never like anything better than teaching. I go into a library, for example, and a library could be entirely different. You have no classes whatsoever, and teachers will come in with their classes and there you are, typing or carding, and your day is just endless. So another field of work seems alien to me. I wouldn't, first of all, I don't have any marketable skills. I don't type. I don't do anything that I could go out and look for another job, something that I think I would be agreeable, at least to give it a chance, to see if it would be a field of work I would like. I just always wanted to be a teacher and I'm afraid that's where I'm going to stay.
Q: Do you think in the future you might consider an alternative to teaching?
R: Yes, (laughs) for the same reason. If I would, I don't have enough ambition to think of a job I'd like to pursue and go to school to get the skills to get that job. So I'm happy staying where I am, even though I have nothing in mind at this point as an alternative. But if something should arise, I know I would need the skills to go into something different.
Q: I'm still not sure whether you would or not.

R: Well, on the basis of all that, I would say no. I would keep it a definite no then. I'm happy doing what I am doing. That's three yesses and a no! (laughs) This is interesting.

This respondent's reluctance to try something new, at which she might not succeed, inhibits her willingness to think of an alternative. In this context, her statement that she always wanted to be a teacher appears even more as a rationalization rather than an objective statement of fact.

The second kind of identity assimilation process was evident in a cluster of statements, all from men, indicating that their work was for them an extension of their personalities and special talents. The statements of these men parallel very closely the theories of vocational choice and development in which the optimal occupation is regarded as one that allows the individual to "implement" his or her self-concept (Super, 1969). When such an occupation is found, the worker can flourish because of the job's potential to fulfill the worker's unique goals and interests. The reason that statements of this nature are regarded as instances of identity assimilation is that they represent an imposition of the worker's identity onto work experiences rather than vice versa. None of these statements convey the impression that the workers changed their own identities in response to the demands of their particular work tasks.

The first example of "self-implementation" is from the interview of an engineer:

Q: How does your work affect the way you think about yourself?
R: One of the things I've, I feel about myself, uh, is that I, I have a very investigative talent, sort of mind, very analytical, and I think that it's a very good decision for me to be in it actually.

His job as an engineer allows this respondent to express his investigative aptitude. Another respondent, also involved in scientific work, saw his job as meeting somewhat of a different need:

Q: You said before that it affects your self-concept or something. Could you talk a little more about that?
R: Well, as because, if I wasn't a biochemist, what would I be? The answer is some sort of scientist, some sort of investigator. Um, why do I want to be an investigator? I'm just the curious sort. I suppose that's really the only reason. Or, I see myself as asking questions and looking for answers.

Another need, seeking order and tidiness, was expressed by a respondent who regarded his work as suiting his personality very closely:

Q: So do you think it affects the way you see yourself as a, as a person, your work?
R: Uh huh, I think so. It, uh, it's very meticulous and I'm like that sometimes, very, everything has to be just so. I'm a little bit of a neurotic, people say. (laughs)

It should be pointed out that the statements of these three respondents may be based partly on identity accommodation. In order to know what one's interests and personality are, it is necessary to engage in a certain degree of self-scrutiny. At some point in their lives, these respondents must have thought about the kind of people they were and what direction they would like to take in their work. In so doing, they would have been engaging in the type of self-analysis that constitutes identity accommodation. Because of this, the form of identity assimilation used by these respondents is considerably more complicated than the case of the teacher for whom work satisfied an ambition that she had "always" held.

Autonomy

In a 10-year research program conducted at the National Institute on Mental Health, Kohn and Schooler (1983) found that the most important work-related factor determining the impact of work on the adult was occupational self-direction, "the use of initiative, thought, and independent judgment in work" (p. 127). Included as a part of occupational self-direction was the rating of the complexity of the work tasks described earlier in this chapter. A second part of occupational self-direction was "closeness of supervision" "a worker's subjective appraisals of his freedom to disagree with his supervisor, how closely he is supervised, the extent to which his supervisor tells him what to do rather than discussing it with him, and the importance in his job of doing what one is told to do" (p. 127). The third component of occupational self-direction was the degree of variety in the work tasks.

Many of the workers in the present sample spontaneously mentioned autonomy as a feature of their work that was important to them in terms that were virtually identical with Kohn and Schooler's definition of closeness of supervision. The main characteristic of this theme was the worker's feeling that he or she could do things "on my own" without having someone "looking over my shoulder." Another related concept was that of "responsibility," or being given the authority to make decisions on one's own. In contrast to the meaning of this word in the context of the family, responsibility in work was almost universally regarded positively, as evidence that the worker was a competent person who could be counted upon not to make a mistake. In this sense, responsibility was another form of self-direction. What was not included as part of the category of autonomy was the freedom to arrange one's own hours or not to have to punch a time clock. These were classified as extrinsic factors determining whether the worker found the job to be convenient and adaptable to his or her demands outside of work.

These two aspects of autonomy, responsibility and freedom from supervision, were often blended together in the perceptions of the respondents when describing the leeway their jobs provided in doing things on their own. This meshing of the two can be seen in the following examples. The first is a local branch manager:

Q: What do you particularly like about your job?
R: Well, for one thing, you don't have any immediate supervision.... And, uh, I like that. I mean, I work harder that way being without somebody supervising me because I, I just can't say. I mean, I gotta be doing something, so, I like that. The responsibility is mine, so, you know, I like that.

Although this man was not strongly positive about the effect of having autonomy on his feelings about work, the second example from a laboratory technician shows greater enthusiasm for the self-direction and responsibility her job permitted her to have:

Q: What do you especially like about it?

R: Well, there's more than helping people. I like the responsibility of it. I don't know if you know about lab work, but you can't make mistakes. It's a very exact and very precise type of place to have to work. And I work alone there at nights. Which at times is lonely but that's not as important to me as the pleasure of working alone and organizing my time. I'll come in and there'll be so much to do at the moment and I'll decide what I'm going to do and how I'm going to do it, and like I like making my own decisions as to how I'm going to do that . . .

This respondent then went on to describe her appreciation of the flexible hours that she had with this job. This feature was often included by others in a statement concerning autonomy, a fact that probably reflects a certain reality of the greater freedom of scheduling and reporting afforded a worker who has autonomy.

One pair of statements concerning autonomy provided an interesting contrast that highlights how the individual's identity can determine how a work situation is perceived. The first respondent was a self-employed man: He gave the following answer as his reason for not seeking different work:

Q: Are you thinking about seeking different kind of work?

R: Well, I'm gonna continue investing, but as far as seeking a different type of, uh, I thought about that last year and I just could not work for someone else. I could not go to IBM or AT&T and work for them. I'm very, I'll make the decisions. If I'm wrong, I'm wrong. It's my problem. It would be very difficult for me to hafta have someone else make the decisions for me . . .

However, the next respondent, who did work at a large company, spoke precisely about the freedom he had to do what he wanted as the major positive feature of his work:

Q: What do you especially like about this position?

R: I got a lot of freedom. I can generally come and go as I please. I have dealings with a supply company which is right over here across the river. I have Berkeley Products on Pleasant Street. I'm gone from my desk most of the day and nobody ever asks me where I went. I have a million and a half dollars to spend a year on supplies and nobody ever asks me where it went. Generally I enjoy the freedom to be sort of, I kind of like to do things on my own and accomplish things on my own without somebody standing right there watching me, making sure that I'm getting something done. Throwing their ideas into what I'm doing. I'd just as soon be left alone. I guess I have a great deal of freedom, and I can disappear for a whole day and nobody will ever ask me where the hell I've—(broken off by interviewer).

The large company that permits this range of latitude bears no resemblance to the previous respondent's description of such a place of employment. The second respondent's situation does not sound atypical for someone working in a large organization with some degree of supervisory power. It is possible that the first respondent's attitude was affected by his lack of knowledge of large corporations, a reluctance to having his identity submerged were he to join the ranks of thousands of other workers, or a fear of not being able to rise above the masses and achieve a position of responsibility in that setting where he could feel competent at his work. In any event, the contrast between the two responses illustrates the impact of identity assimilation on the worker's perceptions.

Attitudes toward supervision were found to be reflected in other ways in the statements concerning autonomy. One automobile worker with a semi-skilled production job had a "you can't get me attitude" toward the bosses that was apparent in remarks about being able to control the rate of production:

Q: What effect on the rest of your daily life does your work as a (name of job) have?
R: I'm not as tired. When I used to be on the assembly line,...I would really get beat....I don't have a set rate. If can do two mufflers a night there's nothing they can really say to me. They don't like it, "you could have gotten some more," but actually they can't tell you what to do because that's the way the contract is written up. I can do about 100 a night, but that's exceeding, usually if I do from 45 to 60, they're satisfied. I can work at my own pace.

Hiding behind the contract was this worker's way of exerting a sense of control over superiors. A much more favorable attitude toward supervision was shown by another worker, a tool machine programmer, whose relationship with the bosses approached that of colleagues:

Q: What do you especially like about it?
R: I just, uh, well, they [bosses] confer with me on jobs or they show me the jobs they're, uh, thinking of taking in and they want to know how much time I think the machine will take to do in...how long you think it's going to take and you have a set hourly rate that you charge for a machine that you are running on that job and they try and quote from another company how much it's going to cost them to make it and it just goes from there...

Being asked to "confer" with bosses indicates a degree of responsibility that this hourly worker found rewarding. The assembly line worker tried to demonstrate autonomy in a more rebellious fashion, perhaps because of a lack of opportunity to have responsibility in any other way.

Frustration with lack of control over scheduling of work tasks was also expressed by other workers who did not have a contract to protect them, as is shown in the following examples. The first is a cake decorator whose job was greatly complicated by the additional tasks she was required to complete in her day's work:

Q: Could you tell me again what kind of questions or doubts you have about the work you do right now?
R: Well, since I started, I was strictly a cake decorator...Um, we obtained a new manager and our sales had gone down, so they're trying a new format where everyone there does a little bit of everything. And I enjoy doing the cakes. I don't enjoy doing these other things that I have to do. And everything is under a clock where they're

trying this new system where by 2 in the afternoon, everything's done. And there's a lot of days where it's physically impossible. And there's days when I go in that I have to fill 80 pies before I can even start my cakes. And it gets frustrating. But if I knew I had to make 80 cakes before I left, that's a little easier.

The image from this description is of a Chaplin-esque character working with lightning speed beneath the tyranny of the clock's hands, but with pies and cakes to assemble instead of machines. This image was apparently not one that impressed the supervisory personnel who made the decisions, though (assuming that the respondent's report was reasonably accurate). A similar image of work piling up, but at a rate entirely out of the worker's control, was conveyed by the following respondent, a worker in a large office whose jobs were rotated according to the work load demands:

Q: What do you particularly like about this? (filling orders)
R: Well, I don't like to be pushed from job to job especially when I have work of my own to do. And I know there's a deadline. Or they say they don't push you, but still you see that work piling up and you do want to get at it and get it done.

Lack of autonomy was not the most disagreeable feature of the job reported by this respondent, but it was clearly one that played a large role in generating a sense of frustration. This worker, unlike the cake decorator, was seeking alternative employment because the extrinsic features of the job were not sufficiently rewarding to keep her from feeling frustrated by her inability to stem the tide of papers reaching her desk.

The desire to create an impression that one has a great deal of responsibility may lead a worker to use the self-justification form of identity assimilation. Without direct knowledge of the worker's actual situation, it is difficult to substantiate the claim to authority. However, a clue can be obtained by comparing a worker's job title with the responsibilities attributed to it by the respondent. The cases excerpted so far come from respondents whose job titles closely parallel the description that they offered concerning the amount of control they had at work. The next respondent, though, was a tool and die worker whose use of self-justification in much of the interview seemed to correspond to his somewhat cryptic statement about the autonomy his job afforded:

Q: . . . did the work affect the way you felt about yourself, the way you regarded yourself as a person?
R: Yes. I earned the respect of the people after a while and, uh, yeah, including engineering . . . if I started a project, yeah, I had quite a free hand with it.

It is not hard to view with skepticism this worker's claim that as a machinist on an hourly wage he was given much, if any, of a "free hand" in projects requiring the expertise of engineers. It apparently enhanced his feelings of competence to claim that he had this much responsibility.

Apart from its importance as a factor leading to intellectual growth, the examples cited here seem to imply that autonomy is a critical factor in the relationship between work and the adult's identity as a competent worker. It is not only that the worker is given the opportunity to use his or her decision-making skills on a regular basis that determines the effects of being given self-direction and responsibility. In addition, the respondents seem to be saying that work that allows them freedom, authority, and control augments their identities as competent persons.

Intellectual Nature of the Work

Apart from its measured complexity on a scale with reasonably objective criteria, such as the "data-people-things" index, work may be perceived by the worker as having or lacking intellectually demanding activities. The intellectual nature of the work was a factor that was mentioned by a far greater proportion of men than women. The workers citing this factor represented a range of occupations, many of which would not seem at first glance to be particularly demanding of a high level of education. Instead, the intellectual features described involved the use of cognitive skills in tasks ranging from manual production to university teaching.

As a starting point for illustrating this subcategory of intrinsic work factors, it is useful to see that a scientific researcher had to say about the intellectual nature of his work:

Q: What do you find attractive about your work?
R: Um, it's intellectually exciting. It's rewarding because I am a tinkerer who likes to find out why things work the way they do . . .

This simple explanation conveys the essence of this intrinsic work factor: the excitement of discovery. In addition, the respondent was able to implement his personality as a "tinkerer," a factor that undoubtedly contributed to his enjoyment of the work. The same feeling was expressed by a part-time student majoring in science:

Q: What would help you decide what to do (get more education or start working after obtaining the associate's degree)?
R: Naturally, getting a job and bringing in more income is appealing to me, but what is even more appealing to me is my quest for knowledge. It's like a drive where I have to know more. I see something and I want to know about this, I want to do that, I want to understand this . . .

Although the researcher and the student were at opposite ends of the academic spectrum they were responding in a similar way to the potential for discovery held in their work.

Another form of this intrinsic work factor was the opportunity that the work provided for creativity. In the case of an engineer, this creativity was expressed in his work in production design. For a metal plate engraver, creativity was found in the opportunity to be artistic. A chef regarded his work as creative, too:

Q: What do you particularly like about it?
R: The creativity of it. You take a raw piece of meat and put it in the oven and you take it out, it looks good, it tastes good.

Although his job is not one that is considered intellectually complex, it nevertheless was perceived as providing a creative outlet by the worker himself. Similarly, another man in a job with little inherent creative potential found his work as a "forms analyst" offered him the chance to be creative because it required structuring new forms to fit the needs of different business operations. In describing his work, the respondent seemed aware of the potential for the job title of his work to imply that it was a menial, boring task. He appeared to be quite defensive about this, claiming that "there's really a lot more to it than a lot of people would think." Apart from this tendency to use identity assimilation regarding the job title, the work itself seemed to consist of tasks that he really did experience as creative. Other respondents expressed similar pleasure at being able to apply their technical knowledge to solving problems at work, such as making machines more efficient and designing circuit boards.

As with autonomy, it appeared that fulfillment of the intrinsic work motivation to have intellectually demanding work was a source of identity enhancement though an accommodation process. In particular, the ability to perform such work enhanced identity through its effect on the individual's awareness of his or her own cognitive skills. Becoming more "alert," better "organized," learning to "think like an engineer," and gaining greater "insight" were some of the effects on their own mental operations that people reported. In some cases, these changes in thought processes had unpredictable effects on other areas of life. A woman whose work consisted largely of being the unofficial complaint department in her job as an office worker in an apartment management firm found that the skills she had acquired in that position led to some unintended consequences:

Q: How does this kind of work affect the way you see yourself as a person?
R: . . . I'm able to put myself in the other person's position. It's like my position is "I'm here to help you and make you believe that I'm on your side and then go to my manager and plead your case.". . . And yet, I can see the manager's point when he says there's no money: "We can't do that, they gotta do it themselves." I'm able to put myself in the other person's position quite easily.
Q: And how does that affect you then? As a person?
R: . . . I believe I can really see the two sides of a coin when I'm in a situation . . . I do that a lot with my husband. And I can see sometimes he gets annoyed with me. When he complains about something, I automatically jump to the other person's, the other side of the situation. I say "Yeah, but look at it from this end." "I don't want to look at it from that end, I'm looking at it from my end, and this is the way it's going, and it doesn't feel right." "Yeah, but lookit, put yourself in the other person's shoes. How would you react to that?" You know, and sometimes that can be annoying . . .
Q: How does this affect how you see yourself then?
R: I tend to think it makes me more open-minded . . .

It is interesting that for this woman, having to handle complaints from tenants did not lead her to adopt the cynical attitude that could easily result from prolonged exposure to the contentious side of human nature. Instead, she saw herself as having become a better person intellectually, even if her husband did not always appreciate that outcome.

Another group of respondents used the process of identity assimilation instead of identity accommodation in response to facing intellectual demands at work. These people had deliberately decided to avoid or fend off any possible avenues of growth from exposure to new information that they could come in contact with through their jobs. Unlike respondents who acknowledged and followed through on the need to "keep up with changes" at work by learning new concepts and skills, these individuals were firmly entrenched in their present approaches to their work. In some cases, this stubborn refusal to engage in further training hampered their professional growth, as was the case of this research associate:

Q: What is it about the job you don't like?
R: . . . I really am not terribly well qualified. If I knew more about computers, it would be very helpful. If I were a statistician it would be very helpful. If I could go and learn how to do those things, but statistics and computers, they're the pits! It doesn't interest me one single bit . . .

This respondent realized that she would be far more satisfied "if I had these other skills," but was not willing to expose herself to finding out more about them. A second respondent, an engineer, realized that "being in engineering you have to keep somewhat abreast of things," including "technical developments" and products and materials. He had not, however, taken any courses outside of work in 10 or 12 years. In both of these cases, a distaste for new and unfamiliar skills and fear of being a failure at mastering them may be behind an identity assimilation process, as suggested earlier. It is also necessary to consider, though, that perhaps their reticence really reflects a lack of interest in the new areas or even for their work in general. The research associate liked "working with people" and was frustrated that her job had been redefined since she took it so that this interest was no longer being fulfilled. The engineer had a hobby that he loved dearly, and was trying to figure out he could become self-employed in a job related to this hobby. Neither person was, then, particularly motivated to expend time and energy in furthering their education in work-related areas.

Work did not always have a positive effect on the individual's appraisal of his or her intellectual skills. Several people had become painfully aware through their work that their education had been insufficient to train them adequately for the job they were in, or to allow them to advance to a more demanding position. Others realized that they were not very "patient," did not "always make the right decision," were "inexperienced," made "mistakes," could "do a better job," were "less sensitive with people," or regretted the lack of better "judgment." In other cases, the effects on the individual's evaluation of cognitive skills were more neutral. This respondent, a self-employed salesperson, acknowledged an effect of work on his thinking, but did not see this effect as either good or bad:

Q: You mentioned that your job is 24 hours, always on your mind. Could you tell me more?
R: Well, as I sit here and talk to you, my brain is looking at your questions. But in the background is a list of the (sales) prospects I want to make sure I contact this week. Around the first of May we agreed that I would contact them. Their names are churn-

ing through my brain. The same thing, when I watch TV at night, and perhaps a character might come up with a name, Greg Smith (name of the interviewer). Instant recall would match it against if I had a client named Greg Smith. It sets me thinking. I can read the paper, watch television, I'm always looking for something.

Other effects of work on thoughts and behaviors outside the workplace were mentioned in a similar way by other respondents: the personnel director who used his skills with people in managing a little league team, the bartender who cut down on his drinking so as not to become like some of his inebriated customers, the automobile mechanic who could repair the home automobile, and the art therapist who gained from his patients ideas that helped him in own paintings. Each of these changes ultimately changed the identity of the worker through its effect on how he or she viewed the world, solved problems, or interacted with people.

In addition to its effects on thought processes, work that is intellectually stimulating is inherently interesting because it involves diversity of mental operations. This may be why production or assembly work is perceived as boring by the worker, as suggested in the following excerpt:

R: . . . But don't put me on a job where I'm doing the same thing over and over again . . . probably all I'll be thinking about is fishing at the end of the day. I won't remember assembling anything. So I have to be active in my mind. It has to keep running . . .

Work that is intellectually stimulating is also perceived as challenging by the worker. This intrinsic work factor is sometimes categorized along with autonomy (e.g., Kalleberg, 1977). However, there emerged in the present sample a small but distinct group of responses all centering around the element of challenge as a factor more similar to problem-solving than autonomy. The first example describes challenge in terms that are interchangeable with problem-solving:

Q: Are you considering other forms of work right now?
R: Funny you should ask that. The best job I ever liked, it didn't hold a lot of esteem as far as other people think, but I managed the pet store over in Tobin's for a while . . . They also owned the pet shop out of the mall so I worked there for about 2 months. The store was a complete upside-down mess so they just hired somebody to be manager there, and I was going to help him out. Straighten up the store and get the clientele back in there and so on, you know. Just make the store neat appearing and so on, right? My specialty is tropical birds. So I thought, "what a challenge" you know? For the first time in my life I can remember, it was the second or third day on the job, I was . . . making breakfast, and I was thinking "I can't wait to get to work and help straighten out that store!" I like a challenge like that. If everything's running smoothly, forget it! I lose my interest. But if something really needs to be straightened out, you know, I loved the job. It was unreal! . . .

This enthusiastic description of the need to clean up a messy pet store shows how solving problems can present a challenge that enhances the individual's sense of competence. In addition, this excerpt highlights the importance of the individual's perception in determining whether a job will be found enjoyable. Cleaning up a messy pet store would not be everyone's idea of the perfect job, but it was extremely challenging to this respondent.

As a business consultant in systems design, a woman who found her work exciting was as challenged by the intellectual demands of her work as by the chance she had to strike a blow for women's liberation:

Q: What is important to you about your work as a systems analyst?
R: Why does it make it important to me? I guess that I get a lot of benefit from that job because I'm learning constantly . . . I think what challenges me too is that most of the time I'm working with men and men that are twice my age and just having to deal with all their biases as soon as they see me, and come out smelling like a rose is really very satisfying, you know.

The need to rise to the occasion when other people present potentially conflicting and critical viewpoints that is apparent in this response was also a factor that the research scientist found to be challenging about the peer review system of research funding in the sciences. In both cases, there is an element of competition involved as well as that of achieving a successful resolution. The taste of success may, in some cases, create a desire for more challenge in one's work. One man in the sample, who was working in an instruments company, found that the success he had achieved stimulated him to seek even greater challenges:

Q: How does your work as an electrician affect the way you view yourself as a person?
R: I like the responsibility related to the job and feel I can handle it and have handled it. Makes me feel good. In that aspect I think I would like to have more challenging, a more challenging job and more thinking now, more responsibility, that's why I'm in school, on the move again.

This example touches upon one of the key features of intrinsic motivation: that it often does not reach an end state where the individual's desires are sated. In this sense, intrinsic motivation is like a need for self-actualization, as described by Maslow (1970). Rather than being aimed at fulfilling a need, after which the motivation diminishes, the self-actualization motive is self-perpetuating. For that reason, it is theorized that an individual can continue to derive satisfaction from work that is not well-paid or given high status if the work is inherently stimulating and challenging. With regard to identity, the perception that one's work is challenging may create a continuous desire for more stimulation rather than a tendency to remain in a state of stable equilibrium. Similarly, lack of challenge may create a situation in which the work loses all intrinsic meaning, becoming entirely a means of earning a living.

Having the Chance to See Results

In addition to being given stimulation and challenge, an important source of intrinsic work motivation is the desire to have the problems one faces be successfully resolved. Also included in this category of intrinsic motivation is the desire to achieve recognition for one's efforts, not in the way of status rewards (which would be extrinsic), but in the form of praise from others (Kalleberg, 1977). Both of these intrinsic work features focus on the ends of one's labors rather than the means through which those ends are achieved. In this way, they are different in quality from the other intrinsic features that are oriented toward interest in the activity itself rather than the product that ensues from that activity.

However, the reason that seeing results is regarded as intrinsic is that it is possible to feel a sense of competence over having completed a job well (so well that others recognize this) without feeling a need to receive monetary remuneration for this effort or a raise in rank. Second, it would be unrealistic for no importance to be attached to completing a project. A worker would not be able to survive for very long in the marketplace without finishing an assigned task. As long as pay or prestige is not the primary aim of the activity, a desire for successful completion may be regarded, then, as intrinsic.

For some respondents, seeing the results of their work was regarded as a developmental process that they could observe and participate in right up until its final maturation. One of the responses of this nature was from a builder:

Q: What in particular is important to you about your work? What's attractive?
R: The satisfaction of being able to take something from beginning to end, and being able to create something. I feel this is very important. I think that's why I put an emphasis on watching things grow. In this case, watching structures grow and seeing a piece of land become a subdivision, you know, people that move into it. Forming relationships with people who eventually purchase the house. I enjoy watching progress.

It is interesting that this statement parallels closely what the same respondent said about watching his children grow (Chapter 4, p. 73). It is not possible to tell whether his attitudes toward his family influenced his attitudes toward his work or vice versa, but in any case, his statement about building houses is a good example of the intrinsic gratification that can be derived from seeing results. Another man, a school administrator, spoke in similar terms regarding the success of programs in his school:

Q: Okay. What in particular do you find satisfying?
R: Well, the ability to develop programs and see them come to fruition with good results. Right now, our reading scores are going up. Our math scores are going up. We're getting an awfully good track record in the competency tests. We're making some progress there. We have some programs in our system that have been designed for honors students . . . and so these are some of the things that you feel good about . . . we have cut our tardiness by 60% this year. We have, in addition to the programs we've developed, I think we've seen some improvement in the attitudes of kids. So this is the kind of progress that you make. Ultimately you know that our so-called "product," the kids who leave our system, are going to be able to function better. . . . I guess this is where the satisfaction comes.

This statement represents a broad form of generativity as well as an expression of satisfaction in seeing a successful "product," because of the interest that it reflects in helping a new generation of young people to start their lives successfully.

Another group of statements come from workers who took pride in having created something that they felt would be enjoyed by or of benefit to other people. These products ranged from baked goods to books to automobile parts:

Q: How do you feel about your work as a baker?
R: I like it. I feel like when I make something and I look at it I feel like I produced something, you know, and people always, people think it's good and I have a good product. I take pride in my work, I try and make, I try to make it as best I can.

* * *

Q: What about this line of work (printing production) do you find particularly attractive?
R: I originally got into it because I like machines . . . [but] after about a year and a half I realized that I was bored with working on the same machine all the time, but I was still intrigued with the process of taking ink and water and turning it into a printed product, something everybody can use all the time . . . that's one thing that really intrigues me, that I can actually go out and create these books . . .

* * *

Q: What do you especially like about (your work in production design)?
R: Well, my particular part of it, well, I like . . . to see a finished product leave well done and to know that I had a part making that product right. It's got to go in somebody's car, whatever, truck, and to me this is important. Making sure everything's safe and everything . . .

These individuals suggested but did not directly state that they felt that their sense of competence was influenced by their ability to do good work. Other respondents openly stated that their ability to accomplish desired goals had a favorable influence on their identities. Two of these are excerpted below, the first from a beautician:

Q: What is important to you about your work as a beautician?
R: That I'm able to make my customers happy, give them what they want. They're paying for my services, so I have to try, you know, or give them, you know, what they want. Make 'em happy.
Q: Why?
R: They're paying for it, you know, it's, you know, their money.
Q: How do you feel about this kind of work?
R: Uh, I like it. I like it a lot. There's sometimes I feel like, uh, I'm almost helping them. People tell me things that they don't tell anybody else, they don't tell their husbands, they don't tell any other member of their family, they don't even tell friends, but they tell me, because they probably figure "Well, she doesn't know anybody that I know, so I feel free to let it all hang out and tell her," you know.
Q: And that feels good to you?
R: Yeah, that somebody would actually, like, confide in me, almost a perfect stranger, even though I see these people, you know, week after week. Every time they come in it's something new or something different. Sure, if I can help them out, I'll help them out.
Q: In that particular area, in what way do you think you've helped them out? Is it just listening?

R: Yeah, I've been told that I'm a good listener. You know, because I guess not too many people must listen or something because they'll always say that "Gee, you're a good listener," or I'll add in a few maybe little solutions here and there and it makes 'em feel good.

It is interesting that the main source of competence this woman reports is not from what she is being paid for (a point that she dismisses summarily) but from her ability to help her customers with their personal problems. In the next excerpt, an electronics technician who is generally very dissatisfied with his work finds the only source of gratification to be the effect on his identity of his ability to do a good job:

Q: How important to you is your work as an electronics technician?
R: On a scale of 1 to 10, squeaking up to a -3... I consider my work, um, you know, very, almost meaningless and it's, you know "Oh, wow! You're in defense!" Gimme a break.
Q: You mean your work is—
R: Defense electronics. Right. And I just, you know, so what?... The thing that my employer makes is a defense goodie.
Q: Is there anything you like about your job?
R: ... I think there's hidden in there, too, in that I tend to be something of a hot shot at it, you know, anything I can do that can shore up a weak ego structure, you know, it's sort of a hidden benefit.

Of course, there is no way of knowing whether any of the workers described so far were as good as they claimed at what they did. It is possible that the respondents presented a glorified image of their success that was not consistent with the objective situation. To the extent that such exaggeration occurs, it represents the self-justification form of identity assimilation. Making a judgment regarding the veridicality of such statements requires, in the absence of external information, a careful reading of the respondent's statement for consistent failure to qualify statements regarding his or her success. Contrast the following two excerpts, the first from a teacher, the second from a clerical worker:

Q: Do you have any questions or doubts?
R: As I said earlier, you always feel you could do more, could do better, could work harder at it. However, I do feel that for the most part I am able to get to the children and give them a good start. I hope so.

* * *

Q: What do you call your position? Clerical worker?
R: That's what I put on my Social Security, but it's actually checking prices. I don't know what you'd call it. Marketing?
Q: I'll call it clerical for the time being. How important to you is your work as a clerical worker?
R: Well, I'm very conscientious with my work. When I do a job, I make sure I do it right, and not have any mistakes.

It is true that the two respondents being contrasted were answering different questions, which may have prompted a more self-critical approach in the teacher. However, the clerical worker never gave any indication, even when asked about questions or doubts, that she actually did make mistakes. She did acknowledge the serious consequences of making a mistake, but did not admit outright to having made one herself. Other statements in the interview add further substance to the judgment that this respondent is using identity assimilation. Her initial qualifications about her job title indicate that she thinks of her job as having greater importance than the requisite tasks would seem to warrant. Second, although she was contemplating alternate employment, this seemed to be originating more out of a sense of self-justification than of an introspective self-appraisal:

Q: How do you feel about this kind of work?
R: All I can say is, the only thing I don't like is, I guess, like everybody else, not getting paid enough for what you do.
Q: How does this make you feel about this kind of work?
R: Not about the work but sometimes you get a feeling about the place, that you feel as though they're not treating you right. You keep asking for a raise, and they say "No, you've reached your level."

This additional information from the respondent tends to reinforce the idea that she has a defensive stance toward her work identity that is captured in her statements about competence as well as her dissatisfaction with not being treated "right." The possibility is not even raised by her that maybe she is not doing as good a job as she thinks she is doing, and that is why her pay and job title are lower than she would like.

The apparent failure of the individual at having performed adequately may, when it is acknowledged, deal a serious blow to his or her identity as a competent worker. This sort of experience was related by one respondent in describing his reasons for not seeking a job change:

Q: Apart from changing companies, why do you feel, though, that you would stay in engineering?
R: I guess the, um, perhaps I'm not the kind of person that would want to take large risks. If you have a certain security in knowing you can do this job well, uh, but there are other, I was in the situation earlier where I wasn't well-suited for what I had to do, so I've had the experience of failing, you might say, not terrible, it wasn't a terrible dead end for me, but it was a little sobering for me knowing that there were certain jobs that I couldn't really handle very well and, uh, so that's, that would be on my mind anyway.

The experience of failure reported by this respondent was one that was so unpleasant that he wished to protect himself from future repetitions. This reaction is consistent with the interpretation offered earlier in the chapter that preference for the familiar may be a form of identity assimilation. The individual who is insecure about his or her competence as a worker may avoid venturing into uncharted territory in which success is not guaranteed. This was also the motivation behind the restaurant worker who had never even tried working in another field:

Q: Do you ever question or wonder about whether you'd like to switch over to a different area?

R: No, uh, in all honesty, I can't really picture myself changing to another field or occupation. 'Cause I've been doing it so long I'm satisfied and content and I can't really see myself switching over. Sometimes I wonder if maybe I should be a little more open-minded or something like this, but I feel that I'm, um, pretty happy, you know . . .

. . .

Q: Is there anything in particular that keeps you from thinking about alternatives?

R: Maybe it's just a little bit of insecurity. You know, trying to, uh, change your field, giving it consideration. *Maybe*, I said it's a feeling of insecurity. I would be afraid of being a failure in another field. As opposed to what I'm in right now. I'm doing good. Very good. It's progress. The only thing I could really say is a feeling of insecurity.

This respondent appears to be using a process of identity assimilation to maintain an identity as a competent worker. What makes his statement a bit more complicated is his awareness of his motivations for not considering change. In addition, his perception of being a success appeared to have some grounding in what he reports as good ratings by his superior and his receiving a good raise once a year.

There were others in the sample who were presently feeling a deep sense of frustration at having their identities as competent workers blocked from realization by virtue of the nature of their job, the company, or the clientele. All three of these elements were present in the work of an administrator in an institution for mentally disabled persons:

Q: What is it you don't like about the job? You said it was bureaucratic?

R: . . . the facilities, the materials you need to work with are not always there. The bureaucracy, the paperwork. The waste.

Q: What about the kind of work you do is important to you?

R: Okay. I'm not happy working with the profoundly retarded, which is where I'm slotted into now. I don't feel they have a future. I think they should be cared for and just made comfortable. And let them grow to what you think their potential is, which is very limited. I find it very depressing to go in and have people send them to class and spend hours at a time and money to try and teach a client who you know will never function above self-help skills. It is such a waste.

Q: So, you prefer to work with autistic children. What is it about that, that is important to you?

R: Well, I feel they have more of a future and more potential to be self-reliant human beings. I think that if we found a way to teach them that that would be an accomplishment, as with the profoundly retarded, the damage is already done. No matter how hard you work with them, you cannot put back gray matter where it does not exist.

Because of this respondent's frustration in working with profoundly retarded persons, she was seeking a job change to work with another difficult group, but one in whom she saw more potential for a successful outcome. Similarly, a case worker who dealt with infirmed elderly persons was also looking for a change, but for her, this was a change to working in supervision rather than providing direct services:

R: . . . I guess for one thing, working with the clientele, with the particular clientele that I have, they're sick people, you know? And for the most part, they don't get better, they are the older, the permanently disabled. It's kind of depressing. The only thing you have to look forward to is death for them, not that they're all particularly terminal, not by any means. People just get sicker and just get worse and there's less and less you can do for them. You know, whereas working with people in the organization (in supervision), I can teach them things, show them things, you know, try to make them better. Bring them up . . .

It is because of the frustration of not being able to solve difficult problems in some human services that, as this respondent said, "the burnout is so fantastic." However, she found she was able to derive feelings of competence from the occasional "thank you's" she received from her clients:

Q: How do you feel about the kind of work that you do?
R: . . . I guess, you know, there's a, you have your nasty people and your nasty clients that you can never seem to do enough for, you know, provide enough you know for, but then for 1 out of the every 25, they'll say "Oh, gee, thanks a lot for doing that." It does kind of make your day worthwhile. It does make you feel good.

Being able to take a more accepting attitude that not everyone can be pleased or not all problems can be successfully solved is this respondent's means of accommodating to the dilemma of feeling frustrated with her work. The same philosophy was expressed by the restaurant worker regarding his clientele:

Q: What do you find attractive about your job?
R: . . . Most people, um 90% of the people, 80% of the people you can always satisfy. There's always that 15 to 20% you know, no matter what you do, you can't satisfy. I think this is normal in any business. It could be a gas station, an ice cream parlor or whatever. I think this is normal procedure, so to speak. You can't satisfy everybody. You try to satisfy the best you can, the highest percentage you can . . .

This respondent did not feel anywhere near the same degree of frustration with his job as a whole as did the case worker, perhaps because the results he was able to see were more under his direct control. The case worker and the supervisor who worked with retarded persons were in situations that they saw as inherently flawed because of the clientele and could not comfort themselves entirely with the cliche that "you can't please everybody." For them, resolution of the situation required a change in their work identities.

Implicit in the individual's expression of a desire to see results is the related goal of wanting to do a good job. If results are achieved, then it means that the individual has competently performed the work tasks required to achieve those results. This goal of wanting to do a good job was intertwined with the desire to see results in one of the examples above ("I had a part in making that product right"). Similarly, a tool and die maker who regarded himself as a "perfectionist" felt "self-satisfaction in producing something decent." A maintenance foreman saw his ability to do a good job as leading to results that contributed to the success of his team and ultimately the whole company:

Q: What do you find rewarding about it?
R: Being able to plan the work so you can see the jobs progress, uh, starting from nothing to getting it occupied, to getting, making sure that it's sound, safe, a good place for other employees to work. Therefore, if I do a good job, and the crew does a good job, we ought to be able to . . . produce a better place to work!

A group of respondents made the desire to "do a good job" explicit in their descriptions of what was important to them about their work, as can be seen from the following statement by a department manager:

Q: How important to you is your job, your work?
R: Uh, the job is important to me. I want stuff to be done right in my department. I don't like to see mistakes. I don't like to see myself make mistakes. I don't want to sound like I think I'm perfect, in my work I do make mistakes, but I care about my job as a job . . .

Note in this response the difference between the narrator's attitude toward his ability to do a good job and that of the clerical worker who gave the impression that she was perfect. The department manager was much more balanced in his self-appraisal, and so would not be considered to be using identity assimilation.

This last respondent's reason for wanting to see things done right was that he felt he had a "responsibility" to the company. For other respondents, doing things well was regarded as a means of achieving recognition by superiors and co-workers:

Q: The job that you have right now how important is it to you?
R: . . . I care that the people I work with feel that I'm capable of what I'm doing, that I'm doing a good job.

* * *

Q: Do you think that your particular job influences the way you perceive yourself in any way?
R: Oh yeah. My first thought in regard to that is if I've done a good job as perceived by my peers and supervision, that really gives me a high. I enjoy that . . .

In other cases the recognition from others was not as positive as was implied in the above two examples:

Q: Well, what do you dislike about your work?
R: Oh, well, these quality control inspectors. They make it miserable. They, I mean, well, just the other night my wife was asking me, what type, what type of guy is he, you know. An inspector. He's an inspector, period . . . all they see is black and white, you know. There's no two ways. There's this way, and that's it. I mean it's my fault, I mean it's up to me. You don't seem to get any encouragement on what you're doing. That's one thing. They tell you everything that's wrong, but they won't ever tell you if you're doing a fairly decent job . . .

The lack of recognition for successful efforts experienced by this respondent coupled with criticism for what he did wrong seemed to be a damaging combination for his sense of personal competence and enjoyment of his work. He did show a tendency to attribute part of his failure to the quality control inspectors, which may represent identity assimilation. However, their criticism of him appeared to have been at least partly internalized through identity accommodation.

In some ways, it is difficult to separate how much of the desire for recognition is for the sake of satisfaction of an intrinsic need and how much is for social acceptance, advancement, or simply a desire to please others. A purely intrinsic need would be the desire to do things well to meet a set of internal standards or, as stated by a salesclerk in the sample: "Anything I work at I try to do well." However, as long as the respondent did not specifically mention status or pay rewards associated with recognition by others, the desire to have one's efforts appreciated by others was regarded as an intrinsic need to perform competently.

The People-Work Character of a Job

The extent to which an individual's work involves meeting people, talking to them, arguing with them, handling complaints, and dealing with specific age groups is a category of intrinsic work involvement that deserves separate attention from other intrinsic work features (Mortimer & Lorence, 1979). Not included in this category are statements about co-workers, because attitude toward co-workers is regarded as an extrinsic job feature in the work literature. The people-work category instead is a set of responses that concern the extent to which one's job involves particular kinds of interactions with people, either individuals or the public at large. It also includes interactions with particular groups of people who are found as clients, customers, students, or colleagues only in this kind of work.

One small but important group of responses concerned the attitude that society has toward the type of work being prepared by the individual. A waitress somewhat defensively claimed that she liked her work despite the fact that "people put waitresses down." An insurance salesperson described a similar prejudice against his work:

Q: What do you find unattractive about it?
R: Unattractive in that it's a product that the public never understands and we end up being about as popular as Nixon. It's a necessity. I try desperately when I work with people to make them understand the pitfalls of the product so that they have a feeling for what they're spending their money on . . . you know, when your awning blows off and you have no coverage for it and it costs you $400 out of pocket, you're going to take it out, you're not going to be happy, and it's an aura that's been for years perpetrated by this industry, so . . .

Another insurance salesperson in the sample described his work as "contributing to society," but discounted this remark by adding "I'm brainwashed, aren't I?" This disclaimer suggested that he too was aware of a general skepticism about the value of insurance to the social welfare.

The second set of respondents who mentioned the people-work factor were those who specifically mentioned "helping" as a mode of interaction with people. A day care director regarded the kind of helping she engaged in as socially useful as well as of benefit to specific individuals:

Q: What is important to you about your work?

R: You're dealing with people and with children and it's very important because of the need for day care with working parents . . . when we're dealing with so many parents, I think that's the most important thing even, to help mothers not feel guilty about doing this (leaving their children in day care).

Other respondents were not in traditional human services, but regarded their work as benefiting others nevertheless. A clerical worker who worked in a records office felt that she was able to help people by making information accessible to them when they needed it.

The third category of people-work statements were those expressing satisfaction or dissatisfaction in working with a specific kind of clientele. Children were mentioned by most of the teachers in the sample as an enjoyable group with whom to work in statements similar to that of the day care director in the previous example. An office worker stated that she enjoyed working with salesmen. Another group of clientele that was given special mention was "customers." The manager of a grocery store meat department enjoyed socializing with his customers:

Q: What do you particularly like about it?

R: I like that I'm with people all the time; you know, I'm uh, you know with customers coming in and talking, you know. I'm with people; most, what I like most about the job is that I'm always involved with talking with people.

However, a salesclerk expressed considerable ambivalence about relating to customers:

Q: What do you especially like about your job?

R: I like the contact with other people I guess, with the public . . .

Q: What do you dislike?

R: When I don't feel so great and having to go in and act as if I feel great. Meeting the public is a hard job . . .

There is obvious ambivalence in this respondent's attitudes toward the public. She had stated earlier in her interview that she liked the idea of being out in the public and "having a change of scenery" from the house. As will be seen in Chapter 7, seeking relief from the boredom of staying at home is an extrinsic feature of work. It was balanced, in this case, against the intrinsic feature of retail sales work, which demands a cheerful and friendly facade at all times.

Other kinds of problems with customers fall under the category of "hassles." Unlike complaints from customers, which may reflect on the respondent's ability to provide good services, hassles occur when a customer is argumentative and refuses to cooperate during a transaction:

Q: Is there anything about it that you don't like (about being a bartender)?

R: That I don't like? Not really, outside of the hassles you get every now and then . . . you
get a drunk every now and then . . .

* * *

Q: What do you find attractive about the work (salesperson in the building trade)?
R: . . . talking with people, and for the most part the builders are courteous and lik-
able. There's probably about 2 or 3% you don't want to see, you know. They're a
real hassle . . .

Another difficulty experienced by a worker in the building trade was of a similar nature, although the people who created the hassles were not necessarily
the customers:

Q: What's unattractive to you?
R: What's unattractive? Um, what is unattractive to me in my work is arguments with
people. Unfortunately, dealing with so many people, everything isn't always easy to
do. Arguments occur. That's one thing I dislike, as well as when people do lie to me.
That's the primary thing I do not tolerate. But that sort of thing happens all the time.

As a contractor, it is likely that the arguments he referred to involved subcontrac-
tors who failed to perform their work on time.
   Another feature of working with people is learning to deal with their vicissitudes of moods, attitudes, personalities, and habits. This was an aspect of work
that respondents in managerial positions were often faced with:

Q: How does your work as a manager affect your opinion of yourself?
R: I think that it's helped me. It's helped me in a lot of ways. You know, dealing with peo-
ple, you have 30 different people to deal with everyday. Learn about life, I guess.
People's problems, how to motivate people, stuff like that.

* * *

Q: How does your work as a manager affect the way you think about yourself?
R: How does it affect the way I think about myself? Well, being a general manager, and
having to relate to so many different people. Each person has a different need, and you
have to try to fulfill that need within the aspect of the corporation and with the aspect
of their job in relationship to your job. So, um, how does it affect *my* life?
Q: The way that you see yourself.
R: The way that I see myself?
Q: Uh hum.
R: Well, I judge myself probably on how well I can relate to the different people. It's a
funny thing to say, but, you know, each time I relate to them, if I can solve the problems that I come across every day easier, it makes me personally feel better.

In both of these cases, the respondents regarded themselves as having become
more knowledgeable about people. This in turn helped them to become better
at performing their managerial functions and ultimately, to feel more competent
as workers.
   As part of this process of dealing with employees, disputes arise that require

resolution by someone in a supervisory position. Having to handle these disputes was, in turn, a feature that a personnel supervisor in the sample found unpleasant:

Q: What do you particularly dislike about your work?
R: . . . I would imagine there are times when you have, this doesn't exactly have to be with personnel work, I imagine it pertains to any kind of a supervisor, when you have to terminate an individual. I think this is one of the nastier things you have to do. And you get to see more of it in personnel than if you're just a department supervisor. You have a disciplinary case in the plant where you might have a fight or that kind of thing. Usually it ends up in the personnel department with a decision being made there. If the supervisors or managers can't come to a decision, you make it for them, and it's not always an easy decision to make. . .

It is not completely clear why the respondent disliked this feature of supervisory work; that is, whether it is the decision-making process or the need to have to take punitive action. However, given the respondent's consistent enthusiasm throughout the interview regarding the "challenge" of the work, it is probable that the "nasty" element of supervision is having to deal firmly with and possibly hurt other people. The need to take such actions may have detracted from his desire to see himself as a "fair" person, an aspiration he expressed in the Values interview. The work in supervision and having to act as a "judge" could potentially lead to a challenging of this identity should the wrong decision be made about a particular case.

Being on the other side of a personnel decision that goes against one's favor is another people-work factor that was difficult for those respondents who experienced it to accommodate into their identities. Instead, they typically used the self-justification or projection form of identity assimilation, or some combination of the two. The case example excerpted below involves exactly this mixture in the respondent's explanation of why he had become stymied in his climb up the corporate ladder and was now in a "meaningless, repetitious" clerical job:

Q: It sounds like you are not very happy about your work.
R: I'm probably about as close to the most unhappy (name of company) person you might find.
Q: What's particularly unsatisfying about it?
R: What's dissatisfying to me would probably make me sound paranoid. I feel I've been totally ripped off as far as progress within my job goes. I unfortunately have many many years of success at (name of company). I stepped on the wrong toes, so to speak, and I'm blacklisted as far as (name of company) promotions systems goes. . . . I had very good success and then I made a rather big error by accepting a transfer into a rather new project area. Unfortunately after I talked to a couple of friends we found out that the people in charge were playing strict favors. These guys were real clowns if you didn't come from the same area they did. No way. Unfortunately, I didn't take too kindly to the situation and let someone else know. . .

The only way that the respondent could manage to preserve his sense of self-respect was by projecting onto the company the reason for having his ambitions thwarted and portraying himself as having acted in a morally correct way:

Q: How does this affect the way you feel about yourself?

R: Well, it affects you to the point that, boy, you're really a stupid so and so for getting into this position and why didn't you keep your dumb mouth shut. But, by the same token, when I shave or look in the mirror, I can look at myself and not say I played the game and owe this guy this and that guy that. I can still face myself in the mirror . . .

It is, of course, possible that the game of corporate politics was so vicious and unfair that the respondent was correct in his behaviors and judgments. However, his identity obviously had much to lose from admitting that he was not really as competent as he liked to believe, and so the identity assimilation explanation cannot be ruled out with any confidence.

The Intrinsic Meaning of Work: Reflections and Qualifications

The major types of intrinsic work factors have now all been described. In most cases, it was possible to rule out potential contributions of extrinsic work factors by making certain assumptions and inferences from the respondent's statements. Interest, autonomy, intellectual stimulation, seeing results, and wanting to do a good job are all features of work that do not have any direct observable payoffs in terms of money or status. Instead, their major value is that they capture a significant feature of the worker's identity: feelings of personal competence. Moreover, the intrinsic features are ones that are specific to a particular match between a given individual and a given type of job. It is the individual's unique qualities that are tapped by work that is intrinsically involving. Conversely, noninterchangeable features of jobs determine whether they will be intrinsically rewarding or intrinsically frustrating. An individual can only have his or her identity engaged in the kind of work that is of personal interest and meaning, and what will be of personal interest and meaning varies from one worker to another.

Left out of the intrinsic category so far are two sets of responses that seem to be intrinsic in nature, but are qualitatively different from the other intrinsic subcategories. The first is a rather small (6 women, 7 men) set of statements that describe the work tasks demanded by the job in positive, negative, or neutral terms. Some of these tasks included typing, paperwork, writing up sales orders, and lifting heavy machinery. There were also general statements such as "the job itself," "something I enjoy," and "the work that I do." Without further qualification, it is not possible to determine whether the "job itself" is enjoyed because of its intrinsic or extrinsic qualities. Similarly, a respondent may dislike work with heavy machinery because it is physically strenuous and exhausting (an extrinsic feature) or because it is boring, manual labor that the respondent finds mentally deadening (intrinsic). These statements were therefore not used for analytic purposes.

The second group of statements presented a much more complicated dilemma. These were statements pertaining to the importance of the work to the individual, to the individual's family, or to society in general. This was a relatively large grouping of statements, with 12 responses from women and 25 from men. In a sense, these statements are the most intrinsic of all, because they define at a very basic level the degree of involvement of the individual's identity in the work that he or she does. However, one is at a loss to categorize these statements as intrinsic or extrinsic because importance may refer to either quality. For instance, work may be important because it contributes to the income of the family, in which case it would be extrinsic, or it may be important because it benefits other people, which would be more of an intrinsic quality. Conversely, work may be regarded as meaningless because it is not well-paid or has low status or because it is inherently boring and mindless.

The decision that was made about these statements was to consider them as having little inherent meaning unless the respondent was describing something specific that could be identified as intrinsic or extrinsic. In many cases, the statements about importance were replicated by other information that was clearly rateable in the interview, and so no data were really lost for those respondents. In other cases, statements describing the respondent's perceptions of the work's importance were regarded as instances of identity assimilation involving self-justification, as in the following case of a woman who was "employed" in the capacity of volunteering her clerical services to her relatives:

Q: With the work that you do, what about that is important to you?
R: Oh, that it's done right. That it gets done. Even though my niece is very intelligent, she doesn't have my business mind. She doesn't have my business experience. That's why I'm doing it now. If I don't do it, it doesn't get done. So I have to do it . . .
. . .
Q: How does that affect the way you see yourself as a person?
R: Well, I feel I'm needed, and if I wasn't there, nobody else would . . . . I think they both depended on me and they both need me and it satisfies me . . .
Q: Do you do anything especially because of your work for (your relatives)?
R: Yes, naturally. I'm giving, well, I'm giving my experience and my support. I like things neat. I can't stand a mess. And it would be in a mess if I wasn't there . . .

The identity of this respondent appeared to rest very heavily on her feeling of being useful and competent in what she did for her family, causing her, perhaps, to present an exaggerated picture of her importance to them.

A number of people who unambiguously hated their work appeared possibly to feel this way because they lacked the opportunity for satisfaction of intrinsic needs, although this was not explicitly stated. There were 1 woman and 7 men who regarded their work as having so little stimulation to themselves or value to society that their jobs were either "meaningless," "just a job," or "a waste of time and money." The responses of two of these individuals are worth examining in detail because of their implications for evaluating statements about intrinsic motivation in general:

Q: How important to you is your job?
R: Uh, my job is, uh, important to me, um, mainly being honest with you, it's a source of income. Alright? It's, it's important to all of us there for the finances. If I didn't get that weekly check on Thursday, I wouldn't be there. You know? . . . It's important mainly because in today's society, uh, in my situation here I'd have to have an income . . .

As it turned out, this respondent's satisfaction from work was very strongly related to his ability to bring home a paycheck and support his family "independently, without anyone's assistance." This earning ability of his contributed to his identity in the family as the "wage-earner" and "head of the house." Apart from this more "intrinsic" form of extrinsic motivation, though, the respondent did make many other statements about his work that reflected intrinsic involvement in his ability to do a good job. However, his candor in describing his underlying work motivation makes it necessary to interpret these intrinsic statements with a great deal of caution. Similarly, another respondent, an owner of his own business, stated that he enjoyed the intrinsic factor of working with and meeting people: "I, I just find this very natural, it's very comfortable, I meet a lot of people and talk a lot, obviously I like to talk a lot." However, all of these factors seem negated by his admission that "the day that I can sell this place for a decent buck and wouldn't have to work anymore, I'm gone."

These respondents may have been representative of many more of the study's participants who were unwilling to admit outright to a lack of work commitment. On the other hand, the respondents may really have been more involved in their work (as indicated by the many statements concerning intrinsic work importance) than they were willing to admit to themselves! Denying the importance or meaning of work may be an assimilative means of coping with fear of the negative implications for identity of admitting that one is not succeeding at one's work. However, this interpretation cannot be verified without more in-depth case studies. Apart from any underlying motivational issues, though, the statements of these two respondents serve an important function. They are a reminder that, whatever its meaning to the individual's identity as a competent worker, a job is performed as a means of earning money.

7
A Spoonful of Sugar

In the movie *Mary Poppins*, the children hear their magical governess sing that "a spoonful of sugar helps the medicine go down" as she whisks about, using her powers to clean up the untidy nursery. The message of this song is that "in every job that must be done there is an element of fun" and all one has to do to enjoy work is find that element. There is a double meaning to this message. On the one hand, the spoonful of sugar provides the extra sweetness needed to transform an unpleasant task to "a piece of cake." On the other hand, once that "element of fun" is discovered, the task activity itself becomes rewarding, and even as mundane an activity as cleaning up one's room can become enjoyable. This principle of having an intrinsic motivation replace an extrinsic one is used extensively in behavior modification, particularly as applied with children. The goal is to have the learner become more motivated by the intrinsic features of the desired behavior (such as keeping "on task" in school) so that extrinsic rewards (tokens or candy) used initially to reinforce the desired behaviors can be phased out eventually.

In this chapter, it will be seen that extrinsic rewards play a very key role in the adult's work identity. This role is different in quality from the role played by intrinsic work factors. Extrinsic factors serve to define the worker's competence in terms of the social indicators of income and status. They are also important determinants of how comfortable the worker feels in the work environment and the quality of life he or she can enjoy outside the workplace.

Unlike the function served by the "spoonful of sugar," though, it will be seen here that extrinsic motivators are not supplanted by intrinsic rewards in the adult's work identity. In some cases, they may even supercede intrinsic ones over the course of the person's tenure in a job. Through a process of identity assimilation, work that was originally regarded as important for intrinsic reasons may come to be viewed as having extrinsic value only. This sequence of events may transpire when the worker fails to have his or her identity as a competent person verified by satisfaction of the intrinsic needs for successful task completion. In order to preserve his or her identity, a worker may downgrade the importance of work to the extrinsic status of being a means to an end and no more than that: "just a job." Identity assimilation may also be used to redefine the importance of work in other ways so that the individual's sense of competence as a person who can earn money and has status is not threatened. These and other mechanisms through which identity processes operate on extrinsic work factors are explored in this chapter.

The Monetary Rewards of Work

All writers on the topic of occupational satisfaction agree that working for money is the epitome of extrinsic work motivation (e.g., Herzberg et al., 1959; Kalleberg, 1977). This factor was mentioned by over half of the men and working women in the present sample. Statements concerning salary fell into a number of subgroupings, though, so the meaning of money to the respondents was not uniform. The majority (15 men, 4 women) attested to the importance of money, declaring it to be the primary or even the only reason for working. Their statements were brief and to the point: "it pays the bills," "we need to establish financial security," "a source of income," "I make a living at it," "a steady income." Related to salary were concerns with security (6 women and 10 men) and advancement in status with its associated advancement in salary (2 women and 11 men). It is clear, then, that the need for a sufficient and steady if not growing income was a major work preoccupation of the men and women in the sample.

In less dramatic but equally compelling terms, other respondents reinforced the statement presented toward the end of Chapter 6 about the relative importance of intrinsic factors compared to the income that work provided:

Q: How important to you is the work that you're doing?
R: Right now, I enjoy the work, naturally I enjoy the pay, to me the most important is the paycheck, I would say. My job is not all that important.
Q: How important to you is your work?
R: How do I, uh, it's, uh, it's very rewarding. It's a rewarding experience for me. Uh, but I certainly wouldn't do it if the paycheck weren't there. (laughs)

* * *

Q: (How are) your ideas about work changing?
R: I want a job paying good money, but I don't want to have to work *that* hard for it.

What these respondents were saying is that if they were going to have to work, they might as well enjoy what they were going to be doing or at least not find it too unpleasant. Unlike the respondents who regarded with grim acceptance their work as a means of earning a living, these individuals were able to find other compensating factors. These compensating factors added an "element of fun" to their jobs but did not supplant the extrinsic features of their work.

A second group of respondents had the opposite attitude toward the importance of earning money. These respondents enjoyed earning money, but did not require it as a means of maintaining their existence. The reason that they did not regard money as having great importance was that they had husbands who were earning relatively high salaries. Their income contributed only a minor share to the total family income. However, even though the amount of money itself was not that important, the fact that they were earning their own independent incomes contributed greatly to their sense of competence:

Q: How does your work affect the way that you think about yourself?
R: Um, well, it only affects me in a positive way. I mean, it's helped me enormously. I could be self-reliant on my own if I had to, and I really need to know that I can do that...
Q: Why is it important to you to be able to depend on yourself?
R: Um, well, for me personally, when Timmy was 3, his father and I separated and were eventually divorced. And I never did have to totally rely on his income completely, but I knew I could at any time. And, um, you know, it's being a child to think that there's always somebody there to take care of you. In fact there isn't. I just like knowing that I can take care of myself and support myself. It's important.

Money as a symbol of independence was also important to another respondent:

Q: Why is work important?
R: ... Money. My own independent money that I make and can do what I wish with. That is very important.

Although not "important," then, in an objective sense of enabling them to live, having access to their own source of income gave these women a sense of freedom and, as another woman said, being able to make "a contribution." For these women, earning a salary seemed to enhance their identity through a process of accommodation as their sense of competence grew stronger.

Earning an income perceived as sufficient could also influence an individual's identity indirectly through its effect on feelings of well-being. If the individual felt as though he or she were earning sufficient income, then there would be no need to use identity assimilation as protection from feelings of being an inadequate wage-earner. In the following excerpt, the respondent spoke of just such an effect of his salary on his well-being:

Q: How do you think your job affects you as a person?
R: Well, um, how does it affect me as a person? I think it affects my feelings about the day, my well-being. If the job goes smoothly, there's no problems, you know, if it doesn't go smoothly—
Q: How about how it affects you over the long haul?
R: I think it does. It, I think, the economy has a little bit of feeling of how I feel. The amount of money, the prime interest rate, it affects the job.
Q: I don't understand.
R: Well, being that we're selling building materials for new homes, and for contractors... whether it be a mortgage for a home or a new building, if the prime interest rate is high and the contractor is going to put on an addition to his store or his building, he is not going to do this when it's high. He's going to wait for it to come down. Et cetera. This directly affects how my business is.
Q: So how successful you are?
R: Right.
Q: Basically the bottom line is whether work is going smoothly and successfully which is influenced by the economy?
R: Yes.

The respondent may be using identity assimilation to a certain extent in his attribution of the reasons for his work going well or not to the economy rather than to his own efforts. However, given the sensitivity of the building industry to interest rates, the respondent's appraisal of his situation is probably quite accurate.

The effect on identity of earning a good living is sometimes difficult to disentangle from the intrinsic rewards of work, since competence in performing one's work is often (but not always) rewarded by a higher salary and possibly a promotion. In the following excerpt, this interdependence is very apparent:

Q: How does your work as a programmer and machine operator affect the way that you think about yourself?

R: Well, it's always a challenge to find out. . . exactly how to go about making a particular piece to make the best time so it's always a challenge of my ingenuity, so it's always like a test for myself. So, in that way I feel challenged I guess. Because the faster you can make them the more valuable you are to the man who is paying you, so if he can see that, he's going to pay you a lot of money to keep making them that way too.

This respondent also had reason to feel an enhanced sense of identity because of his knowledge that he would be progressing to a higher level position than he presently held ("I know the promise that's going to be there so I just have to kind of grin and bear it for now"). Unless he was using identity assimilation to exaggerate wildly the amount of encouragement he was receiving from his superiors, his self-esteem would soon be destined to rise along with his job level. Another respondent, who already had achieved what he regarded as a high-status position in the military, reflected on the effects of this on his identity:

Q: Does your job as an officer affect the way you see yourself as a person?

R: Well, I suppose, of course, being a commander or an officer, you're given more responsibility and, of course, I would have to say that I, you enjoy the responsibility, being looked up to. I'd be a liar if I'd say it's nothing. . .

In the same breath, the respondent mentions both an intrinsic factor (responsibility) and an extrinsic factor (being looked up to) as something he enjoys. These two factors cannot be disentangled in any simple way in terms of the identity accommodation process they stimulated in this man's feelings of competence.

Failure to receive what the worker regards as adequate recognition or compensation for efforts on the job can lead, conversely, to an identity assimilation process in which the intrinsic values of work are downgraded. The respondent rationalizes failure to receive promotions or raises by claiming that the work really is not that important, in comparison to other aspects of life. This rationalization protects the individual's sense of competence from being negatively affected by his or her lack of advancement and success. This process was evident in the attitude of a worker in a social agency who was given the same heavy work load but not the higher title and larger salary of employees who had a college education:

Q: What effect on the rest of your life does your work have?

R: It used to have a lot more than it does now. I think, um, well I guess it's true in probably any type of position you have. In the first year, you really are all gung-ho work. Going in on Saturdays and staying late, working through your lunch hour, impressing everybody, and that's really very important. And then you kind of get to along the line there, things aren't going quite your way, or it just came to a point for me, where I think, uh, again, my house was kind of a big thing to me . . . I kind of came to a point in life where I said, you know, what do they care? They really don't . . . The work is going to be there again tomorrow morning. It's just going to get done one way or another, maybe a little bit slower. It's not important to me! I enjoy coming home and painting the outside of the house, or scraping it, fixing something, you know, putting up some wallpaper. I'm much more satisfied. So I said, well, you know, I'll give it my 100% from 8:30 to 5, but before that and after that, I really don't want to know.

This respondent seemed to be using her house as either an outlet or as a justification for her loss of interest in work. The lack of organizational recognition of her efforts seemed to have led her to the point of changing her attitude toward work from intrinsically to extrinsically oriented. The statement in the interview that preceded this excerpt was this description of her situation:

R: I get appointed to every single committee, I get a double case load and everything but [don't have the title] you see, because, and of course they don't pay me as much either, because I don't have the degree. And I can see their point. It's an important thing, it's extremely important, but I just feel if I'm capable of all the other responsibilities [as people with the title], well, I don't know, it seems like well, I ought to be an equal. Or I shouldn't be doing all these extra things.

In order to prevent her identity from being negatively affected by this lack of regard for her competence, she effectively withdrew the involvement of her identity in the intrinsic features of her work.

Another group of respondents showed a different kind of juxtaposition in the effects on identity of intrinsic and extrinsic work factors. These were the respondents who regarded money as important so that they could "pay the bills," but were more interested in seeking personal fulfillment, either through their present work or through an alternative. One was the military officer excerpted above, whose enjoyment of life in the service and belief in the value of what he was doing for his country made him "willing to make a few sacrifices in terms of salary." Two other respondents, both of whom were involved in part-time college studies in engineering, felt that money would be important, but not as important as being interested in their work. However, others lacking the luxury of being able to take such a position felt that they could not seek other employment because of financial limitations. Because they were in jobs that either paid well or paid just enough to cover their financial obligations, these respondents felt they were unable to make a move into a job that would be more interesting but offer less remuneration. In the following excerpt the respondent, an assembly worker, presents an image of quiet desperation as he regretfully describes what he would really like to be doing:

Q: What is an average work day like for you?

R: Boring.
Q: What sorts of things do you do?
R: I'm really not interested in doing this. I was more happier at my other job. It was the kind of work that I enjoyed doing. Each day, each project, was more of a challenge for me. This just strictly is routine work.
Q: Are you thinking of changing?
R: No.
Q: What keeps you from going back to that?
R: . . . the pay isn't there . . . I could get a job in that but it's only half of what I'm getting now though per hour.

This respondent, at the age of 51, described himself in the Age Identity interview as "one year closer to retirement." It is not difficult to understand why he regarded himself as marking time until he could be relieved of the job that he disliked so intensely. This respondent's attitude toward his work seemed to be a relatively straightforward case of dissatisfaction with a job that, compared to one he truly enjoyed, was boring and repetitive. However, another respondent's bitter unhappiness with her job as a typist seemed to reflect a fairly heavy reliance upon identity assimilation to cope with her situation:

Q: What kind of work do you do?
R: It's a specialized kind of typing on a computer terminal. It doesn't involve a lot of original work, but there was a long training period, just applying the procedures and knowledge.
Q: How important to you is the work that you do right now?
R: It's important solely as a, for the money that I'm working for. I'm not involved in it, intellectually or emotionally.
Q: Does it have an effect on the way you feel about yourself?
R: Well, my present job has not been good for the way I feel about myself. The conditions that they have, it's not the kind of situation that's conducive to self-confidence, which I think I could use a little more of. I think I do feel proud or gratified that I'm able to, it's a challenging job, and, well, I'm really contributing to the family's income. Not by choice, however. (laughs)
Q: What are you, or are you considering any other kinds of work?
R: I haven't narrowed it down to a field. I would really like to become involved in maybe 6 years in something that be a career to me, interesting, that I could really participate in and enjoy being productive. My interests don't seem to be related to the job market right now. I'm very interested in history, research, teaching, I think an affiliation with a library or university would, probably starting at this point in time and my past record, it may not be practical, many of those things. But hopefully when the children are older I can reach a point where I can be working, investigating those areas.

There are two different lines of evidence that converge in suggesting that this respondent was using identity assimilation in her description of her current work and, correspondingly, her interest in future work. By putting her ideas for alternate work into the future and keeping them vague and unexplored, she did not have to concern herself with the risk of actually taking steps to pursue that interest. Conversely, any experiences of failure on her "challenging" job that threatened her identity by weakening her self-confidence could be discounted as due to her basic lack of interest, claiming that what she "really" wanted to do was something different, anyhow. Her self-attribution of an extrinsic orientation enabled her to justify her continued employment in that position without having to change her identity as a competent worker. It also allowed her to enhance her status within the family through her economic contribution, a contribution that amounted to almost one-half the family income.

An interesting phenomenon that took place over the course of the interview adds to this account of identity assimilation. The respondent continually revised downward her estimate of how long she planned to wait before seeking other work. Her first estimate of the time it would take for her children to grow up was 6 years. Later in the interview, she pared this estimate down to 4, and then to 3. It was as if she was trying to convince the interviewer (and maybe herself) that she really was going to follow through on this plan of entering the world of academia. Not the least of the respondent's motivation to do so may have been to impress the interviewer, herself a student in one of those fields, with her intellectual interests. Further evidence for the respondent's need to present herself as a person with academic abilities was her description of her job as being difficult to learn, if not original.

This case was the most extreme representation of the identity assimilation process in regard to an extrinsic work factor. It is certainly plausible that other respondents who had visions about what they could accomplish if it were not for their need to earn a living were using a similar form of identity assimilation. Nine men in the sample, for instance, expressed the classic American dream of wanting to start their own businesses or become self-employed. One of these respondents, who had grown disgusted with corporate politics (he was described in Chapter 6), was waiting for the right moment financially to move across the country and open a small business. However, his admission that it was a "pipe dream . . . but that's what keeps you going" suggests an introspective quality not consistent with the use of identity assimilation. The respondent's frank admission of his lack of "particular talent or ability in anything" further suggests that he was not using identity assimilation in his aspirations for self-employment.

Seven of the other men who were entertaining ideas about starting their own businesses, whatever their reasons for doing so, appeared to be fairly realistic about this possibility. Some hoped to be able to devote more time to a hobby (writing, woodworking, antique cars, computers) that they could turn into profit. Others were contemplating extensions of their current jobs into related fields so that they could make more money or have more autonomy. However, these men did not plan to abandon the jobs they were holding, unless their own enterprises were successful. These visions of having their own business may have been "pipe dreams" also that enabled them to cope with their present situations, but they seemed well grounded enough in reality. For one of the men in this situation, though, "coping" seemed to involve identity assimilation in order to maintain an identity as a competent worker:

Q: Does your job affect your feelings in any other way?

R: Well, I wish that I, like I said, that I had more time, and as far as a job, I think I am doing a good job, and I hope that someday that they see the job that I'm doing, that I get a little bit more ahead or something.

Q: A promotion, you mean?

R: Promotion-wise, yeah.

Q: Have you had any promotions recently?

R: Well, I've only been with this company for about 8 years.

Q: Oh, I see.

R: And, uh, I think I've done pretty good for 8 years because there are guys there, they've been there longer than me and they're so, I think I've been pretty lucky on the job.

Q: Have they mentioned anything to you about a promotion or suggested anything to you?

R: Well, they say that if you do a good job for the company you eventually get promoted.

Q: Have they in any way told you that you've done a good job?

R: Not lately, no. They just, well, they tell me I do a good job, but, uh, it isn't when things come up, you know, and by then there's nothing, so . . .

The way that this respondent was able to rationalize not having been promoted is an excellent illustration of identity assimilation. His concern over promotion seemed to be as much a function of the meaning this promotion would have as far as recognition as of the salary increase that advancement would bring. By being able to attribute his failure to advance to the excuses of not having been at the company long enough and not being at the right place at the right time, he was able to avoid having his disappointment invade his sense of competence. This respondent's vision of starting his own business was very tentatively worded as "nothing serious, really." It is perhaps because identity assimilation was effectively reducing his feelings of self-doubt that he did not have a strong need to focus on the coping strategy of striking off on his own.

Another case was that of a man who, medically disabled at the time of the interview, was reviewing his past employment history in terms that suggested he was using identity assimilation to avoid facing threats to his identity from feelings of inadequacy in his work. This case is worth considering here because of its demonstration of how identity assimilation can affect reconstruction of the past, and because it demonstrates that extrinsic work factors can have a bearing on identity. The respondent's use of identity assimilation in reconstructing his past was evident first of all in his defensive attitude toward his lack of education. This is the respondent described in Chapter 6 who claimed to have been given a "free hand" in designing projects, even though he was a tool and die worker rather than an engineer. This is what he had to say about his education:

Q: Was there anything you particularly disliked about your work?

R: Yes, there is something. Every time you changed jobs you dropped 3 or 4 grades and you have to prove it to the next company that you went to. See, um, I went to one year in high school, but I done it by choice, and when I went into the service I was interested in aircraft, and, uh, they wouldn't let me get into pilot training because I had one year in high school. (laughing)

Q: Not enough education?

R: Ah, that's everything. I, all my life, I've had education thrown at me until I've had it up to here. Because what it ended up as, is I took the test [presumably for pilot training] with two-year college graduates. I passed the test and they didn't, which doesn't say much for the college. . . . I ended up after I'd flown my 40 missions in the service and came out and did those, I went into preflight, I was in officer's training, and the war ended. All it tells me is, uh, what happens to the college graduate who didn't make it, and somebody's father paid the way through, I don't know. (laughing)

Q: So, one thing you disliked about your work was that every time you changed positions, for different companies you dropped down.

R: Yes, if you, if you have a college degree to get a job, you usually present your diploma and it'll get you a job, it opens the door . . . show a diploma . . . they know you went to college and that's it. So that's some of the frustration, you can't climb and your foreman's not going to make you the general foreman over your foreman . . .

The respondent's gloating over his passing the test that college graduates did not combined with his resentment over his inability to get better jobs suggest that the respondent was using the self-justification form of identity assimilation to make himself appear to be competent despite his lack of education. His assertion that he attended one year of high school "by choice" adds further weight to this argument. With regard to his desire to have his own business, and the role played by economic limitations in that, it is necessary to turn to the Values portion of his Identity Interview:

Q: Do you have any doubts or questions about your values as they are now?

R: Uh, if, I think everybody's a good Monday morning quarterback. I think that there are things I would have done differently if I had to do it over again. Not too much, but some.

Q: What values would you change, then?

R: My values would have remained the same. I would never have worked for a large organization. I would have started my own business and go down the drain if I had to. But at least if I went down the drain, it would be my own doing, not somebody else's.

Q: But I was wondering specifically about your values. Would you change any of those?

R: Not really. Still, if you have a family, I think you're obligated to that family and . . . the place you work . . . they are paying you and as long as you work there you should try to give them a day's work or whatever. That's my value.

The evidence for identity assimilation in this segment is the respondent's use of his family responsibility and duty to his employer to justify not having started his own business. By using this form of identity assimilation, the respondent could engage in wishful thinking about what he might have accomplished had he worked on his own, without taking the blame for not having done so. His discouragement about his lack of education may have played a role in this self-justification process as well. Had he worked for himself rather than a large company, his poor education would not have stood in the way of his achieving higher paying positions. As in the military, he could have advanced on the basis of his own abilities rather than on the basis of a diploma.

As a final note, it is interesting to point out that this respondent was one of many (5 women and 14 men) who regretted not have had more education.

However, not everyone who mentioned their low education did so in a negative way. Two respondents regarded themselves as extremely fortunate because they were able to get and keep jobs that normally demanded a higher level of training. One of these, a metal plate engraver, observed that: "I think for a guy with my education, that I've really done pretty good. In the job that I'm doing, you could have a degree in commercial art." Of course, advancing beyond one's educational level is a common occurrence, often forming the basis for fictional and nonfictional books and movies. The existence of such mobility further strengthens the interpretation offered here that blaming failure to succeed in terms of status or income on lack of education can be a form of identity assimilation.

This analysis of identity assimilation seems to have gone well beyond the original topic of monetary rewards in work as a form of extrinsic motivation. However, what must be remembered is that financial pressures formed the backdrop for all of the responses excerpted here concerning identity assimilation and accommodation. No matter how desirable a position that offered opportunity for greater intrinsic work satisfaction appeared, it could not be contemplated unless the respondent could be assured of financial success or at least financial security.

The Conditions of Work: Creature Comforts and Convenience

The extrinsic work factors that formed the second largest grouping of responses concerned the "where and when" of work. The setting in which the work takes place determines much of how the worker will feel during the day. Kalleberg (1977) used the term "creature comforts" to describe the extent to which the work environment provides for the individual's physical well-being. In addition, whether work allowed the individual to feel mentally stressed or relaxed is another factor adding to the worker's perceived comfort. The convenience of work describes the "when": whether the hours are compatible with the worker's outside interests and responsibilities, and whether there is any flexibility for the worker to adapt his or her schedule to the vicissitudes of other needs and interests. These factors are extrinsic because they are not particular to any one kind of job, and because they do not involve the work activity itself. However, it will be shown that they can both produce and demand direct involvement of the worker's identity.

CREATURE COMFORTS

The Physical Environment

One of the basic distinctions between types of work environments is whether the work takes place outdoors or indoors. The relatively harsh and long winters would seem to make outdoor work in the upstate New York area less than attractive for most of the year. Nevertheless, there were several respondents who expressed a distinct preference for being in the open air instead of an office. One man's preference for outside work was expressed in particularly strong terms:

Q: Do you think there's anything special about this work that makes you feel a certain way as a person?

R: I think it does. I can't see myself working unless I was working on the outside. If I was working in a factory or doing a 9 to 5 inside somewhere I'd go crazy.

Q: What do you like about working outside?

R: It gives you a feeling of a lot of freedom, and it, uh, you know, you don't have anybody, you work out your own schedule at your own pace. It gives you initiative, pride, to do more where if you are inside you're just putting in time on the machine . . .

Working outside meant, for this respondent, not just the physical conditions, but also the intrinsic factors of having autonomy and freedom from supervision. His identity as a competent worker was, in this way, indirectly influenced by the quality of the work environment. A second respondent attributed part of his dislike for his job as a construction worker to the physical discomfort he experienced due to having to work outside in the cold:

Q: Would you say that overall there are more things you dislike about the job than you like about it?

R: No, there ain't too much, just about the only things is if you have to go through the winter, the cold weather, wear work gloves, have trouble breathing.

His discomfort was so great that he was considering leaving construction work:

Q: How likely is it that you'll actually leave construction?

R: I don't know. I'm getting older now, I'm about 43 now, and I figure in a while I'll get too old to be going in and out of the cold and putting in electric ducts and different things, you know. I'm going to have to change and get something. The thing is about it, you know, you get stuck on the job and you ain't got the money to take off and be off long enough to go around applying for different jobs . . .

That the financial rewards of his job were of primary importance to this worker was indicated early in his interview: "it's the money that's most important, not just the work." The fact that he had to work outside made an otherwise well-paying job disagreeable, but it did not seem to impinge at all on his identity. In contrast, the conditions within the physical environment of work did represent a factor that directly influenced the identities of other respondents. One case in which this effect was particularly strong was that of a woman who worked in a factory in which heavy equipment was manufactured:

Q: What is it about the work that you don't like?

R: I have to use a lot of hammers and screwdrivers and drills, and my hands get cut up a lot, like, you know, the fingertips, and . . . working with the oils, it gets your hands very rough and your hands don't look nice, don't look feminine, maybe I shouldn't use the word "feminine," but they just don't look nice. It is basically a masculine job . . .

Q: How does your work affect the way that you think about yourself?

R: Well, it makes me think, I don't want to do it all my life. Even though it's an upgraded job, and it's paying good money, I would like a different kind of job. I would like to keep my feminine status. I'm not a liberated woman.

R: (My) job is basically a masculine job because you're doing a lot of bending and lifting. Some of those parts are heavy, you cut your fingers, no fingernails—fingernail polish is out. You'd have to put it on twice a day. Before you go to work and when you come home!

Apart from the heavy work involved in her job, this respondent was sensitive to the fact that the job's physical environment made it impossible for her to keep up her appearance in a way that would be consistent with her desire to appear feminine. Her unhappiness over this was so strong that she was even willing to give up the job's high pay and high status if necessary, in order to find work that was less dirty.

Considering the number of workers, particularly men, whose jobs brought them in contact with heavy equipment, electrical components, and chemicals, there were relatively few who regarded the danger they were exposed to through their jobs as something to be concerned with. As would be expected, those who did report on this aspect of the physical environment were displeased about the risks that their jobs entailed. The next excerpt is from the respondent described in Chapter 6 who worked in electronics on defense contracts:

Q: What do you particularly dislike about your work?
R: . . . The other thing is the environment; the working area I work in. When you stick a probe into a power supply you do it very gingerly. You could be sent across the room or cooked if you're not careful. And then, I don't know how to explain this, but the military, when they want equipment, they want to make sure it don't break. So you have to put it on a gigundus steel table, rock it up and down, push it into this great big box that is a refrigerator and an oven all in one and you can't, you know, I went to my doctor. He said "You're on your way to an ulcer. I want you to quit smoking, quit drinking, quit your job!" It's the environment. . . I found the industrial complex, there was something just not quite legitimate about it, you know, . . . it's got to stop.

This respondent's distaste for the military in general appeared to have been reinforced by the kind of risks he was forced to take in conducting work for them. Both he and the female factory worker, although responding to what appear to be extrinsic characteristics, could also be seen as reacting negatively to their situations due to intrinsic reasons connected to their identities.

The involvement of identity took what appears to be the following form. The attitudes of these two respondents toward their situations reflected the assimilation by their own identities of their perceptions of the work environments they inhabited. A woman who did not care about looking feminine would not, for instance, care about the fact that she could not wear nail polish. The electronics technician perceived the risks he was taking in terms of his overall dislike and distrust of the military establishment. Furthermore, both individuals were resisting incorporating the identities that would be consistent with their environments (she a masculine identity; he that of a defense contract worker). The inner disequilibrium they were experiencing between their identities and their environments could very well have been the key factor accounting for their outward dissatisfaction. In the case of the factory worker, the disequilibrium was leading her to seek a new environment more consistent with her identity. The electronics technician intended to remain in his present occupation, citing personal reasons as inhibiting him from considering a change.

The extrinsic feature of the job conditions may also involve factors related to the individual's identity through the accommodation process. This would occur when the worker feels that there has been a change in an aspect of his or her appearance or behavior in a feature relevant to identity. The most notable of these effects observed among the respondents were the effects of work on their bodies. A woman who worked part-time as a waitress noticed changes in her appearance as a result of her exposure to food:

Q: How does your work as a waitress affect the way you think about yourself?
R: Right now I'm very unhappy with myself because I've gained so much weight. Is that what you mean?
Q: Is that related, do you think, to your work?
R: Oh, not really. It's just the fact that being in the restaurant, everytime someone says "let's try something" I'm probably one of the first ones to be in the line to try it.

Despite her disclaimer that gaining weight was not "really" due to her work, it is apparent from the rest of her answer that it was. Another woman in the sample, the beautician described earlier in this chapter, did not regard her work as having much effect on her behavior outside of work. The one exception was in regard to her physical appearance:

Q: What effect do you think your job might have, or if it doesn't have any effect at all?
R: Not really. I wouldn't say so. There's no effect. Aside from, uh, outside of work, if I know I'm going to be someplace, let's say, out socially, I'll try to, you know, look good, dress nice, you know, make sure I look good in case anybody might say, you know, what do you do, or where do you work? You know, I want to, if I'm promoting myself for my business, you know, I'll make an extra special effort to look good, make sure everything is perfect. Because if you're promoting yourself or trying to build up business you have to look good. You have to look the part.

Both of these women were describing different aspects of their physical appearance. The strength and agility of the body were factors discussed by men in regard to their work. Men who had active jobs, requiring lifting of heavy boxes or equipment, commented favorably upon their ability to stay "in shape" because of their work. Several other men, whose jobs were sedentary, lamented over the opposite effect:

Q: How important to you is your work as an engraver?
R: Oh, it's not that important, you know, it's a job. And it's a good job. It's not a hard job, and it's not an easy job. It's not a physical job at all. Like, well, I've been programming now for 18 years. And before that I was in the physical jobs, that of outside labor and landscaping, and doing the muscle work. Stuff like that. Which in a way, I wish I was still in. I'd be in better shape than what I have, you know . . .

The importance of physical fitness to this respondent's identity can be inferred from his description of the effects of age in the Age Identity portion of the interview (his age was 43):

Q: How does your age affect the way you think about yourself as a person?
R: Well, my mind says yes, but my age say no. I mean, I played slow pitch. I really
enjoyed baseball. I was never on a winning team, but I just enjoyed going out there and
playing. I played on this one team for 10 years. Okay, it does have an effect. I've
noticed in the last 2 years, since I've hit the 40 mark, my triples are doubles, my doubles are singles, and my singles are outs... I'm running slower...

The importance to this respondent of physical fitness meant that spending his
days in a job requiring no physical exertion was taking its toll on his identity as
a person with athletic prowess.

The physical conditions of work are not, then, simply the presence of walls,
work materials, demands for physical labor, and temperature. Instead, the physical environment can have a very potent symbolic meaning to the identity of the
worker, both as a stimulus for identity accommodation and as a set of features to
be interpreted through identity assimilation.

Pressure

Another form of "creature comfort" is freedom from mental stress or pressure
in one's work setting. This kind of comfort is in part of a function of the nature
of the work itself, and whether it involves decisions that have important implications. It is also a function of the rate at which products, services, or information
must be produced, and whether this rate is so high that it taxes the individual's
resources. Pressure may be created, in addition, by the attitudes and behaviors
of one's co-workers, especially a supervisor. Although the extrinsic work factor
describing co-workers and superiors is considered as a condition in its own right,
there is some overlap with pressure. In the present discussion, other people at
work are regarded as contributing to pressure when they place numerous
demands upon the worker and create an atmosphere of tension.

Before describing the kinds of tensions that result from work task demands,
another kind of pressure more related to the work environment must be considered. This is a factor usually described by respondents in a positive sense
because it is seen as a desirable feature of the environment in which work is performed. The worker may appreciate the work environment because it provides
relief from the boredom that would otherwise be experienced if the worker had
to remain home all day. As one might guess, this is a factor more frequently mentioned by those women who have the choice of working or staying home. In
Chapter 8, it will be seen that homemakers are very much involved in this sort of
thinking. Among the sample of working women and men, four women and one
man described their satisfaction with work in these terms. The following excerpt
illustrates the nature of this extrinsic work factor, and also the way that it
becomes interwoven with the intrinsic factor of stimulation:

Q: How important to you is your work?
R: Uh, very... It is important. I like to be out now that the kids are out. I don't like to
be home for 8 hours a day.

Q: Why is the work important? Specifically why?

R: Specifically, to use up my time. I am not a big leisure time person. I can read a book for an hour and love it, but that's it. I can't everyday do that. . . . And seeing other adults and other people. Because I have been in the house for a while, with the kids.

Q: How would you feel about yourself if you did not work?

R: When I didn't, I would get very uptight. I need this time to be out. . . . I think you need to be outside your own four walls to realize what's going on.

Q: What would you do differently if you did not have the work that you have?

R: If I wouldn't have any job at all? I'd have to learn to do something with my time, rather than just sit around. I've gone through the crewel bit when I was home, and the embroidery bit, sewing bit, and I did all these things in short periods and never got involved in something.

Q: So, it would have a major effect.

R: Oh yeah. I'm not good with time on my hands.

This respondent found the pressure of the work environment in contrast to the boredom of the home to be a major source of gratification. It also appeared to enhance her identity, since work provided her with the stimulation to become involved in interesting activities. This particular combination of intrinsic and extrinsic factors will be examined in the next chapter, as it was a major theme of the women who were not employed outside the home.

The kind of work that in and of itself seems to create the most pressure is that in which actions must be taken that have life-and-death implications for other people or for the worker. The first case is of a hospital worker:

Q: What do you particularly dislike about (your job)?

R: Uh, there's a couple things. One is the tension. I don't mind the responsibility, but the tension is unhealthy. Usually when somebody comes in and they're bleeding or hemorrhaging, or there was an accident or whatever, or they can't be cross-linked, they have some weird antibody, um, and it's important that they get blood right away and there's just no way to get blood right away. You can do everything that is possible to do and still you can't get it as fast as they need it. It's very frustrating to get, have a request come in and know that they would have liked the blood 2 hours sooner. And then the phone rings, and why isn't it ready or this or that, you know. There's a lot of tension.

Although this respondent's job did not involve having to make major decisions that could affect the lives of her patients, her job did involve playing a role in a process in which lives could be saved or lost. A second source of stress was keeping up with other people's demands, a factor that is considered in more detail shortly.

A job may also create pressure if the worker knows that a false move could result in severe injury. This was a problem noted by the electronics technician described earlier in the chapter, who was afraid of getting "cooked." In that case, the respondent seemed to be referring less to a perception of pressure than a perception of the physical environment in general. Another respondent who worked in construction felt more directly a sense of pressure from the potential dangers of his job:

Q: Does being a construction worker affect what you do in the rest of your life outside of work?

R: ...Being in construction work you gotta go to bed 8, 9:00, you know.

Q: You need your rest.

R: You gotta have that rest, because too much happening, too many electric, you're going to dig down that hole, ain't nothing but electric in there, you don't know what's in your hand, you gotta be watching it all the time.

The pressure of having to keep on guard for possible danger affected this respondent not only in his working hours, but also influenced his thoughts and actions outside work. Another respondent, whose work tasks required constant scrutiny for visual details, reported a different kind of effect on his personal life:

Q: What effect on the rest of your life does your work as an engraver have?

R: Well, none really. The only effect that it has on my life is eye strain. . . . And I think if I wasn't doing this job, I would be, uh, more alert at night. And able to stay up to watch the 11:00 news. I peter out pretty good at about 10:30.

Although not as dramatic an effect as that described by the construction worker, in both cases there was an undesirable change reported in the worker's personal habits. Other respondents reported effects on their personal lives due to the stress they experienced on the job, stress that was due to the amount of responsibility their work involved. While having control and authority is a feature of a job usually thought of as intrinsically rewarding, it also creates pressure that invades the worker's outside life. In the next section, the trade-off between responsibility and time demands off the job is specifically examined. For present purposes, what is considered is the trade-off between the self-direction of being in a position of authority and the pressure of making sure things go smoothly. The following excerpt, from a school director, illustrates how a position of responsibility can be stressful in this way:

Q: What kinds of things do you do in your job?

R: Since it's a fairly large operation, I have about 20 employees under me whom I have to hire myself. We deal with 150 children, so that means 150 children plus their mothers and fathers. Three hundred parents, so there's a lot of P.R. work. I'm in charge of keeping the budget for the operation, bookkeeping. I do have clerical help, but you have to be on top of it yourself. I order supplies, you know.

Q: How important to you is your work?

R: I get, um, a great deal of satisfaction out of the job. It's rewarding to me. There is quite a bit of pressure with it because I have the position all alone. . . . Because I've been the director for 4 years and have been able to hire staff, I have quite a responsible staff and things run quite smoothly. But this is a job keeping on top of things and making sure—but I get real satisfaction out of seeing something like this run smoothly or mesh and things go along, because I am in charge and control that part. It's rewarding and it's frustrating sometimes, when things go wrong, but it's been more rewarding than frustrating.

Although the balance of rewards and frustrations was positive, this respondent was seeking other work offering higher salary and fringe benefits. The pressure she was experiencing was not, she felt, adequately rewarded in terms of income:

Q: What do you dislike?

R: I dislike the pressure. Sometimes the responsibility that I feel it's on me and also the fact that if somebody saw my job description, I'm sure if I told them what I get paid for it, it makes you very angry . . .

It appeared that this respondent was taking a fairly objective view of her situation, neither exaggerating her importance nor unduly attributing her low salary to external causes outside her control. Instead, this was the case of a worker who was involved in her work for intrinsic reasons. It was the lack of equity that she perceived between the extrinsic factors of pressure and salary rather than insecurities over her identity as a competent worker that was causing her to look elsewhere for employment.

Another source of pressure is fulfilling the demands of the job communicated by other people. The pressure in this kind of situation is not only due to the need to complete the task successfully, but also to be able to do so in a limited period of time. The cake decorator described in Chapter 6 addressed this source of stress directly:

Q: So when you talk about doing other work, you would be interested in those for other kinds of reasons?

R: Maybe something a little less demanding. My job doesn't sound like it, but it's a pretty high pressure job. Specifically, around graduation time when I have, say, 60 cakes a day to do and just one person doing them is sometimes physically impossible. I would go in and work a 20-hour shift and sometimes that just gets to be a little much. And a race against the clock.

This sense of time pressure becomes even more stressful when the worker has to take orders from different people, all of whom have the authority to request that their orders be carried out immediately, as was the case for this secretary:

Q: Is the work that you're doing satisfactory?

R: . . . I don't mind typing. I like to type, but I don't like it 8 hours a day. And my job now that they've increased the firm when I started from 2 men to 5, it's becoming more typing. The typing that is involved is "Can you do this? I have a meeting in 15 minutes." More pressure. You know, "it isn't already late, can we get it out today?" You know, now I have 5 men I'm typing for, 5 different personalities, and I find just that I don't want to do this forever.

Time pressure can be stressful not only when the worker has to meet the demands of many other people, but also when the work pace is unpredictably variable. A grocery store department manager observed that "every so often it's a feast or a famine—you may be busier than hell and the next day nothing; it's sometimes a little hard to schedule." The worker in this situation cannot even prepare at the beginning of the day for what is to be expected of his or her performance.

As will be seen in the next section, control over the scheduling of work hours can have an intrinsic as well as an extrinsic component. With regard to the rate at which work is performed during work hours, it appears that there is a similar blending of the intrinsic and the extrinsic. The extrinsic component is clear enough: it is physically and mentally tiring and unpleasant to have to work at a rate of speed that overburdens the worker's intellectual and physical resources. It is probable that the intrinsic reason for time pressure being perceived negatively is that the rate at which the worker must perform his or her duties is a concrete indication of the amount of autonomy that the worker has in general.

A statement that some workers used to characterize the freedom from supervision they had in their jobs was that there was "nobody looking over my shoulder." Not only did this autonomy give the workers the opportunity to determine *what* they would do, but it also gave them the chance to determine *when* they would do it and at what pace. For most kinds of work, more autonomy is associated with more responsibility and hence more pressure to make the right decisions. However, the autonomous worker also has the advantage of possessing greater power to exercise self-determination over his or her rate of mental or physical labor. Rather than being the agent of superiors or co-workers to produce something that will meet their needs, the worker is producing at a rate consistent with internal standards. When internal standards are substituted for external ones, the motivation becomes intrinsic. The outcome of the individual's efforts can therefore have a direct bearing on his or her identity as a competent worker.

CONVENIENCE

One of the most notable effects of industrialization on modern society is the loss of control by individuals over how they delegate their time (DeGrazia, 1971). Jobs vary, however, in how much flexibility individuals have in determining their own work hours. To a certain extent, flexibility of scheduling may have effects on the individual similar to those of the intrinsic factor of occupational self-direction. However, the difference between the flexibility of hours and flexibility of tasks is that the ability to set one's own working hours (beginning and ending times) is thought to have its major influence on what the worker does outside of work rather than during the course of the working day. It will be seen here, however, that time is like the physical environment in that both can have a symbolic meaning to the worker. Time is given this meaning through interconnections between the demands of work and the worker's identity.

The respondent with probably the worst hours of anyone in the sample was a production worker on a rotating shift schedule; in his own words:

R: ...I work on rotation. I'm not on any one trick [shift], A [8–4], B [4–12], or C [12–8] any more than 2 days. Except on the weekends. So I work Monday, Tuesday, A, Wednesday, Thursday, B, Friday, Saturday, C. And the next week will be different from that...The hours are terrible, and changing tricks. I got out of work last night at 12 midnight and I'm going in tonight on C trick.

This schedule was hard even for the respondent himself to keep straight:

Q: What is the average work day like for you?
R: Well, get to work at 8, 4, or 12, okay? (laughs) Take A trick, a regular day, okay? I set the alarm at 6:30, get up at a quarter to 7...get to work about 7:30...go to my machine...so I do that and then it's time to punch out...go straight home...

eat . . . watch a little TV . . . hit the sack about 11, 11:30. When I do the B trick, it's not too much different from that. . . . So today on the B trick, I get up, we got up late today about 9:00, and we ate, got ready, came here, and then we'll go home . . . and after that I'll have something to eat . . . and then about a quarter after 3 I'll go to work. Wait a minute, today's not B trick! But I'll talk as if it were.

Needless to say, this respondent was fairly preoccupied with getting a job that was "straight days." He was taking on an additional job part-time at home that he hoped to build up enough to make up the differential in pay between "trick work" and straight days. The other alternative he was considering was data processing:

Q: What about data processing is attractive?
R: Well, I'll tell you the honest-to-God's truth. I don't know that much about it. Uh, I know there's more opportunity not in data processing but in the programming aspect of it, alright? Data processing. Processing, that's all it is. Just take data and "Whsssh!" There is a very good demand for data processing at (name of company). So my uncle's with computers, data processing, so I really don't know what the work is like . . . I can learn to like almost any job I go into . . .
Q: So what would be the main reason for pursuing data processing?
R: To get into a straight A trick. I wouldn't have to be working the shifts all the time.
Q: So, there's nothing in particular about the activities, it's the hours.
R: Right.
Q: Increased salary?
R: Yeah. See a job is important to me, right? As far as, I like to enjoy what I'm doing. Okay? And right now I moderately enjoy what I'm doing. Okay? But I don't think any less of myself doing this, you know, than Job A, or Job B, or Job C. You know?

The scheduling nightmare represented by this respondent's job then, was not perceived by him as having any impact on his identity. He regarded the trick work as a temporary nuisance, enabling him to earn a higher salary than straight day work until he was able to advance to a more skilled position with the same pay on a regular shift. A less straightforward interpretation of the respondent's answers may be offered, though, that is consistent with the lack of insight form of identity assimilation. Respondents who deny any effect of their work on their feelings about themselves may be trying to keep from thinking about the implications for their identities of the type of work that they are doing. It is not only confusing and bothersome, but somewhat demeaning, to have to take on a job with difficult hours in order to earn sufficient income for one's family. Moreover, the type of job that the respondent held was one that he regarded as extremely boring, a judgment that is consistent with his description of the work tasks. Rather than admit that he was in a job requiring little skill and a high degree of routinization, he could protect his identity by negating the effect of any kind of work on his feelings of competence.

For some workers in jobs where they could enter and leave on their own recognizance, having to punch a time clock symbolized the very essence of dehumanization, turning the individual into a "number." However, there was surprisingly little reference among hourly workers to this feature of their jobs. Instead, being able to punch "out" seemed to give them the psychological reassurance that they could leave their work "at work" and do what they wished with the rest of their days. These punch-clock workers may have been using identity assimilation to avoid attributing to themselves the dehumanizing qualities described by the salaried workers. It is more likely, though, that the freedom from invasion of work into their time off the job was seen as compensating for the loss of individuality represented by the time clock. The following response provides some insight into this process:

Q: What do you especially like about your job?
R: Well, it keeps you busy. Uh, I go to work at 6:15 in the morning and I get out at 2:15 in the afternoon. People say "How can you go out so early in the morning?" Well, I'd rather go out early in the morning and get out early in the afternoon, and then you have some time in the afternoon for yourself if you want to do something like cut the grass. Especially when you've got work to do around the house. You've got daylight when you can do it, and the snow starts, it's really heavy in the wintertime here, you get home at a halfway decent hour when you don't have to buck the traffic and be around it at 7:00 at night. I done that once, and never again.

Not only did the job permit him the freedom not to have to think about his work after he left, but it also gave this respondent the opportunity to complete his household chores at his convenience.

For the salaried workers, having responsibility and autonomy in their work often went along with being able to determine their own working hours. It also meant, though, that one was under obligation to be available at a moment's notice to handle any emergencies. Several respondents in positions of authority or responsibility provided graphic illustrations of these kinds of situations. One was a school administrator who normally worked 14-hour days, either doing paperwork at night or going to meetings. In addition, this person's "free" time activities were often unexpectedly interrupted:

Q: It sounds like you spend a lot of your off-time involved in school?
R: Oh, yeah. It's all part of the overhead . . . And if I have a social engagement and something comes up at school or maybe a calendar's been changed because something came up and they had to postpone it and put it on a different day. It doesn't really matter what that is short of, you know, I don't know what. I will cancel anything on my calendar to make sure that I'm available for that school event. That's all. It comes first. I've given away theater tickets, I've cancelled trips, I've done all kinds of things to make sure that I'm going to be available . . .

In reading this excerpt, it is necessary to suspend the usual disbelief attached to such extreme statements, which normally would be regarded as showing identity assimilation. Although the respondent does portray a "holier than thou" image through much of the interview, there are also frequent enough admissions of inadequacies ("I make mistakes," "I'm not perfect!") to discount the interpretation that most of the statement is an attempt by the respondent to give a biased self-portrayal. The response is also consistent with the nature of the person's job, and with descriptions by others in the sample with similar kinds of responsibilities.

Another type of worker who has autonomy but little time flexibility is the one who has no set hours but whose salary depends on how much he or she is able to sell or produce. If such a person is sufficiently motivated to earn a high income, all available hours of the day, going well beyond the normal work day, will be given over to work activity. This was the case of one self-employed salesperson:

Q: What's an average work day like for you?

R: Well, last week it was horrible. Two weeks ago, I was going probably from about 9 to 9 at night. Sometimes Saturdays are a good time to see some of my clients who are on the road. I work 24 hours a day. My main thing is to get a prospect. I don't care what time it is . . .

Q: Is there an average work day, in terms of starting at a certain time, doing certain tasks?

R: No, I don't walk in, I do not punch a clock. I do not quit at 5:00. I do not go home. I cannot go home and have dinner and wash my mind completely. I live my job 24 hours a day.

This respondent was a high achiever (he was the Boy Scout leader described in Chapter 4) and so his ability to earn essentially as much as the number of hours in the day permitted was something he saw as positive:

Q: How important to you is your work?

R: I like the sales job because it gives me the flexibility and I'm compensated directly to my effort. If I worked for a large industrial firm, my raises would come only upon reviews, which would be every year, every 6 months, every 18 months. Here, my only judge is myself. So I like my job. I think I've got the whole wide world.

However, he was not always successful in drumming up large sums of money, and described as undesirable the fact that his salary was "either a feast or a famine." Of course, this is the risk of a job with no guaranteed income but potentially an infinitely large pay-off if circumstances are favorable. It is perhaps this element of danger that drew the respondent to this kind of work. He may be looking for ways to test and then reconfirm his identity as a successful salesperson. However, his approach to his family life bears some reexamination after hearing what he said about his work. It is difficult to imagine how, as he claims, "the family comes first." This inconsistency suggests that he is using identity assimilation in one of these spheres of his identity. The most likely conclusion from considering both interviews is that he sacrifices his family identity for the sake of his work rather than vice versa.

Another type of worker whose position of responsibility can lead to unpredictable schedules is one who has responsibility for people's lives. Physicians, particularly obstetricians, are usually thought of as falling into this category. There were no physicians in the present sample, but there was a respondent who had a similar kind of responsibility and similar kinds of schedule interruptions in his work as a hospital supplier:

Q: What effect does your job have on the rest of your life?

R: Well, uh, it's never completely out of my mind. I mean, you don't know when something may go wrong, at a hospital. And then, it causes you trouble. That's always subconsciously, subconsciously there. 'Cause I, all week you have emergencies, I have to run out, no matter, 24 hours a day, you know, you don't, you have to take care of it, and being able to take care of it, that bothers me sometimes. You know, we haven't had that for a long time, but that stays with you, you know. If anything unusual should happen. . . . They'll call me, so naturally I'll have to get over there. They'll be in Syracuse, but hoping nobody dies or, you've got a life to consider, that's the thing. It doesn't bother me but, you know, it's there. Especially if the phone rang during the night. If I was in bed. And that's what I would think in my mind, something is wrong.

Despite his assertion that the responsibility "doesn't bother me," his response describes a situation in which there seems to be a great deal of interference in his everyday life. His attempt here to deny the importance of being called on in emergencies is similar to another statement of his earlier in the interview in which he negates the amount of stress from other sources that he appears to have been under. The company that he works for had, since he was hired, undergone rather massive changes in its organization. In addition, the government's increasing efforts to regulate his industry have led to proliferation of regulations that the respondent found difficult to keep pace with. He did not have a college education, and knew that he was really underqualified for the job compared to the new "younger guys" with better qualifications who had been "brought up" to handle the changed demands of his profession. In fact, the main reason he could not change jobs was that at his age (57) and with his education, he would not get "anything near" his line. This is also the same respondent whose critical performance evaluations from the quality control inspector (see Chapter 6) were distorted through identity assimilation so as to fault the inspector rather than himself.

After describing the recent changes in his company and his problems in keeping up with them, the following exchange with the interviewer took place:

R: . . . since then . . . I just don't let it get to me.
Q: Great.
R: I haven't taken a thing for an upset stomach or anything since then.
Q: Fantastic.
R: Well, I've had three operations. Ten weeks I was in the hospital. Doctor said I should've been dead. But since then, so I've—
Q: Because of the job stress?
R: Yeah, it's that kind. But the hell with it, you know.

His physical symptoms attest to the extent to which his job, despite his denials, does in fact "bother" him. One interpretation of his problem lies in understanding his illness as arising out of a long-term psychological disequilibrium in which identity assimilation has been his predominant means of defending against threats to his identity as a competent worker. Identity assimilation may also have altered the respondent's perception of the intrinsic and extrinsic factors in his work. His underlying belief (which identity assimilation keeps him from admitting openly) that he failed miserably on most counts except being able to keep his job may have led him, over the years, to devalue his job's intrinsically rewarding potential and see it now as something to be tolerated until he can retire. At the same time, in order to maintain a favorable identity as someone of importance (if not competence), he may have given greater emphasis to his responsibility for people's lives than his position warrants. A similar line of reasoning would apply to the high value he places on having freedom from direct supervision.

This interpretation could have been arrived at by a variety of routes. The key phrase "it doesn't bother me" set off the present analysis because of the glaring inconsistencies in the respondent's statements about time demands in his job. With respect to time flexibility as an "extrinsic" factor, the implications are that it can have very deep connections with dynamic processes taking place in some of the fundamental aspects of work identity.

The People Factor

In Chapter 6 a "People-Work" factor was described that was intrinsic to the nature of the work task. The extrinsic counterpart to this factor is the "People" component that is not inherent to the type of occupation in which one is employed. The kinds of extrinsic "People" factors to be considered here may be found in connection with any job, because they are not inherent to the job's clientele or mode of working with people. Instead, the extrinsic factors pertaining to people have to do with co-workers and superiors and the extent to which they liked or disliked.

In developing this subcategory of extrinsic work factors, it will be seen that there are ways in which the "People" factor may have implications for the individual worker's identity. The identity processes of assimilation and accommodation are involved in the perception of other workers and their effects on the worker's identity. In addition, the results of relationships with peers and supervisors on the job can have ramifications for the worker's sense of competence.

GETTING ALONG WITH CO-WORKERS

The people who work at one's place of employment may be thought of as being a part of the social environment. Like the physical environment, the social environment's quality contributes to the worker's overall sense of well-being. If one's co-workers are perceived as friendly and cooperative, the workplace will be that much more pleasant and enjoyable. Conversely, having co-workers who are competitive and hostile, or just not very willing to interact, is something that detracts from the quality of one's work experience. Of course, whether co-workers are perceived in a positive or a negative light may depend heavily upon the worker's identity assimilation processes. A worker who is insecure and defensive about his or her abilities may regard with suspicion even the friendliest of gestures from co-workers, believing them to be concealed overtures to gain power and influence. The worker's perception of co-workers can also influence the worker's own social behaviors. A worker who likes co-workers is more inclined to behave in a considerate and cooperative manner. An individual who is plagued with insecurity and fear will probably not be very open and sociable.

The behavior of co-workers not only affects how the individual feels about the workplace, but may also influence the individual's identity. For at least one-third of the day the worker interacts with the co-workers in his or her immediate work environment. Their actions and reactions to the individual can serve as a frequent, if not potent, source of information about how desirable or undesirable are the worker's personality and habits. If the worker is able to maintain the respect and cooperation of these people who are seen day in and day out, it provides evidence to the worker that he or she is a good and likeable person. This evidence can enhance the worker's sense of interpersonal competence, or ability to get along with people (Foote & Cottrell, 1955). In addition, the reactions of other workers to oneself can provide valuable information that can be used outside of the workplace to enhance family and other love relationships.

Co-workers can be important for a third set of reasons. If a group of workers gets along well, the chances are much greater that their work productivity and quality will benefit. Each member of the group thereby has the opportunity to enhance his or her own sense of personal competence as a worker. Unless the work setting is one in which competition is so fierce that there is no benefit to working for the benefit of the group, co-workers who cooperate also stand a better chance of being considered favorably at the time of salary raises, bonuses, and promotions. Co-workers who have favorable regard for one another may also stand to gain in their personal lives by the friendships that they establish in the workplace that carry over into off-work social activities.

The statements made by the present sample of respondents were expected to contain these elements regarding co-workers. As it turned out, the reasons enumerated by respondents for liking or disliking co-workers as people were for the most part brief and superficial. Most of the statements about co-workers were simple descriptions of them as "nice," "challenging," "marvelous," "terrific," "my best friends." The respondents were generally content to let such brief phrases suffice without any further elaboration.

Of the three negative statements about co-workers, two provided some insight into the nature of the speaker's identity. Both respondents used comparison with their co-workers to make a point about a positive feature regarding themselves. The first complained about specific behaviors of his co-workers:

Q: What do you dislike about (your job)?
R: The females that I work with. I guess that I probably shouldn't say it like that, but I seem to have, well, to look at the majority of women as being largely frustrated females because of the work they have to do. I don't like to hear people crying. I always look at it as whatever territory comes with the job, if you have not already prepared yourself to handle it, you start preparing yourself to be ready for any changes that occur. And I see [them] as not able to make some of the changes.
Q: So that aggravates you?

R: No. I laugh at it. I dislike it because I don't like to hear them squawking about it. They remind me of a bunch of insecure teenagers. Instead of being the mature professionals they are supposed to be. I can see there being disagreements over aspects of the job, but not as much as I've heard over the past two and a half years.

This statement includes some sweeping generalizations about women as well as criticisms in particular of the lack of professionalism of this respondent's co-workers. Although he may be quite accurate about the lack of professionalism shown by the women with whom he works, it seems to be fairly obvious from his description of women in general that the respondent is using identity assimilation as a basis for interpreting the co-workers' behaviors. In particular, the respondent uses self-justification in describing his ability to distance himself from the job, an interpretation consistent with a subsequent response in his interview:

Q: How does your work affect the way you think of yourself?
R: It doesn't too much. It makes me feel good that I know I can walk into my place of employment every morning with a smile on my face and nine times out of 10 walk out of it at the end of the day maybe not with that same smile but with a big smile on my face. I can begin the day with a smile on my face and end it with a smile.

Although the respondent attributed the smile on his face to a lack of "outside pressure," it also appears that his self-description serves the function of making him appear to be a cool professional compared to his "immature" co-workers.

Another respondent used the comparison with his co-workers to make a point indirectly about his own approach to his job:

Q: What do you find unattractive about (your job)?
R: ... I find that generally the people in this business, my contemporaries, are generally assholes . . . A lot of them think they do more than they really do, you know, the end-all answer, next to God or the Pope or somewhere in between there. They're not. They provide a function, a service the same way that a guy who sells TVs does. They have all kinds of high-class names for what they do, brokers, er, they're peddlers, you know, the "sanitary engineer," the guy who cleans the shit out of the bedpans.

This rather gross statement seems designed to make as graphic as possible the distinction the respondent sees between himself and his fellow salespersons. It is less a comment on his co-workers as individual people than a reflection of his own identity. At the outset of the interview, he responded "I'm a peddler," when asked what his employment status was. In describing his co-workers, the respondent used, then, what seems to be self-justification to avoid attributing to himself the undesirable features of his colleagues.

With the exception of these two men, the topic of co-workers seemed to be less important and to have less relevance to identity than was expected. The majority of statements about co-workers were associated with pleasant but not particularly strong affect, and no particular involvement of identity. There also were no sex differences in the incidence of mentioning the social aspects of work, suggesting that women and men were equally likely to respond to the opportunities for affiliation with co-workers provided by their jobs.

BOSS-EMPLOYEE INTERACTIONS

The boss-employee relationship is unlike other co-worker interactions because it is, by definition, contaminated by a power imbalance. The people in a working relationship in which one person has authority over the other cannot interact as freely or as openly with each other as can two equals. The supervisor is continually evaluating the performance of the supervisee, and the supervisee knows this. The supervisor is also dependent on the supervisee to perform work tasks efficiently so that the group effort reflects favorably on the supervisor's managerial skills. Moreover, the supervisor is regarded by the supervisee as someone who represents the "company," with all its strengths and weaknesses of policy. Conversely, the supervisor feels the need to maintain this image throughout interactions with supervisees.

The responses of supervisors regarding their supervisees were almost entirely positive in the descriptions of their attitudes and efficiency. Some statements testified as to how well their supervisees worked together as a group, as in the following excerpt:

Q: What do you especially like about (your work)? You mentioned people, for one thing.
R: Okay, the people. We got a good crew, real good. Everybody gets along well, it's almost like birds of a feather. Everybody is pretty easy-going. Even though there is a little petty friction, overall everyone works well together. Everybody's been psyched (laugh). Uh, it's a good working environment.

This response is a statement not only about how well the crew works, but also how well the members get along. Another respondent described the cooperation of his supervisees in terms of how they related to him personally:

Q: Are there other things about it you find attractive as well?
R: . . . it's also satisfaction in knowing that the guys I've got working underneath me like me. They don't think that I'm a prick. I won't jump down their throats if they do something wrong. I tell them that they did it wrong. I find I get better results. That makes me feel good to know that they like me and think of me as a friend just as much as they do a boss. I think that's the trouble with a lot of places. People just don't know what their boss is. If they get a chance to cut your throat, they're going to do it. I figure if you can keep the people working for you happy, they like you, they're not going to cut your throat.

It was important to this respondent to be liked as a "friend," not because he felt friendly toward his supervisees, but because it gave him better results in managing them. It is also possible that in his eagerness to be liked by his supervisees, he exaggerated the extent to which they did to be consistent with his identity as a good supervisor. In contrast, another respondent found it difficult to manage his small staff of female employees who worked in his bar because of the intrusion of personal factors into the relationship:

Q: How do you feel about your work?
R: . . . I have employees now, full-time employees for the first time. They're all women which, you know, it's difficult to manage them sometimes. All the problems and love

affairs and everything else. You gotta be more or less the father and talk to them and so on, but other than that it's interesting.

Apart from the negative attitudes toward women that this statement reveals, it is apparent that the respondent preferred to maintain a greater distance from his supervisees. It is possible that he really enjoyed the role of "father," which is why the women who worked for him disclosed their personal problems. Identity assimilation may have prevented him from acknowledging that his desired identity as a supervisor was incongruent with his actual behavior with supervisees.

All of these respondents had a relatively limited range of authority, since they each had only a few people whose work they supervised. The fact that their supervision consisted in large part of direct interactions with their supervisees is probably what accounted for the importance of interpersonal factors in their relationships. In contrast, two of the respondents with larger staffs to supervise commented more impersonally about the working potential of their supervisees. One of these was a school administrator who generally was pleased with the performance of staff members:

Q: What do you find satisfying about (your work)?
R: ... We have a pretty good understanding. It's tougher these days than it used to be. Contract kinds of things, you know. And I don't get the contract waved in my face as often as my colleagues do in other schools. And I really do. I tell you. I have really a very fine bunch of people working in that system by and large. Right now I've got 140 some-odd professional staff members in that system. If anybody were to say to me, you know, you can get rid of any ones you want, I probably would start with one hand and have some fingers left over. 'Cause you know, they're good people, and if they need a good kick in the rear once in a while, so do I. But that's what we, you know, appreciate about each other, you know, lack of perfection, but the continuous striving for it that keeps us going.

Being able to supervise as large a staff as this requires more than just good feelings among individuals. As was evident in the statement of the respondent, it also involved the contractual relationship between the administrators in the school system and the labor union to which the staff belonged. This was an aspect of the relationship to which the respondent had mixed reactions. In the above statement, there appeared to be no problem. However, the situation was not quite so rosy, as was evident in the subsequent response:

Q: What do you find unattractive about your work?
R: ... Uh, enforcing some aspects of the contract. Having some of the aspects of the contract waved in my nose and people complaining about minutia. You know? Like somebody complaining about "If you set up the schedule this way I'm not going to have my free period tomorrow." And I'm saying "There's 180 school days. So you're going to have 179 free periods this year instead of 180! What's the big god-damn deal?" You know. It's that kind of crap, you know, that I don't particularly care about.

Having to play the "heavy" with the staff was a role that was not consistent with the respondent's identity as a person who was able to manage the staff on the basis of fairness and equality. Arguing with employees about contractual details was also unpleasant because it represented a direct affront to the respondent's perception that the staff was motivated to work out of a sense of obligation to their teaching.

Although they differed in their supervisory duties, the respondents who spoke of the nature of their relationship with supervisees seemed to share a common element with respect to the meaning of their work for identity. The quality of this relationship, whether it was personal or professional, seemed to be regarded as a direct reflection of the supervisor's competence. The tendency for the supervisors in the sample to report that these relationships were consistent with their identities probably reflects a tendency toward identity assimilation. Regardless of how accurate their self-portrayals were, the extent to which these respondents valued having the cooperation if not friendship of their supervisees indicates that, to them, the boss-employee relationship held a deep intrinsic meaning.

Turning around the boss-employee relationship and examining it from the point of view of the supervisee brings to light another set of feelings and ideas in this complicated relationship. Those respondents who dwelt at any length on this relationship reflected on a variety of features. Since there were so few who mentioned this factor at all (4 women and 4 men), it is doubtful that all or even most of the possible perspectives have been gathered. From the available responses, some very preliminary statements can be made about the association between attitudes toward supervisors and work identity.

There were basically three divisions among the eight statements from supervisees concerning their supervisors. The first concerned whether the supervisor or employer was a "nice" person. One respondent was particularly enthusiastic about her supervisor, who employed the respondent as a research associate:

Q: What do you particularly dislike about (your work)?
R: (not having summers off). . . Aside from that, minor gripes, which is true of any job. But my boss is an exceptional man. I enjoy working for him.
  . . .
Q: Are you thinking about seeking different work?
R: No, hopefully not as long as my boss stays with the company.
Q: Do you have any questions or doubts about your work?
R: No, I can't think of any.
Q: Why not?
R: I suppose I have one question, a possible doubt, and that's if my boss will remain with the company, and that one never knows, really.
  . . .
Q: What is it about this particular boss that you have right now that would. . . make you question about staying (if he left)?
R: One thing, I've worked with him for a good number of years, so you kind of know the person pretty well and what they expect of you. And he's always been fairly easy, you might say, that's not a good word, does allow you freedom as long as you get your work done. If he needs something then you will make sure you get it out no matter what hours you have to work. That kind of person may be hard to replace. He seems to be pretty fair.

What initially appeared to be a statement regarding the supervisor's "exceptional" personal qualities turned out, on further explanation, to be related to something quite different. This respondent's devotion to her supervisor clearly reflected her gratitude that he gave her flexible working hours, not her appreciation of his general kindness or brilliance, or any other inherent quality of his. The respondent had described in another part of the interview her ideal situation in having the freedom to take a two-hour lunch if "you've got your work done" and make up for time during the day in attending to household emergencies by working at night. It was, then, the convenience of her work that made her thankful to have this particular supervisor. The other respondents who used the word "nice" to describe their employers did say what about them was so pleasant. The research associate's response excerpted here suggests that such apparently "personal" statements may not be so at all.

The supervisor's ability to manage was a second dimension underlying statements about the boss. It is this quality of serving as a resource and leader that is described in the work literature under the heading of "supervision" (e.g., Kalleberg, 1977). In the present sample, those who referred to this feature of their supervisors provided some interesting clarifications of what good supervision meant to them. The first was the research associate described above who ended her comments about her boss with reference to his ability to serve as a resource:

Q: You said you didn't have any particular doubts about being a research associate. Why not?

R: Because I guess I know what I'm doing and I've done it for a number of years. And any area that I'm doubtful in, I can go to my boss and straighten out that doubtful area.

Being available to provide assistance when needed was a feature of the employer mentioned by another respondent in almost identical terms. Although it was not stated directly, by providing help when needed, the supervisor makes it possible for the worker to fulfill his or her job duties effectively. A supervisor who does not know the answers or is not there to share in solving problems when they arise places the worker's feelings of competence, as well as the worker's potential of advancing on the job, in jeopardy. It is somewhat surprising that, given its importance for the supervisee, this factor was not reflected in the statements by any of the supervisors in the sample about their work. The only observation that came close was a school director's frustration over not having the financial resources to pay the staff adequately. In this sense, she was commenting on the short supply of institutional resources at her disposal. However, neither she nor any of her peers seemed to have insight into this factor as it applied to their supervisory ability.

Personal leadership qualities were the factor described by two men in the sample, both of whom were reacting negatively to their own supervisors. These two men, who worked for the same large company, had similar complaints about their bosses, but for different reasons:

Q: What, if anything, do you dislike (about your work)?

R: The boss!... He's about as dynamic as a soft summer breeze.... We get along reasonably well. I wouldn't run things the way he's doing it for sure.

The primary source of this respondent's dissatisfaction was his inability to advance in the company as far as he would like. He attributed his lack of advancement to "vagueness" in his division in general, and lack of a strong person in charge, specifically. This type of rationalization is one that suggests that the respondent is using identity assimilation. By criticizing his boss, the respondent can attribute his failure to advance to something other than his own lack of competence. The respondent's attitude toward seeking change reveals more about how this process is operating:

Q: What are you doing to try to work this out for yourself?
R: I'm talking with supervision, two levels above me, just trying to find out where I stand. Putting my cards on the table, tell them my concerns, and try to find out what's probable to happen over what time period. Explain what I'd like to be able to do, what I'm looking to do and if that doesn't seem, if they think there's going to be a conflict between what's probable and what I'm looking to do then it would cause me to make a change in my career.

This "change" in his career would be starting his own business as a freelance consultant or moving into the computer area within his company. The evidence for identity assimilation is the disparity between the respondent's description above of how he is laying his "cards on the table" and the retreat from this position of strength when the question of change is directly confronted:

Q: How about the other alternatives (freelance consulting, computers)?
R: I would say right now that's not a feasible thing for me to do right now. Things would have to really get bad for me to put that into a higher probability of doing it.

In this follow-up comment, the respondent's dissatisfaction about his supervisor has been transformed into a less serious concern not really that bad "right now." He has used identity assimilation to protect himself from the possible threats to his sense of competence that a career move would entail.

The second case of criticism of the boss's leadership skills comes from a man in the opposite kind of situation. This respondent at the age of 27 describes himself as in training for a higher position, in a job that is "a proving ground for supervision." He has no reason to doubt that he will advance into supervision because of the nature of the work group of which he is a member: "As existing supervisors move to other positions, they fill them out of our group." This respondent does use the self-justification form of identity assimilation in his description of his work attitudes: "I'm part of a dying breed of Americans that really care at all about what they're doing." This respondent's complaints about his own supervisor come not from a position of weakness, as was true for the previous respondent, but from a position of relative strength:

Q: What do you particularly dislike about (your job)?
R: Generally my boss. I don't really appreciate him. I got a real jerk for a boss and he has absolutely no leadership qualities at all. He's the wrong person in the right job. He

doesn't belong there at all. A supervisor in this group has the ability to move out and be a general supervisor, so it's like his proving ground for the next step up. A lot of other people would do well in that position if they put some effort into it. He's the kind of guy that if you ask him a question about work, he'll answer by asking you if you went fishing that weekend. There's absolutely no direction or leadership in the guy at all. He's very nonsupportive to all of his people. I find it very difficult to work with someone like that.

Given the nature of the group that the respondent is a part of, it is hard to imagine how such a poor supervisor could be assigned to it. Instead, it might be argued that it is the respondent's projection of his own identity onto the situation that is responsible for his uncompromising approach to his supervisor. As a supervisor "in training," the respondent is eager to demonstrate his own leadership skills. He is therefore looking for ways to assert his own supervisory authority, and expects to find similar behavior in the person serving as his own superior. Any evidence of leniency or friendliness on the part of his supervisor is regarded with derision by the respondent as a sign of weakness. The respondent's use of identity assimilation prevents him from recognizing the need of a supervisor to temper the control over supervisees with concern for their own interests and needs for autonomy.

In both of these cases, then, the criticism levied against a superior can be interpreted to be a direct outgrowth of the respondent's use of identity assimilation. The nature of the criticism reveals one worker to have an insecure view of his own competence, and the other to be overly confident about his own leadership qualities. Neither respondent shows any sign of having accommodated their identities to the situation. For two other respondents, identity accommodation was the predominant process involved in the boss-employee relationship. In these cases, positive feelings toward the supervisors were the result of the favorable evaluations the workers had received about their performance. These evaluations served to strengthen their own identities as competent workers, as can be seen in the following excerpt:

Q: It sounds like your work is pretty important to you?
R: Yeah, well, they treat me good, too, you know, I don't mind working there. You know, I guess everybody these days is saying "Take this job and shove it," or whatever, but I'm feeling pretty good about where I'm working now.
. . .
Q: How does your work affect the way that you think about yourself?
R: . . . I'm certainly doing okay, well I must be if he [the boss] is asking me to time jobs and how long it's going to take. He must know that I know what I'm doing . . .

The respondent's perception that he is being treated "good" seems to be directly related to this appraisal of how well he thinks his boss regards him. It is not possible to tell how accurate the respondent is about his boss's attitude. The use of self-justification in describing his motivated attitude toward work (comparing himself to everyone else's poor attitudes) suggests that this respondent is using identity assimilation to a certain extent. However, the respondent also seems sensitive to the supervisor's actual behaviors of giving him autonomy in deciding on how much time to estimate for a particular job. Another respondent regarded her boss favorably for a similar reason—that by giving her "challenges" he was showing how much "confidence" he placed in her. As a result, the respondent claimed to be "discovering all kinds of potential that I didn't know I had."

In both of these cases, what the respondents were accommodating into their identities was intrinsic in nature since autonomy and challenge are two of the primary intrinsic work factors. The relationship between boss and employee had, then, moved from the extrinsic to the intrinsic realm and so it had the potential to have a direct effect on the respondents' identities as competent workers.

With these analyses, it can be seen that the attitude of the worker to the supervisor is not a simple manifestation of an extrinsic orientation. The boss-employee relationship, when viewed from the perspective of the employee as well as the boss, can serve to stimulate the identity processes. The overtly expressed attitude of the worker toward this relationship may signify whether identity assimilation is used to avoid attributing negative qualities to one's identity as a worker, or identity accommodation is used to incorporate new information about one's competence. The boss-employee relationship, like the other so-called extrinsic factors, therefore has the potential to invoke powerful processes that tap into the foundation of the worker's identity.

8
"Just a Housewife"

The title of this chapter is taken directly from a homemaker's self-description in the opening response to her Work Identity interview:

Q: What is your current employment status?
R: Do you mean am I working? No, I'm just a housewife.
Q: Do you consider yourself to be a full-time homemaker?
R: Yes.
Q: How important to you is your work as a homemaker?
R: Very important. It's all I do.

What kind of identity would stimulate the self-description contained in the above excerpt? Is it the identity of someone who believes herself to be competent? Is it the identity of someone who believes her work performs a valuable service? This interview excerpt captures the essence of the contradiction in terms that many of the full-time homemakers in the sample described in defining themselves as workers. Without a paycheck to show for their efforts, they did not have the external validation of themselves as workers that paid employees receive. However, the activities that occupied them for 8, 10, or 16 hours a day to the exclusion of anything else certainly qualified as "work."

This chapter concerns full-time homemakers only. Women who worked part-time were included in the portion of the sample described in Chapter 6 and 7. The decision to use only full-time homemakers in this chapter was based on interest in the special problem created for an adult's identity by taking on this role. A full-time homemaker is working full-time in an unpaid position at work that is not considered to be of particularly high social status, especially given the emphasis on the "modern" career woman. The full-time homemaker therefore does not have access to the usual intrinsic sources of competence or extrinsic routes to high social esteem.

The dilemma of the homemaker has been extensively written about in feminist writings and in the empirical literature (e.g., Ferree, 1980; Oakley, 1974). What makes the present analysis different is the focus on the homemaker's identity as a worker, and on how what she does during her everyday activities reflects on her sense of competence. The intrinsic and extrinsic work factors described in previous chapters on work identity are discussed simultaneously in the analysis of homemaking, with greater attention given to intrinsic factors.

Variations on these themes are examined as they apply to the special situation of the homemaker. Other work features unique to the homemaker interviews are also introduced.

The processes through which the homemaker relates her identity to work will be found to be as powerful as those found in the sample of paid employees. The identity processes are given additional force in the homemaker by virtue of the ambiguities that exist in her status as an "employed" worker.

The Work of the Homemaker

Although anyone who is a homemaker would stringently disagree, the homemaker's daily activities are not usually reported as "work" in the conventional sense. The U.S. Department of Labor does not even list homemaking that is not paid in its extensive *Dictionary of Occupational Titles* (1977). However, like her colleagues who are paid for their labor, the homemaker is given a job to do that has associated with it specific kinds of tasks. The tasks that the homemaker must carry out in the course of her daily work constitute intrinsic characteristics of housework. Her motivation to perform these tasks will be determined by how interesting they are to her; that is, how much they stimulate her mind. The other intrinsic features of housework are the extent to which it allows self-direction, and the potential it has to allow the homemaker to see the results of her work. The homemaker's sense of competence is determined by the extent to which she feels she has successfully performed work that is interesting to her and how much control she has over what she does in the course of her work.

The homemakers in the present sample described their work in terms that captured the main elements of the intrinsic work identity theme: the interest value of their work, their sense of self-direction, and their ability to see results. Some of these intrinsic factors bore an intimate relationship to factors considered as extrinsic in the context of paid employment, such as the work environment, the flexibility of work hours, and the amount of time pressure. In addition, a subcategory of intrinsic work factors that applied strictly to homemakers was the belief that their work was important for reasons that were specifically intrinsic in nature.

As was true for paid employees, some homemakers used identity assimilation to justify their own self-importance or to avoid thinking about unpleasant ramifications of their work. Other homemakers appeared to be using identity accommodation to change their identities in response to experiences in their work. One important determinant of whether identity assimilation or accommodation took place with regard to the intrinsic work factors was the meaning that the homemaker attached to her title—whether it was "domestic engineer," "full-time homemaker," or "just a housewife."

The Tedium of Housework

The interest value of homemaking, according to all 5 of the full-time homemakers who mentioned this factor, is basically quite low. The following excerpt is representative of the attitudes expressed toward housework:

Q: What do you particularly dislike about your work?

R: What do I dislike? Defrosting the refrigerator. (laughs) That's one of the things I really hate. What do I dislike? Well, I guess it's repetition all the time, doing the same thing, you know, after a while you just get to do the same things over and over.

As can be seen from this excerpt, the key reason for the inherent boredom of housework is the repetitive nature of the tasks that are performed with the same materials and the same motions day after day. Because they are so repetitive, they do not engage the homemaker's mental activity, which was seen in Chapter 6 to be one of the main features of work that is regarded as stimulating. In the words of one respondent:

R: To me, working at home, I don't really have to use my brain. I don't have to sit there and really use my brain the way I'd like to. You have to think somewhat, but not the way you do at work.

Cooking was the one homemaking activity that offered room for variety and creativity. However, the knowledge that cooking meals was something that "had" to be done every day, along with the rest of the homemaker's tasks, detracted from its potential to be intrinsically interesting.

SEEING THE RESULTS OF HOMEMAKING

The Unending Nature of Housework

Several homemakers who regarded their work as boring elaborated on this perception in a way that suggests another reason for its lack of interest value. Housework is never "done." It is repeated over and over without having a definite end point or a definite outcome. As a result, the homemaker cannot derive the intrinsic rewards of seeing a project through to completion. The connection between housework as boring and as unending was made clear in the following excerpt:

Q: How important to you is this work?

R: I enjoy most of it except the cleaning. I might as well be honest. I don't enjoy the cleaning that much. If it stayed clean when you did it, but I get into a routine. Same thing over and over.

The reason that things do not stay clean is that "someone comes along and messes it up." Usually the "someone" is a child:

Q: How important to you is your work as a homemaker?

R: ... When I'm folding clothes and it's all nicely cleaned, dried, folded, it's great. The next day, when it's all on the floor, boy do I get upset! And I say, "the heck with it." Shut the door. I don't want to see it. My 10-year-old especially, his room. Four cyclones are in there everyday, helping him . . .

Taking care of a young child all day long can lead to a similar sense of frustration of not being able to see an end to one's work. Not only does the child's presence interfere with the homemaker's ability to complete her work, but the child itself presents continuous demands for care:

Q: What do you particularly dislike about your work as a homemaker?

R: The fact that it seems like a vicious circle and you never get things done. It just seems like when you have a little baby you always have to be on your toes. He is going through a stage now where he is into everything. It feels like I get up in the morning, and it seems like I tell him to stay away from things all day long. Sometimes it's like I never get out of the house.

Despite this continued potential to have one's sense of identity as a competent worker put to the test, there was a fairly sizeable group of 7 women who felt that they did get to see the results of their efforts at home. Two of these women specifically referred to the effects of this sense of task completion on their identities, one at some length:

Q: How important to you is your work as a homemaker?
R: It's pretty important to me. I want to make sure everything is just so. . . . As far as the boys, they don't know what it is to eat store-bought cookies. They won't eat them. Because they're so used to me doing it.
Q: What is important to you about your work?
R: I hate a dirty house myself. I hate everything all cluttered. And being a homemaker, I train the boys. When they get done, they are to pick up their toys. I like everything just as Mike does. It's not spotless, but it's not cluttered, either.
Q: How do you feel about this kind of work?
R: It's really something that has to be done. I can't tell you I enjoy it, because I don't enjoy it, cleaning, doing dishes, ironing. It's just something that has to be done.
Q: Do you have particular feelings about that?
R: I have a feeling, like, enjoyment or something? I just, I just. Hm. I guess when everything's done and everything's so, it's a very satisfying feeling. That everything is just the way I want it.
. . .
Q: How does your work as a homemaker affect the way you think about yourself?
R: Well, it makes me feel very good about myself. I don't feel bad about myself at all. Maybe it's certain things I do, such as different things that I usually don't do around the house, gives me satisfaction, makes me feel like I've accomplished more than just the usual day-to-day activity. Mike's really spoiled me in a lot of ways. It makes me satisfied knowing that it would be hard for somebody else to do all the things I do for him.

This response provides a complicated mixture of identity accommodation and identity assimilation. On the one hand, the respondent derives feelings of competence from her reported success in keeping the house uncluttered, making cookies, and spoiling her husband (but not her children). This effect of her homemaking experience on her identity suggests an accommodation process. Further evidence for accommodation is the respondent's willingness to admit to imperfections in her situation. Were she using identity assimilation, she would deny the existence of any problems. On the other hand, there is a lack of qualification that suggests the self-justification form of identity assimilation in the respondent's description of the outcome of her homemaking efforts.

In order to resolve this paradox, some additional information about the respondent is needed. It is helpful to know that this is the same respondent who described housework as being a fairly mindless activity ("I don't really have to use my brain"). It is also important to realize that one of the chief sources of satisfaction she experienced in her previous work as a computer programmer was: "having a program that didn't work, having it work, having it run, just the satisfaction." She felt that she could not go back into computer work, because it would be too time-consuming and she would not be able to spend enough time with her children at home. However, she deeply regretted this loss: "I was sorry I left it. I really enjoyed doing it."

Given this additional information, the respondent's situation can be more clearly seen as involving identity assimilation as a means through which she can present a positive image of the effectiveness she has as a homemaker. This intrinsic reward, one that was important to her in her previous work, serves to make up for the mindlessness of her daily activities. She can then gain a sense of competence by accommodating into her identity the view of herself as someone who is achieving the intrinsic rewards of having accomplished something in her work.

Being Appreciated

Another intrinsic work factor associated with seeing results is receiving recognition from others as acknowledgment for the success of one's efforts. One woman who commented specifically on this factor captures almost perfectly the legendary failure of children to appreciate the work of their mothers:

Q: What do you particularly dislike about your job?
R: Well, there are some days when it does become lonely, or I shouldn't say lonely, I shouldn't say bored because I'm not really bored. I really don't think it's drudgery. Well, I imagine it would probably be the fact that I'm taken for granted. Let's say the garbage could overflow and no one would dump it, or the dog may need to be fed, and yet he's everybody's dog, and everybody relies on mother to do it. It's this type of thing that some days I feel that they're taking me for granted. They know I'm not going out into the work force, and every once in a while I hear one of my sons say "Well, you don't do anything all day long." They don't seem to realize, I think, if they didn't have clean clothes or their beds weren't changed or something like that they might realize that their mother does do something. But most of the time they don't. I don't think men feel that a woman does a day's work.

There are elements of identity assimilation in this response, including projection (regarding men), and denial (regarding the boredom of housework). However, the respondent has touched upon the essence of a very critical aspect of the homemaker's work identity: that she is simply not appreciated. Lack of recognition for her tireless efforts and endless sacrifices adds to the boredom of her work to devalue her sense of competence. Moreover, the general social attitude that is represented by the behavior of this respondent's son is one that can haunt the homemaker's everyday life, placing her in a position of having continuously to defend the worth of her work. From this defensive position emerge statements based on the identity assimilation process. In the words of another respondent:

Q: How does being home now and doing housework affect you as a person?

R: It affects me fantastically, to be honest with you. As the children are getting older, they'll say "Mom, why don't you go back to school?" "Why don't you further your ambitions in different areas?" And I say I'm enjoying it after all the years of tending. I am just enjoying the freedom not to take on the commitments, the daily commitments, at this time.

Q: So you have a fair amount of freedom?

R: And I'm enjoying the freedom, to read if I wish, to do what I wish to do. . . . [but] I worry about judgments from the children. "Mom's laying down," or "Mom's whatever," you know. "Everytime we catch Mom she's laying down." And this bothers me, because there are many times that I will accomplish something and then lay down, but they're not aware of that. So I do have a definite guilt reaction at times, I have to defend myself. "I scrubbed the walls yesterday, but you weren't home when I scrubbed the walls." It's a defensive, it could be a defensive feeling.

This mother of 8 children, with her youngest a preteenager, was just reaching a point of emerging from a period of heavy child-rearing responsibilities. Her children not only did not appear to have appreciated her efforts (from her point of view, anyhow), but on top of that criticized her for not doing more.

The position of the homemaker, because of the lack of intrinsic or extrinsic recognition attached to it, is therefore one that places an enormous strain on a woman's identity as a competent worker. However, there is an important compensating feature for this lack of recognition, one alluded to in the previous excerpt. This compensating feature is the ability to work without direct supervision and set one's own pace.

BEING ONE'S OWN BOSS

During at least the hours of the normal working day, the homemaker is her own supervisor. The fact that she is employee as well as boss helps to make up for the fact that her work tasks, as the employee, range from the routine to the unpleasant.

For the homemaker as compared to the paid employee, the intrinsic factor of freedom from supervision is even more difficult to separate from the extrinsic features of flexibility of hours and the pace of scheduling. The one variable factor in the homemaker's duties is not so much *what* she does as *when* she does it. The discretion that the homemaker has in deciding on the order of her work activities means that she can arrange her schedule to suit her convenience. For most paid workers, the two factors are not quite as intimately tied together.

The combination of flexibility and autonomy evident in three of the homemaker's responses is apparent in the following excerpt:

Q: What do you especially like about your work as a homemaker?

R: Maybe the hours. (laughs) Your time's more or less your own, you can judge, you can do more or less what you want to at any time, you can get it done during the day, you can do it at night, nobody there to watch over you and press you for time.

The extrinsic features of this statement are its reference to time being "your own," and not having anyone "press you for time." The intrinsic feature, signifying occupational self-direction, is having "nobody there to watch over you." The seven homemakers whose statements concerned the scheduling of work tasks all had formed this association between intrinsic and extrinsic factors. It was as if the existence of a flexible schedule was for them a symbol of their ability to control their work in the home.

There is, however, a price to be paid for this autonomy and flexibility, apart from the fact that the homemaker has to perform many menial and repetitive chores. This is the penalty associated with the fact the work is done at home. The work can therefore expand almost infinitely to fill the entire waking day because there is no work place from which to "punch out." As a result, the woman may feel that she "never gets a break" and has no time for her own leisure interests. Although several women expressed relief at not having to "punch a clock," others would probably have been glad to have this opportunity. Two of the homemakers in particular mentioned the limitation on their sense of personal autonomy of never having time to themselves. Another feature that detracts from the homemaker's ability to exercise her autonomy is the fact that she must accommodate her duties in the home to the curricular and extracurricular needs of her children. As observed by one respondent, "Even though when you're a mother, you say you're your own boss, but you're not always because you still have to bend for whatever ways something happens to go, and that happens a lot."

Because the responses concerning autonomy and freedom from supervision were either dominated or strongly contaminated by the extrinsic feature of time flexibility, it is not clear to what extent the intrinsic factors alone influenced the identity of the homemakers. In addition, no homemakers described their work as "challenging," as a position of high responsibility, or as involving high-level decision-making ability. The usual positive effects on the worker's sense of competence of having self-direction would therefore have only a very limited potential to enhance the homemaker's work identity. Instead, other sources of compensation were sought by the homemakers in trying to define an identity for themselves as competent workers.

The Importance of the Homemaker's Work

Clearly the most significant intrinsic aspect of the homemaker's work identity was that it served an essential function for her family's welfare. Virtually all of the homemakers in the sample (15 out of the 17) defined their work as "very" important. "Importance" was not accepted as an intrinsic feature in the rating of the work identities of paid employees, since its meaning was ambiguous. For the homemakers in the sample, though, the meaning was unquestionably intrinsic, as will be seen in the transcripts excerpted below. Because of its intrinsic value to the homemaker, the perceived importance of her work served as a central defining characteristic to her identity as a competent worker. Furthermore, it was the intrinsic rewards of homemaking that made it possible for the homemaker to put up with lack of recognition for her continued performance of her repetitive and frustrating work tasks.

The risk in defining one's work as "important" is that there is the tendency to use identity assimilation in the form of self-justification. There was ample evidence in Chapter 6 of respondents who claimed their work to be of great importance but whose identities appeared instead to be based on insecurity concerning their own competence. The homemakers seemed to be at least as defensive, if not more so, about their sense of importance. As noted earlier, the homemakers were in this defensive position almost by definition. They felt they had to justify the need for work that is undervalued by society in terms of status and pay. They also felt a need to justify their own importance in contrast to the more highly recognized accomplishments of the career woman. For these reasons, almost every statement of importance had associated with it one or more forms of identity assimilation. This is not to say, though, that all the homemakers were unable to consider their situations from other perspectives. Even those women who defended their sense of importance with identity assimilation were using identity accommodation in varying degrees to evaluate whether their situations were really optimal. These cases are examined in the next section.

The first statement concerning importance is almost a textbook example of identity assimilation in its combined reliance upon self-justification, rigidity, and projection:

Q: How important to you is your work as a homemaker?
R: Very important. Everything I do is very important. Everything I have is very important.
Q: You feel very strongly about that?
R: Yes, I do. I've always felt that way. I was married when I was 18 years old and we had our oldest son that very same year. I've always felt that way, always. My husband is that way. We are just that type of people. There's nothing more important than our family.

This case was one of the most extreme, but not atypical in quality from other assimilative statements concerning the importance of housework. The next excerpt represents one of the more interesting variants of this type of process:

Q: How important to you is your work in the home?
R: . . . It's very important. It's my life!
Q: How do you feel about this kind of work?
R: What do you mean, how do I feel? Do I feel sometimes put down by it or whatever?
Q: Whatever.
R: Hm! That's interesting. I certainly do not feel any negative feelings about it. I enjoy it. I think if I didn't really enjoy it, if my family wasn't important to me, I think I would try to find outside work to do if I was that unhappy or unfulfilled. But I'm not unhappy or that unfulfilled. So I, you know, I find this very, this is a work of my own choosing, you know . . . this is a job, I do enjoy doing it, otherwise I wouldn't be doing it, with as much of my full-time attention as I am giving it. So I feel it's very important and I like the way I'm doing it and I'm happy with it.

The variant on the identity assimilation process apparent in this woman's interview excerpt is how she "reads" into the interviewer's question a possible criticism of the importance of the homemaker's work. The fact that it is apparently on her mind suggests that it may be something she has thought about but not allowed herself to confront fully.

In contrast to these almost defiant statements about the importance of the homemaker's work were the self-doubts expressed by the next respondent:

Q: How does your work as a homemaker affect the way you see yourself?

R: At times, I feel very unimportant because I think you hear things on television, the radio, about people doing all these great things, interesting things. And you think, "Oh, my gosh, here am I in this house. Is that important? What am I missing? There's a big world out there and here am I in this house."

Q: What effect on the rest of your life does your work as a homemaker have?

R: I don't know how to answer that. I guess maybe I don't have the enthusiasm and I'm not going to do the things that were so important to me. And if they slide and take a back seat, it's not going to bother me, where before it would have. I thought it was my job and I did it.

This respondent is the same one who in Chapter 5 was found to be undergoing a major identity accommodation process in adapting to the "launching" of her children from the home. Her intense self-questioning of her identity as a mother shows up here to have spread to her identity as a worker and she was, in fact, taking some very preliminary steps to find outside employment. What stands out from her excerpt, though, is her application to herself of what she hears about career women "success stories." Unlike the previous respondent, whose use of identity assimilation kept her from questioning her importance, this woman's sense of importance is deflated by such negative self-comparisons.

These examples of importance were fairly general statements without a clear-cut explanation for why the homemaker's work was or was not important. Other women in the sample were more specific about the importance to them and their families of their work.

One specific reason cited by the homemakers in the sample for the importance of their work was the need to take care of their children themselves. The mother of two young children (6 and 2 years old) described her importance as fulfilling this need:

Q: How important to you is the work that you're doing right now?

R: Very important. I think, um, having children who need you to be here. Not only to watch them grow, but to help them grow. They need their mother rather than being in day care. Or being with the child part time or something. Being with the children, and helping them and teaching them, giving them the love and security that they need... Because the children, when they're small, need to be home with their mothers. That's pretty much the most important part of staying home.

This is a fairly straightforward statement, with only a slight hint of self-justification ("rather than being in day care"). In a later response, this form of identity assimilation is elaborated upon, along with some projection:

R: I know people, I see people around in the neighborhood who are not, you know, they have children, but they push them off to a day care center or a baby sitter, trying to make a few extra dollars. The government takes half of that and, um, I just can't, I can't understand why, someone would want to do that. The children didn't ask to be born. I think people that I see like that should think about what they're doing to their children.

The belief that "other people" are not treating their children well by sending them to day care centers was a common form of projection to emerge in the responses concerning the importance of caring for children "oneself." Another respondent added to this criticism of working mothers her observation that without the mother there to watch the children, the children fall prey to a variety of misfortunes and evils:

Q: How important is it to you to be home? It sounded like it is pretty important, I wonder if you could elaborate on that a little bit.
R: Well, I guess it's because I've seen what happens when the mother isn't home and I'm still convinced that this has been the right thing for me. I don't, neither my husband nor I, have family in the area, and when our children have been sick, I've been the one to take care of them. I haven't had to go off and leave them in a day care center when they've had a sore throat or other disease. I know many women who have gone back to work after their children have been in school for the most part of the day, and I've seen the children come home and do things that I'm sure their parents were not aware of. They are things that I would not want my children to do. And I think the only reason these children did them was because they knew they could get away with it. And I think that my children are no better than these other children, they'd do the same things with the temptation. And I feel that being here, not only have they been able to come home and relate what they've done during the day, but it's been a factor in preventing them from doing things they might have done that society doesn't approve of.

In the first part of her statement, this respondent touches upon a very real problem that working mothers face, particularly those who do not have family living close by. However, the judgment remains for this respondent that her statement represents identity assimilation (self-justification and projection). This is because her children, at ages 18 and 22, are no longer dependent upon her to watch them at home when they have colds and if they were going to yield to immoral temptations, they would not have to wait until she left the house to do so but could go out on their own.

Another respondent who echoed this respondent's desire to do what she could to ensure her children's welfare was more balanced in her assessment of how much she was needed to care for her youngest child, 16 years old at the time of the interview:

Q: What do you especially like about being a homemaker?
R: I guess I like being here still when the last one comes home from school. And see, when I was young, my mother worked out of necessity, so I was alone a lot, and this was always important to me that I'm here when they come home, right up to the last one. Although I'm sure he doesn't need me, but I think that in my mind that's important. See, now to him, probably that's not. Even 'till he gets out of high school, he has 2 more years. There's something there, you don't go home to a cold house.

This homemaker's statement contrasts sharply with the previous respondent's in its open admission that she was fulfilling her *own* needs, not those of her child's, in staying home with him. This statement is also free of the criticism of working mothers evident in other homemakers' assertions regarding their importance. What this homemaker is bringing out in her response is the desire to fulfill her own intrinsic need to do something that she thinks is important: provide a good home for her children. This desire, albeit often overlaid with identity assimilation, forms the basis for the second category of statements representing the intrinsic importance of homemaking.

For some homemakers, creating a "clean and healthy environment" in which the family could have a "comfortable living" was their main sense of purpose in life. Often, this desire to provide a "pleasant existence" for the family's well-being overlapped with a family identity based on similar intrinsic concerns. The association of their affections and concern for the family with the routine demands of their work gave the household tasks a great deal of symbolic meaning. The responses in this category of importance statements made it clear that it was this symbolic meaning that allowed them to put up with the other frustrations they felt:

Q: Okay, so the working at home, how does that affect the way you feel about yourself?
R: Well, it makes me feel good . . . my husband . . . likes to come home and have a nice house.
Q: How difficult or easy is it for you to get things running the way you want to?
R: There's days when it's easy, and days when it's hard. (laughs) Um, it's just something I start out doing. I know every day when I get up that I have "x" amount of things to do in the house, and I just do 'em.
Q: What kinds of things would you need to do to feel that things were coming out smooth?
R: Um, well, they like a clean house. You know, they like it vacuumed, picked up, cleaned. Um, clothes, they like their clothes washed and things like that . . . They like decent meals every night. It's not Burger King. Or, you know, Kentucky Fried Chicken. They like to eat at home, they like a good meal. Um, I have a lot of conveniences, too. You know, microwave oven . . . So there's a lot of things that really help out. Convection oven. So, it's not really that hard a task. (laughs)

There appears to be a sincere intent on the part of this homemaker to do things that will make her family happy and well cared for, and her self-description is not particularly beset with self-justification. If anything, she was trying to show that her job was really not that bad, a belief she reinforced by commenting on the extent to which her husband and children helped her:

R: . . . I'm not saying that I run around and do everything. My husband is the type of person who will pitch in. The children . . . do whatever they're asked to do. Like if I do the wash, they take it upstairs . . .

Where identity assimilation did come into play in the statements of importance that fell into this category was when the respondent seemed to use her husband's or family's attitude toward her as a justification for not working outside the home. It was often difficult to tell whose need was being served when a homemaker said she could not consider getting paid employment because her husband wanted her home. This is an issue that is examined further in the next section.

The third category of importance statements concerned the responsibility of having to do household tasks and care for the children. Unlike the meaning of this term as a component of occupational self-direction, the word "responsibility" as used by the homemakers meant that there was "no one else" to do it. In this sense, responsibility was a dubious honor. Having a paid job with responsibility means that the worker has a certain degree of autonomy and moreover, that the worker has earned the respect of the employer to take on high-level assignments. None of the homemakers, as mentioned earlier, described their responsibility in this way. The need to have the job done contributed to an intrinsic sense of importance, but it did not have attached to it connotations of recognition and respect of having "earned" the right to do the work:

Q: How do you feel about this kind of work?
R: I don't know. I think it's important. Somebody has to do it, if you didn't do it. If you weren't home to do it you'd either have to have somebody come in and do it, or if you work, somebody to help you. I think it's important to everybody in the family, because if you're not there to do things like washing and stuff, you have to get it done somehow.
Q: Do you have any particular kinds of feelings about this kind of work?
R: Just that you get kind of tired of doing it after a while. That's about all. The same thing, you know.

The lack of enthusiasm for the actual work tasks she performed was not incompatible with this respondent's sense of the importance of her work. It is even possible that the knowledge that the job would have to get "done somehow" is what detracts from the interest value of household tasks. The complete lack of choice that the homemaker has about her work tasks is the very antithesis of occupational self-direction.

To another respondent, though, having household responsibilities enabled her to justify her work in the home as a "job":

R: I don't consider all the time that I'm home as free time for me. I've got responsibilities here. And my responsibilities are just like your responsibilities to go out and work in the morning. I feel like when at 7:30 in the morning everybody leaves here, that's when my job starts. Maybe I'm thinking wrong, but I feel that I'm home, yet I'm working, and yet the time is not my own. I don't sit down and read books, because I feel that this is my job. Maybe I'm not getting $500 at the end of the week for my job, but I still feel that it's my job.

This statement was made by the same homemaker who felt that her sons did not appreciate her work. In the response excerpted here, she appears to use the self-justification mode of identity assimilation to assert that her work is important, despite the lack of recognition she receives, and despite the lack of an income. Were she not able to justify her work as a "job" by citing the responsibilities she has, this respondent would be bereft of a sense of competence. Two other respondents similarly emphasized the resemblance between their work and a "job," by pointing out that "everything runs on schedule." These statements provided an interesting contrast to the larger group of enthusiastic endorsements of work scheduling flexibility. Both sets of comments, though, share the quality of attempts to arrive at a sense of having compensation for the uninteresting nature of the homemaker's work.

In reviewing the three categories of importance statements, it appears that the one category least influenced by identity assimilation is the second, in which care and concern for the family form the basis for a feeling of being needed. Of course, the belief that one is "needed" may be influenced by one's desire to perceive oneself as needed. Whether one's family feels this way may be another matter. With only the respondent's perspective represented in the interviews, this possibility cannot be tested unless the respondent chooses to speak more candidly on the issue (as one did). Regardless of what actual service the homemaker's work fulfills in the home, the fact is that, without a sense of commitment to her work's importance, the work is in and of itself not sufficiently rewarding to be intrinsically motivating. If the homemaker is to have a sense of competence, given that she is tied down to this set of circumstances, identity assimilation may be an adaptive mechanism. Where it becomes less than adaptive, though, is if it prevents her from seeking alternate sources of competence that would not involve a disequilibrium between identity assimilation and accommodation.

Finding Alternate Sources of Competence

A strange inconsistency emerged from the descriptions by the homemakers of their questions, doubts, and thoughts about alternatives to their work. Although almost all of the full-time homemakers in the sample regarded their work as very important, all but three of these were thinking of finding paid work outside the home. How could it be that these women, apparently convinced of the worth of their unpaid labor, were so ready to join the ranks of paid workers? In answering this question, it is possible to learn not only about the motivations and identities of the present group of homemakers, but also to observe some principles regarding the identity processes. There was considerable variation among the 14 homemakers in the seriousness of their intent to find alternate work. This variation seemed to be related to the degree to which they were prepared to engage in a critical evaluation of their identities as homemakers through identity accommodation.

It can be assumed, in the first place, that those homemakers who were seeking alternate work to meet a currently unfulfilled intrinsic need are more intensely engaged in identity accommodation. This is because they are directly challenging the extent to which their identities as competent workers were being expressed through their work as homemakers. In contrast, concern with finding alternate work that would be extrinsically rewarding does not negate the potential of housework to provide the individual with an identity as a competent worker. Seeking alternate work for extrinsic reasons therefore presents a less serious need for identity accommodation, and a less intense process of self-reflection.

This logic of evaluating the extent of identity accommodation by considering the degree of concern a person has with satisfying intrinsic needs could be applied to paid workers as well as to homemakers. However, the analysis is more straightforward in the case of homemakers. Because they are currently not receiving any salary, they can consider alternatives without being limited in any way by concern over what they might lose by giving up their current employment. In addition, because so many homemakers shared the concern about doing "important" work, they were a relatively homogeneous group with respect to this intrinsic work factor.

THE NEED FOR A PAYCHECK

The desire to seek outside employment for pay was the sole object of only three of the homemakers. One of these women was on the verge of seeking a divorce, and the other two were trying to contribute to the family income. The attitudes of these women toward homemaking were consistent with the expectations that they would not be likely to be engaging in a process of questioning their identities. In one case, identity assimilation was used to avoid just such a confrontation:

Q: Can you imagine anything at all that would cause you to question the importance of the work you do in the home?
R: If I was unhappy at what I was doing, I would probably question it more. I think if I was, I suppose if I had a friend who was, friends will do this sometimes. They'll say "I'm doing this or that." You might say "Well, gee, I'm not doing this or I'm not doing that" and you might go home and start to question "Is this really what I want to do or why?"

. . .

Q: What would keep you from making a change now?
R: What would keep me from doing it?
Q: What would keep you from making a change? You're talking about getting part-time work, but your work at home will be number 1.
R: Um hmm.
Q: What would keep you from making a change now? Or in the future making home number 2?
R: My husband would. These questions. I don't think I understand them very well! (laughs)
Q: You're doing fine.
R: I sound like a very boring homebody! (laughs) It's just these are, I feel these are the people that I love. And I want them to be happy. And I know what it takes to make them happy, so I do it.

Throughout this excerpt, the respondent uses various forms of defensive rigidity. By describing her reaction to "friends" who are "doing this or that" in the conditional sense, she avoids saying that *she* actually has this reaction. However, the fact that she mentions this possibility suggests that it is really not very far removed from her thoughts. Then, following a quick disclaimer, she restates her basic position using self-justification to show how important her work really is.

Even though she is considering part-time work, she seems determined not to let this detract from her sense of commitment to being a homemaker.

Escape From Boredom

Other extrinsic factors besides salary were given as the primary reason for seeking work by four of the homemakers. These factors were all based on the desire to escape from the loneliness and boredom of the house environment; in the words of one respondent: "just to get out and get away." Although boredom might be considered an intrinsic factor to the extent that it reflects the routine nature of housework, Kalleberg's (1977) classification system, used in the present analysis, regards "escape" from the home environment to be an extrinsic work factor. However, seeking work that would be "with people" was regarded as signifying the "people-work" intrinsic factor described in Chapter 6.

Another related extrinsic factor was the desire to get out of the house so that the respondent would have the opportunity to get "dressed up." Several working women had mentioned this factor as an advantage of working versus staying home. From the homemaker's perspective, the opportunity to wear the clothes of a working woman was part of the mystique of getting out of the house and into the "real" world:

Q: So, you're staying that now, being home, is not very fulfilling for you?
R: No. I get bored staying at home, day in and day out. I don't like doing housework everyday. I like being out in the world, you know.
Q: You'd really like that.
R: Right.
Q: Would you feel a lot better about yourself?
R: Yes.
Q: When you say it helps you keep your sanity, what does that mean?
R: Well, at home day in and day out, you don't dress the way you ordinarily would if you were working. You don't fix yourself up, ordinarily, like you would if you were going out in the public or whatever. You'd just have a different outlook on life, you'd just, I don't know, to me you want to look nice. Being home, doing housework, you say, "Well, why should I dress up to do this?" Clean windows, why should I look nice to do that? You'd get dirty doing it anyway, so. At work, you want to look nice, everybody else looks nice, so you want to look nice, too.
Q: Getting dressed up makes you feel differently?
R: Yeah.

While clothing may be considered part of the worker's response to the work environment, it seems to have meaning in its own right for its effects on one's identity regarding personal appearance. Clothing is also a symbol of one's work status, as represented by the distinction between "white" and "blue" collar workers. For the homemaker, it may be a symbol of higher status and self-respect afforded to the woman who works for pay, whose evaluations by others are partly influenced by her appearance. While the homemaker could get "dressed up," if not for cleaning the windows then for going out of the house on errands, favorable evaluations of her appearance by others would not have any particular rewards attached to them. Moreover, without an independent salary, she may have difficulty justifying the heavy expenditures needed to maintain a fashionable wardrobe. If she is working, then she has the means as well as the reason for keeping up her appearance.

Because they are extrinsic factors, the lack of stimulation in the homemaking environment, along with the general attitude associated with wearing clothes suitable for housework, may not directly influence the homemaker's sense of competence. Accordingly, a desire to work based on the need to escape the household milieu may not pose a serious threat to the homemaker's identity as a worker. However, escape from the constraints of her house can represent an attractive alternative as a way to improve the homemaker's general well-being.

THE NEED FOR STIMULATING WORK

For the 7 women who were seeking work to satisfy intrinsic needs, the admission that housework was not sufficiently stimulating posed a potentially serious threat to their current identities as competent workers. By describing themselves as seeking work that was "challenging," would be something "important" that "I would enjoy," and would have more "potential for growth," they were clearly taking the risks of exposing their insecurities about their sense of competence now, as homemakers. The process of identity accommodation used in examining an alternative was generally mixed with a fairly heavy dose of identity assimilation because of the risks of exposing this weakness. One of the women in this group of 7 had used identity assimilation throughout most of her Work Identity interview to justify her sense of importance. Just prior to that, however, at the end of the Family Identity interview, she described a crack in this armor of defenses:

Q: What effect does being a full-time wife and mother have on the way you feel about yourself as a person?
R: As a person? (pause) Well, I guess I'd have to be honest and say that there is that small portion of me that feels it's not doing what I was trained to do years ago. You know, I'm not being fulfilled in one small quarter of my life, because being a wife and mother, in that what I want to be has superimposed, um well, has taken over any aspect that I could have time for in my life . . . So as a person, I would like to be a more personally self-expressed, in ways that I don't feel I can be as a wife and a mother . . . As a person, I'm fairly happy, but I do have, you know, moments every now and then of wishing I could do something else in addition to what I'm doing . . .

Throughout the rest of the Family interview, the respondent continued to assert that whatever else she would do, she absolutely could not "give up anything that I'm doing with the family now for the sake of a job." Despite her clear interest in the "fascinating" work activities in which she had been engaged before her marriage, and recurrent "frustrating moments in my own mind," the respondent kept returning to her need to avoid "sacrificing" her time with her family. Added to this sort of defensive rigidity was a series of good excuses, but excuses nevertheless, attesting to why she has not been able to get part-time work before. By the time the interviewer began the Work Identity interview, the respondent had managed to suppress completely her reference to this desire for part-time work, and never brought it up again.

Other homemakers who were facing up to their lack of intrinsic involvement in their work also appeared to use the defensive rigidity form of identity assimilation in order to keep their questions from penetrating too deeply into their sense of competence. Their rigidity was expressed, in some cases, in ways similar to the respondent just described; that is, having a good "excuse" not to follow through on their desire to seek other work. Some of these excuses were patently transparent ways of downplaying the seriousness of their questions about homemaking. The following excerpt was taken from the interview of the woman whose children failed to show appreciation for the work she did at home and who had described her work as a "job" because of its "responsibility." According to her account of her desire for outside work, she had a strong interest in a job that would allow her to satisfy her desire to fulfill a "people-work" form of intrinsic motivation. The following is the excuse she used to justify not seeking such work "at this time":

Q: How seriously are you considering part-time work?
R: Well, one day I consider it, the next day I don't. My sister called at 7:15 this morning and said "I've got a bushel of beans for you to freeze." Now that's my morning's work tomorrow. So, every time I think about going out and applying for a job, something comes up.
Q: What are you doing to try to work this out for yourself?
R: Not much, except going to school [typing school]. If something does come up I might. I might not. You should be asking me this in January or February.
Q: Why is that?
R: In October I'm busy with birthday parties, dinner parties. Thanksgiving I cook dinner for 20 people, have Christmas shopping . . . [etc.]

Her "busy" schedule provided this woman with a perfectly good rationale for not having the time to job hunt. Other women attributed their inability to look for work to their husbands, as is illustrated by a homemaker also interested in satisfying the "people-work" factor in a job outside the home:

Q: Are you thinking about seeking different work?
R: . . . My husband pretty much likes me to be home . . . I don't really go and look because I know my husband doesn't like it. He says I have done enough in my life, it's time to relax.

By setting their husbands up as scapegoats for not being able to seek employment, these respondents are then free of having to examine their work motivations and, ultimately, their identities as homemakers.

Perhaps more realistic, but just as defensively rigid, were excuses that revolved around lack of training, the futility of earning money that would be heavily taxed, the labor market, and the problems of finding part-time work. Related to this was the tactic of enumerating such stringent criteria that there would be no danger of actually finding a job that met all those conditions. One respondent, who felt that her "growth potential" was limited as a homemaker, was brushing up on her typing skills as a first step toward finding outside work:

Q: It sounds like you're fairly serious about this.
R: Yeah, I don't know, my husband kids me, he says I've been going back to work for 10 years now, but after you're out of the work crowd you can't get right back in. You have to try to prepare yourself.

. . .

Q: Are you doing anything besides having gotten a typewriter to try to work this out for yourself?
R: No, not other than typing, I can't say. That's about it.
Q: You haven't actually started looking.
R: No, I haven't. I look in the want ads, under part-time, just to see if there's anything close, what the hours would be, and a lot of them don't say where they are. They have to be downtown for me, or someplace close around here. Part-time jobs, there's not that much.
Q: What do you think you'll do to try to work this out for yourself?
R: Well, I don't know. I may go down to the stores and put my application in for part-time help. If something would come along, if it was the hours I wanted, I might take it, but I don't want it if the hours aren't good for me. Also depends on the buses.

It is not difficult to imagine how the respondent's husband came up with his observation about the intensity and seriousness of his wife's job search. A similar set of obstacles was arranged by another respondent, one who was really intensely unhappy with her work as a homemaker. Although she realized that she could not "command a wage," this respondent still set up the unrealistic condition that she would not work for minimum wage under any circumstances. This constraint would effectively keep her out of the job market indefinitely unless a most favorable but improbable turn of events took place.

These cases of identity assimilation bear a great deal of similarity to the kinds of attributions made by full-time workers that their poor salary or lack of advancement was due to their poor education rather than to their lack of competence. In the case of full-time workers, such rationalizations serve the purpose of protecting their work identities from admissions of incompetence. In the case of homemakers, assimilation is used partly to avoid having to take a close look at their identities as homemakers, but it also serve the function of protecting them from risks of failure in the outside world. Some full-time workers used this kind of defensive rigidity to avoid risking possible failure in new and unfamiliar kinds of work. For the disenchanted homemaker, it is even more threatening to consider another area of endeavor, because she has no alternate source of competence on which she can fall back if she is not successful at her new work.

Another perspective on the rigidity of these homemakers can be gained by examining some of the statements of women who were intent on finding outside work because they needed to begin earning money as soon as possible. One of these was a women who felt that there was not "much choice" about her finding work, because of the difficulty she and her husband were having in meeting the normal expenses of a family:

R: ... You can only turn your heat down so much. You can only drive just, you know, like, less. There's only so much you can do. And after a point where it's still eating up more and more of the family income, something is going to, you can't cut that much more out...

Although she did not have a particularly rigid attitude toward the importance of her work as a homemaker, this respondent had no desire to seek outside work for any reason other than this financial need. Now that her youngest child was entering kindergarten, the respondent had her first real opportunity to combine her work as a homemaker with work outside the home for pay. Unlike the homemakers whose desire for outside employment was based on dissatisfaction with the intrinsic features of their work in the home, this woman was willing to accept a job that was less than perfect:

Q: How likely is it that this is going to happen?
R: Well, providing... that there is a need for what I'm going after, I may have to make a stepping stone. I may have to, like I said, shovel hamburgers at McDonald's until something comes along. Just because I'm ready for the world doesn't mean the world's going to be ready for me...

It is perhaps because of the relatively high degree of security that this respondent felt toward her identity as a homemaker that she was able to consider almost cheerfully the prospect of working at an unpleasant job strictly for money. Since she was not seeking an alternate way to define her sense of competence as a worker, she could openly confront the possibility of having outside employment that would not be commensurate with her training or interests.

The analyses presented here of the women whose desire for outside work was based on intrinsic factors may appear to be cynical because of the interpretations offered of the respondents' "excuses." The purpose of these analyses was not to denigrate the sincerity of the respondents, but to point to the inconsistencies in their approaches. It is very doubtful that these inconsistencies were deliberate or even within the conscious awareness of the respondents. Instead, the inconsistencies represent a real ambivalence over questioning and challenging a part of their identity that was very central to their sense of competence for most of their adult lives.

Reflections on the Homemaker's Identity

Returning to the questions posed at the beginning of this chapter, it is now possible to provide some tentative solutions to the paradox of the homemaker's identity. She is engaged in daily work that has little inherent interest, with the possible exception of cooking. Her work receives no pay, and little recognition in the way of thanks from her family, high regard from her working women friends, or status in a society turning its attention to women who are success stories in jobs ranging from those of the astronaut to the candidate for vice president. As far as seeing the results of what she accomplishes in the home, it is very difficult for her to have the feeling that she has "finished" a project. Even when something as close to a project as the spring cleaning is completed, there is the certain knowledge that the same drawers, closets, attic, floors, walls, porch, and yard will need the same treatment in a year's time.

As compensation for the routine and unrewarding nature of her work, the homemaker has the power to decide on how she will allot her time and energy, and to set the criteria for successful job performance. However, this freedom is limited by the homemaker's commitments to her family and their own schedule. As the only parent who is home during the day, except under unusual circumstances, it is incumbent upon her to provide transportation, meals, and attention to her children according to their needs.

So far, the conclusions based on analyses of transcript material are in agreement with the results of other research on homemaking (e.g., Oakley, 1974; Vanek, 1978). What emerges from the present analyses of homemakers concerns the processes they engage in to arrive at and maintain an identity as workers.

What allows the homemaker to continue with her work year in and year out is her conviction that the health and emotional well-being of her family depend upon her work. The cleaning she does, the meals she prepares, and the services she provides, when regarded as symbols of her love for her children and husband, become more tolerable. Even if they do not press upon her their appreciation of her work, she can console herself in the thought that she is doing what is best for her family, and that they are happy because of the work she does in the home. In order to arrive at and maintain this state of selfless gratification, though, the homemaker must translate her efforts into socially meaningful terms by convincing herself of the importance of her work. This conviction must be strong enough to withstand challenges and direct attacks from others who regard with condescension and derision the work of the homemaker. It is from this conviction that the homemaker can extract her sense of competence as a worker. However, extensive use of identity assimilation is required to protect this vulnerable identity from internal and external attacks.

The unique features of the homemaker's identity have some important implications for the identity processes. The identity assimilation process can function for many years as the predominant mode through which the individual interacts with the environment as long as the person's situation remains fairly constant. However, as children grow older, as society's attitudes toward working women change, as friends and neighbors go off to work, the stability of this situation begins to be threatened. Under these influences of changing circumstances, the homemaker may begin to use identity accommodation, allowing herself to think about doing work that would be personally interesting and challenging. As soon as these thoughts take on any degree of seriousness, they have the potential to undercut and undermine the identity as a competent worker that the homemaker has taken so long to build. Her reaction, then, is to revert to identity assimilation in order to minimize the likelihood of her following through on her outside interests.

Some women successfully break through even this secondary line of defense from identity assimilation. It may be that only when their extrinsic needs for pay become greatly exacerbated can they rationalize their move to the outside world without challenging their identities as competent homemakers. In any event, having made this move, they become like the women who are the part- and full-time workers described in Chapters 6 and 7. What they found, when they entered the work world, was that conditions were not as glorious as they had imagined: employers failed to give sufficient recognition or remuneration, work could be dull, the environment could be unpleasant, and the paths to advancement were not always open. In addition, like their male counterparts, they found it necessary to forge an identity that could integrate their identities as workers with their family identities. The outcome of this process for both men and women is the topic of the next chapter.

Part IV
Integrative Themes

In this final section of the book, an attempt is made to look across separate areas and to derive a sense of the adult as a total person. Part of this process involves looking at the relationship between the two areas of identity studied separately so far: family and work identities. In examining this relationship, an idea can be gained of how the adult maintains a sense of continuity in moving back and forth between the two primary modes of his or her waking life. It will also be possible to gain an understanding of the extent to which men and women vary, if at all, in their adventures and perspectives in combining the worlds of work and family.

The analysis of the Values portion of the identity interview is also integrative, perhaps the most integrative of the analyses in the entire investigation. The adult's purpose in life and identity about how he or she is fulfilling this purpose are the concerns of the Values interview. These concerns are what give the adult's life its meaning and what provide an impetus to the adult's entire identity. In their thoughtful responses to this part of the interview, the 94 adults in the sample rose one step above the daily issues of their work and family lives. They provided an overarching view of how their identities in those areas fit into their life's larger scheme.

The Values Identity material was also integrative in the sense that there was a two-way link between the respondents' identities as expressed in their daily lives and their overall sense of purpose in life. The work and family lives of the respondents could be seen as a reflection of their identities concerning their values. At the same time, their values reflected their experiences in their daily interactions in the work and family spheres. Without the additional insights provided by the statements concerning values, these interconnections would never have been discovered. The discovery of these interconnections makes it possible to view the adult's identity as a complicated mixture of the lofty and the practical.

9
Family and Work Identities: Conflict or Compatibility?

The man or woman with a family who works outside the home for pay has a double identity. One identity is dominated by emotional commitments to the people who represent the objects of strong attachment. The other identity is one based on objectivity, professionalism, and productive labor in which human relationships are overshadowed in the ruthless bargaining for individual profit and success. However, the adult's double identity is not quite so dichotomous as this. In Part II it was shown that the adult's family identity includes preoccupations with the practical and monetary concerns of maintaining the home unit's viability. The opposite was found to be the case in the adult's work identity. In Part III it was shown that this work identity often is based upon humane considerations for the feelings and needs of co-workers, superiors, and subordinates. Therefore, both of these complementary concerns of individual enterprise and family relationships contribute to the adult's identity in each of the two areas. However, it still stands that the adult's family identity, even in the extrinsic domains of family life, is dominated by feelings toward family members. The adult's work identity, even with its basis in intrinsic factors that determine competence, is still grounded in the facts of economic necessity. In the present chapter, direct connections are sought between the themes that jointly serve to define the integration of these two modes of human existence and adult identity.

There are differing positions within the adult development literature concerning whether family and work are compatible with each other, or whether they are destined to be diametrically opposed and in constant competition for the adult's sense of priorities (see Marks, 1977, 1979). One position is that adults have only a limited amount of time and energy to devote to their family and work activities; if work takes up too much of the worker's resources, there will be a "drain" on the worker's participation in the home. The more interesting, involving, and encompassing of the worker's identity is work, the more exhausted and pressured will he or she be in nonwork hours. In addition, the adult with a heavy responsibility to work will stay at work longer hours, and be likely to bring home work to do in the evening and on weekends.

The opposite to this "drain" or conflict model of adult work and family relationships is the "expansion" or compatibility model. Rather than detracting from the worker's home life, it is the premise of the compatibility model that work that keeps the adult interested and enthusiastic will heighten his or her interest and enthusiasm for home-centered activities. If the worker is committed enough to the importance of having good family relationships, he or she will find that the time and energy available for the family can expand indefinitely. Implicit in the compatibility model is the idea that the happier and more productive the adult is as a worker, the better he or she will feel. These good feelings and energy will carry over into the realm of family relationships.

The conflict versus compatibility model debate has obvious implications for adult identity and the integration of family and work positions into the adult's total identity as a person. In a test of this model relative to the identity of blue-collar men in traditional male-breadwinner families, Gaesser and Whitbourne (1985) found that a work identity based on extrinsic factors was positively related to scores on a test of marital satisfaction. In other words, men who were involved in work as a source of income were happier in their home lives. Their work was for them a means of supporting a family, and the more important work was for this reason, the better they felt about their marriages.

The present set of identity interviews allows for a more complete description of the work-family identity relationship on a more varied group of men and women than the Gaesser and Whitbourne study could yield. The basis of this description is the set of statements that concern the respondents' perspectives on how their work and family identities are interrelated. These statements were drawn from both the Work and Family Identity interviews of the 77 adults who were now working or previously had worked for most of their adult lives. In analyzing these statements for the purposes of the present chapter, it was assumed that an identity in either area that had its basis in intrinsic factors reflected a deeper involvement of the individual than an identity based on extrinsic factors. This assumption follows directly from the intrinsic-extrinsic distinction as it has been treated in the work identity area. By analogy, this distinction should have a similar application in the family areas as well.

The real test, then, of the conflict versus compatibility models of work-family identity relationships is whether the individual could maintain intrinsic involvements in both areas simultaneously. If this were possible, then it would support the compatibility model. If the conflict model were correct, on the other hand, an intrinsic identity in one area could be maintained only in the presence of an extrinsic identity in the other. The analysis of this test offered here cannot be definitive, but may suggest which of the two possible models holds more potential for further, quantitative study. An exploratory analysis is also provided of the processes of assimilation and accommodation as they cut across the two areas of the interview. These identity processes proved to be a key linkage in the underlying dynamics that integrate the work and family areas.

Sources of Conflict Between Family and Work Identities

Although usually thought of in terms of a one-way valve (from work to family), the "drain" model does allow for the possibility of the valve opening up in the other direction as well. In fact, it may be very difficult to determine the origin of the "leak." A worker whose family identity has lost its intrinsic meaning may begin to regard it from a more extrinsic standpoint. At the same time, he may gradually come to relocate more of his identity into the intrinsic features of his job. Conversely, a worker who is failing to derive a sense of competence from the intrinsic features of her work may gradually come to define a larger share of her interests around the intrinsic qualities of the family. Work for her would then become an almost totally extrinsically oriented enterprise. If one were to study the identities of these individuals at any single point in time, it would not be possible to tell on which side the drain originated. All that would be observed would be a disparity between the extent to which the identities of the individuals were intrinsically involved in work and family.

The identity processes also enter as complicating features into this imbalance. The failure to have one's identity as a competent person verified in work may lead the adult to use identity assimilation in order to avoid applying this negative information to the self. Thus, the individual can redefine the situation so that it appears that work had never been a central focus of identity compared to the family. In order to avoid having to attribute the failure at work to incompetence, the individual can use the ready excuse that it was the strong family identity that had detracted from a lack of work achievement. A similar type of self-justification process could apply to a family identity that had become devoid of intrinsic gratification.

Conversely, a change in the work-family imbalance may tip the scales in the other direction through the identity accommodation process. The worker whose family identity was mainly an extrinsic one because of heavy intrinsic involvement in work may discover, as in the song "Cat's in the Cradle," that he has lost the affection of his child. This may trigger a change in the way a worker defines his family identity so that it becomes increasingly intrinsic.

Before progressing to some of these more complicated issues, analysis of the conflict model begins by examining cases of conflict between the time demands of family and work. This is the model's most straightforward and clearly analyzed form and has the least potential for the overuse of identity assimilation or radical changes in identity through accommodation. At the next level of complexity is the incompatibility of behaviors between family and work. Finally, the analysis of the conflict model proceeds to the head-to-head confrontations of work and family identities. The roles of the identity processes prove to be much more significant in these last cases, which is partly what makes them so complex.

TIME COMMITMENTS

The worker whose job requires him or her to work weekends, evenings, or both is in a conflict situation of not being physically capable of being two places at once. Three of the respondents in the present sample had work in the food and restaurant businesses, which required them to be present on weekends and evenings. There was no reason to suspect that these conflicts reflected anything other than a simple acknowledgment of an inevitable and unpleasant feature of their work, as can be seen in the following brief excerpt:

Q: Does your work affect the rest of your life in any way?

R: Sometimes.

Q: How is that?

R: Well, sometimes you may feel like being home on weekends with your family, but you can't do it because you've got to give a party and you have to be in there, but other than that, not really.

This respondent's need to work on weekends does not seem to relate particularly strongly to his identity in the family or his identity as a worker. A similar case was the "trick shift" worker described in Chapter 7, whose strange and irregular hours made it difficult to have a semblance of a normal home life. However, since his wife did not work, this situation did not detract from the quality of their relationship. The respondent's efforts to find alternate work that he could perform "straight days" was his means of resolving the situation.

In some cases, heavy family involvements are shown to detract from the worker's ability to put in enough hours at work. Usually, the worker lacks the discretion to reduce his or her working hours because these are set as part of the job. The one type of worker who has this option is the secondary wage earner in the family, particularly one with a part-time job. In the present sample, the respondents who fit this category were all women. One of these part-time working women illustrated the family-to-work identity direction of the conflict model, showing how a heavy investment of time spent in the family can cut down the time available for work:

Q: Do you have any doubts or questions about being a homemaker or being a mother?

R: No.

Q: Why not?

R: Because probably as I mentioned before, I love my home, and I love being here. I really enjoy, I like to cook and I like to clean. I like to wash clothes and hang them outside. It's kind of a thing I do everyday. In fact, my one daughter said to me today, asked me if I wanted to go out tonight, but I said no, a lady was coming to interview me from the University and she said "Are you going to get a job, Ma?" My husband was sitting over there and he said "What would you think if your mom went to work full time?" And she asked, "Are you really going to?" I said, "No, Beth, I think I have enough here. At my particular point in life I don't think I could handle a full-time job." Then she laughed. She really thought I was going to be interviewed for a full-time job.

For the purpose of analyzing the family-work time relationship, the fact that this respondent's identity was primarily extrinsic in orientation is not a critical factor. The main point here is that the respondent's dual time commitments were mutually exclusive.

As a footnote to this excerpt, the respondent's description of her husband's and daughter's reaction to her interview appointment provides an interesting contrast to the reactions of full-time homemakers to their family's attitudes. There was not a trace of the defensiveness that was shown by those women over their children's desire for them to work. It is possible that the respondent in the present example felt secure enough in her identity as a part-time worker to be unthreatened by challenges to her work identity from her family.

BEHAVIORS AND ATTITUDES

A negative interaction between the behaviors and attitudes characteristic of home and the work place is the next higher level after time in the degree of psychological involvement the individual has in each of these spheres of activity. Having to perform the actions or take on the ways of viewing the world that are inherent in one set of roles and circumstances may prove to be detrimental or inappropriate if these same behaviors and attitudes are shown in the other setting. This level of involvement is regarded as not affecting identity because the behaviors and attitudes associated with work and family activities are assumed not to be acutely personal or deeply penetrating.

Conflict in the direction of work to family at the level of behavior and attitudes could be seen quite clearly in the statements of respondents who found that they did not want to continue actions at home in which they had engaged at work. This type of conflict was exemplified by the cake decorator:

Q: How does your work affect what you do in your everyday life? Does it carry over?
R: It shouldn't carry into my life, but on days when it's frustrating, naturally I bring it home with me. It's the type of job where you should be able to leave it behind you when you walk out the door, and there are days when it's frustrating that I do bring it home. But I do less baking, that's for sure. I don't bake cakes at home. (laughs) I try to do very little baking.

After having made 80 cakes a day and more, it is not surprising that this respondent was not eager to make any at home. The other component of this respondent's statement, that she brings her mood home with her, was a common feature throughout the interviews. This respondent's description was somewhat unusual because she was able to identify such a specific behavior, in addition to an attitude, that represented a deleterious effect of work on her behaviors with her family.

There were few respondents who openly admitted to letting the attitudes or behaviors that they associated with their home lives detract from their work efficiency. It may be that perception of the need to assume a "professional" stance in one's role at work is so strong that it really does restrict the family-work conflict that would otherwise run in this direction. On the other hand, the desire to appear as a mature and rational worker unaffected by the strong emotions more suitable to the home led the respondents to suppress any such admissions to the interviewer. One of the exceptions was a woman who disclosed that the status of her relationship with her husband either improved or dampened her spirits at work:

Q: How does the importance of your husband affect the way you feel about yourself?
R: I think it has almost everything to do with the way I feel about myself because I feel that if things are going well here, and we're communicating, and I'm happy and satisfied here, it affects my attitude when I go outside and lock that door. But if I'm upset and all angry, it's hard to lock that in the house and then go out and be somebody else. I might not exhibit all those feelings, but I know there's pressure. There have been

times when I've been angry and upset about things that didn't go exactly as I thought or hoped they should, and I've left home in a kind of down state. And I think it's reflected in your associations with other people. It's not that I go out and grab the first person that I see and try to take out on them all the frustrations I should've taken out on my husband, but maybe it makes you withdrawn, you just don't feel like being involved, maybe fighting as hard if you're working or something, you know, because things aren't as they should be.

There was no sign that this respondent was having serious concerns about her marriage and so the effect on her work of her mood state at home did not seem to be associated with any deeper level identity issues. This carry-over of mood seemed to have some effect on her work behaviors (not "fighting" as hard), but not in the same specific way as the cake decorator's work affected her baking at home. A better example of transfer of specific behaviors from home to work that was regarded as a conflict was in the case of a school administrator, whose attitudes toward his family were extremely positive:

Q: How does your family relationship affect the way you see yourself as a person?
R: How does it affect the way I see myself as a person? Gee, I don't know. I know it affects the way I deal with other people on the job. I probably tend to extend a bit too much probably at times the idea of "we're family and let's work this out." I deal with a lot of kids and I deal with a lot of adults and I suppose that's maybe where it has its greatest effect. In terms of how I perceive myself.

Although he does not say this in so many words, one may read into this statement the possibility that he has gotten in some unpleasant or uncomfortable situations as the result of being either too close, too confiding, or too trusting of the good wishes of an adversarial party. Whatever the incidents that prompted this response, it is clear that it is based on a perception that the behaviors he felt free to exercise at home were not appropriate in his work setting.

IDENTITY

At the most complex level of a work-family conflict is the incompatibility of identities in these two areas of life. It is at this level that the individual's deepest commitments are felt, where incongruities between basic orientations will create anxiety and unhappiness, and where the identity processes become most critical as a way of restoring a sense of equilibrium. Analyses of the work-family identity conflicts are the most complicated of all, because of the interplay within and between the identity processes in the two areas where such powerful forces and emotions can be aroused.

It is not always clear, as was pointed out earlier, what is the direction of influence: from work to family, or the reverse, or maybe even back and forth. In the analyses of these conflicts, inferences can be made about the source of the work-family identity imbalances, but these are quite tentative without any direct observations about how the situation developed over time. Because of the complexities in the analysis at the level of identity, there will be at least two examples selected for each type of conflict: work to family and family to work. The examples selected illustrate different variations on how identity involvements in one area can change as a result of alterations in the other.

Work-to-Family Conflicts

The possibility for work identity to detract from the individual's family identity was alluded to by 11 respondents who used this phrase, or a variant of it, in describing the effect of their work on their everyday lives: "I leave work at work." Implicit in this phrase is the acknowledgement that overinvolvement in work is a threat to one's family life that must be avoided at all costs. Whether this phrase reflects the respondent's identity as a worker and a family member is difficult to determine without further explanation from the respondent. Nevertheless, the prevalence of this concern is evidence of a conflict in "reverse" between the two potentially disparate sets of psychological involvements.

Much more convincing evidence in favor of the conflict model were the cases in which the respondents specifically addressed the deleterious effects of their identities as workers on their identities as family members. These effects included but went far beyond clashes in time commitments and behaviors. In addition, these effects, because they pierced so deeply into the individual's identity, also involved considerable use of one or both identity processes.

The first case is a very cryptic statement from a woman with a relatively high-power position in a small company who has received encouragement to "go after challenges" from her employer. This is the same respondent who described, in Chapter 6, the pleasure she derived from "smelling like a rose" after successful confrontations in her dealings with male executives. Given the reported effects that this "discovering" of her "potential" had on her work identity, as well as perhaps her behavior, her reflections on the effects on her marital relationship are not totally unexpected:

Q: What effect on the rest of your life does your work have?
R: ... The only negative thing that happens is that I think sometimes it makes for a little competition between my husband and myself, because he is part owner in a business, and I'm in the field of guiding business people, and I think sometimes he thinks I'm stepping on his toes. It's a very touchy area which is beginning to smooth out.

The reason that this particular work-family conflict is being used here as an example involving identity is that it is obvious from most of her interview that the respondent has gained a greater sense of competence as a result of her successes at work. Her identity as a worker is, furthermore, almost entirely based on intrinsic features (seeing results, challenge, interest). The effects on her marriage may or may not reflect changes that have taken place in her family identity, though. The respondent simply does not provide enough information to determine whether or not she perceives a difference in her interactions with her husband from which might follow changes in the nature of her involvement with him.

In contrast, a second respondent, in a similar situation with regard to having undergone recent positive changes in her identity as a competent worker, was much more clearly undergoing a serious reevaluation of her family identity.

Pregnant with her first child, she found herself in a situation at work where: "My job is just, within the last 4 to 5 months worked into a position where I've been allowed to do more of what I want to do." She claims to have been told by her superiors "You do have the ability, and here's a chance to prove yourself." The respondent found herself, because of this recent accommodation in her work identity, reevaluating her earlier decision to commit herself entirely to the care of her child:

R: ... and all of a sudden it's like I like to work and I don't want to leave it, but I want to have a baby too and stay home, so yeah, it's kind of unique. It would be a lot easier for me to stay home if I hated the job.

As it turned out, the respondent decided to fulfill her commitment to her new work identity after all, because she had in effect already made up her mind to return to work. She claimed that part of her reason for doing so was financial:

Q: It sounds like you're still open about (going back to work).
R: Trying to.
Q: What do you mean, "trying to"?
R: Well, I just, with the financial situation the way it is, I'm blocked into pretty much needing to bring some sort of income home and I think once the child is here and I'm back at work it'll be easier for me to see do we really need as much as I make the whole week? Or can we get by with my working 2 days a week? Would that keep me equally satisfied, or more so?

In this excerpt, the respondent appears to be using identity assimilation as a way of justifying her decision to return to work while protecting her commitment to the as-yet unborn child. However, she has apparently accommodated to the change in her work identity, acknowledging that work really is important to her. She was willing to admit that staying home would have been the unrealistic solution to her dilemma:

Q: How difficult is this decision going to be?
R: I'm not sure ... The decision to go back to work once I had the baby was difficult to reach. I guess I wanted to think that maybe by then Richard would've gotten another raise and we would have enough for me not to go back to work. And then the more we talked about it and seriously looked at things, I guess I realized that was just a fantasy, and I had to face reality that if I wanted to work, a lot of other women do too, so I guess I would.

The "fantasy" to which she is referring is the belief she held earlier that she would have been happy with the identity of a mother totally dedicated to her child. Having come to grips with her need to satisfy her strongly intrinsic identity as a worker, the respondent has made a deliberate decision to arrive at an identity as a mother that would involve a less complete commitment of her identity.

The third case to be considered is one that also involves the work-to-family direction of conflict between identities, but this conflict requires considerable examination before its source in the respondent's work identity is revealed. The respondent is a man whose involvement in his work as a supervisor over a small department was based on the intrinsic factors of autonomy, responsibility, and seeing results. He perceived himself as underpaid due to the "high overhead in that business," and was currently looking for a job with a higher salary in a large company in the city. Despite his current extrinsic dissatisfaction with his work, his work identity was based on intrinsic factors. He therefore was considered highly involved in work. With respect to his family, though, his relationship with his wife was steadily deteriorating into frequent arguments, and at least once a week he seriously considered separating from her. The most radical step he had taken was to sleep in the car one night. What was preventing his actually entering into a separation was his concern over his young children. He hoped that if he found a higher paid position, the arguments might cease. However, one of his goals in finding a higher paid position was being able to support his developing a hobby in which he was deeply interested into a profession in which he could be self-employed. Clearly, then, he was headed toward even greater intrinsic work involvement, were he to follow through on this plan.

The situation just described suggests a strong work identity combined with a family identity whose quality was rapidly diminishing as a source of intrinsic satisfaction, at least his identity as a husband. The respondent's method of assimilating this work-family conflict was to attribute most of the blame to his wife for her bad temper:

Q: Do you have any other questions or doubts about your marriage? Your relationship with your wife?

R: Yeah, she's, I don't know, maybe I am too, but to an extent, she's temperamental. . . She flies off the handle. It's tough for me to deal with that. . . . I'm not used to that. I'm used to someone talking it out with me. It might be emotionally involved, but to the extent that we're restrained some. But she flies off the handle. It's tough for me to deal with that. I think "What did I do to deserve this?" You know? That's the toughest aspect for me to deal with. And it's a tendency to make my attitude, like, well, maybe I should just think about myself. You know, I've given her 100% and that means a lot to me for somebody to just talk nicely to me. That's important. . .

Q: So, does that affect your feelings about being a husband?

R: Yeah, I think that, for all I've given, is this any way to treat me? It may be self-centered, but that's the way I feel.

From this excerpt, the respondent's use of self-justification was quite apparent in his interpretation of his wife's behavior, although he had made a perfunctory acknowledgement that some of the blame may be his. The thrust of his comments, though, is that he is the recipient of behavior he does not "deserve." He also uses identity assimilation in other parts of the interview to minimize the extent of his marital problems: "Louise is just a little bit nervous; you know, probably no more than anyone else on the average. . . ."

The respondent himself attributes the primary source of arguments with his wife to their financial problems: if he could earn more money, they would argue less frequently, as he states obliquely in this response:

Q: You think at some time in the future you'll have some type of resolution?

R: Hopefully, yeah. . . . Well, she pays the bills, so as far as that's concerned, she looks at it and she gets concerned and we've had a lot of, you know, I tend to stay calm . . .

Not only would the couple have fewer arguments about money were he to earn more at his work, but he thinks they would be able to have more time together, as is apparent from the continuation of the above excerpt:

R: . . . So, monetarily, if I could become financially independent, a lot of that will change because, for one, we'll have more time together . . .

On the surface, it appears from the continuation of this statement that having more time together would help their situation in giving them more of an opportunity to work on their troubled marriage:

R: You know, things happen, and spending the time together, the more time we spend together, things get better when we have time to work them out . . .

However, having more time together may not be completely desirable from the standpoint of their marital relationship, as he himself is aware:

R: . . . but then again, we'll have more time to argue.

If it is not having more time to be together that the respondent desires, then why should he be so anxious to have his wife quit her work? The reason is that she and her husband work different shifts so that they can share child-care responsibilities:

R: That's one thing about our marriage. She's been working all kinds of different hours. Okay, it's tough, we're always scheduling each other, you know, and I have to coordinate everything and for like 3 and 4 days at a time we'll see each other for 20 minutes in the morning and 20 minutes at night and a half hour when we're dead tired and frustrated from the day.

By "coordinating everything," the respondent seems to be alluding to his responsibility for watching the children and cleaning the house, as can be seen from this statement that came in response to an earlier question:

Q: How about being a husband? Your relationship with your wife. What's important to you about that?
R: Sharing things 50–50. That's really important. Try to have any sense of right and wrong. You know, certain things, like, just, do the kitchen, do the housework, wash all the clothes. I can't see sitting down on the couch, watching ball and drinking beer, you know. Definitely, I think it should be 50–50.

Her having to work, therefore, has led to no small inconvenience for him. If he could earn more money, his wife could then take over more of the household responsibilities, or at least child care. This would enable him to spend more time on his own "creative projects," the work he would most like to pursue, and the reason for his desire to become "financially independent." In other words, there are really two factors operating in his desire to make more money. One is that it would allow him to support his family on entirely his own income. Having freed his wife from her work, then he would have time to devote to his "creative projects." Early in the Family Identity interview, the respondent alluded to this "selfish" interest in his own projects:

R: . . . I have a tendency to be that, because, you know, I'm into so many different things and there's only 24 hours in a day . . .

Later, in the Work Identity interview, he reveals his goal of spending more time on his personal, "creative" interests:

Q: So, it sounds like what you really want, deep down in your heart, is to be a writer.
R: Okay, I like producing shows, tapes, you know, entertainment. I like producing entertainment. And that's what I would like to do. I wouldn't necessarily want to have to depend on that for, you know, that's almost a hobby. Instead of having 10 hours a week to do it, I'd like to have 30 hours.
Q: . . . You don't see that as becoming an actual career?
R: No.
Q: You'd just like to have more time for it to become a hobby?
R: More time to put into it, whatever it becomes. Do you know what I mean? I'm not actively pursuing it any longer. You know, at one time when I was in school I was actively doing that. But, um, . . .
Q: So, just so I understand more clearly, right now you've applied for a job at (name of company), mainly because that would be an opportunity to have work-study, work and get training on the job, too.
R: Right. And additional income.
Q: And additional income.
R: So that I can make investments . . .
Q: Okay, you mean stocks and bonds and things like that?
R: Real estate.
Q: So, I sense it's not so much the job at (name of company) that you're interested in, but it's a means to an end.
R: Right.
Q: You don't really have any particular field outlined or specified, you know, like the graphics arts department, or whatever.
R: Not, okay, in that sense, yeah, I'd like some electronics training. Just to know it. (laughs) That'll help me as far as my creative projects, understanding the world I live in now . . .

Here, then, is the real cause of his work-family conflict. The respondent's desire to pursue his intrinsic interests in his work have led to frustration with his responsibilities at home and has probably contributed to some of the arguments with his wife. It is undoubtedly inconsistent, though, with his identity as a "calm" person to get involved in heated disputes. When these arise, therefore, he uses self-justification to claim almost total innocence in the whole matter. Identity assimilation may also prevent him from recognizing the effects of his intense desire to devote more time to his passion for creative work on his deteriorating marital relationship, and the weakening of his identity as a husband.

Other respondents in the sample did, however, appear to recognize how their deep intrinsic involvements in work had interfered with their involvement in their family identities. This could be seen in the case of one respondent who was currently separated from his wife. Throughout his working life, he had taken on a series of different jobs, sometimes moonlighting, in order to support his interest in the arts. His retrospective account provides a striking parallel with the current circumstances of the previous respondent:

Q: What effect, if any, does your work, your current position, have on the rest of the areas of your life that you've identified: family, the avocational pursuits, social, and so on? Does the work—

R: The job that I had had a very negative effect on the family in many respects. Most of my jobs did. After I left that laborer's job, which I only had a week, I became a waiter. I've been a waiter before. I became a waiter and was quite successful at it. I was a waiter for, oh, about 3 and a half years. I became an officer of the waiter's union, and I earned a lot more money than I had as a laborer or as a worker at (name of company). It was during that time I began studying and made my interest in music become a career. And even then, I worked overrealistic, because waiters served meals to other people while their own family is eating by themselves, alright? And the holidays when I made the most money I'd be away from home Christmas or New Year's Day or Mother's Day, my family would be somewhere else. So that had a negative effect. The best thing was when I was just teaching, except I wasn't earning, I wasn't able to support my family as a teacher so I continued to be a waiter. . . . But this (current) job especially has interfered with my life, because it took me away from home a lot, I did a lot of travelling, and I was out a number of nights every week at . . . meetings . . . and I think it had a negative effect on my family relationships. A time when my two daughters were growing up and moving out of the house, my wife developing a career of her own, and there wasn't enough time for us to get together. Traveling out of town sometimes she was out, and, you know, suspicion was really going on and that kind of thing. So I think, yeah, there was a lot of negative effect . . .

The identity accommodation process that this respondent appeared to be going through in reevaluating the effect of his work identity on his family relationships may have been given impetus by his recent marital separation. In addition, though, the respondent had recently suffered a major setback at work when his department was reorganized and he was apparently given a reduction in authority. This change was perceived as a demotion by the respondent:

Q: How does your work affect the way you think about yourself? The way you feel about yourself as a person?

R: At the moment? Well, I'd say until recently it, um, I felt very good about myself. I accomplished many of the goals I set out to do, many of them were a real long shot . . . Reorganization of a large structure like this . . . always puts a lot of stress on the person's self-concept . . .

Part of the respondent's reaction to this stress was an attempt to hold onto his identity of himself as a competent worker through self-justification:

Q: . . . Um, so I would say in general, I'm at peace with myself. I don't allow myself to get annoyed with the local equivalent of "losing the key to the executive washroom," that kind of thing. There are people who, if we're talking about budget cuts, are unemployed in this field. I'm not unemployed. . . . What I lack and what I think the company lacks as a result is my ability to help this company in which I've invested a lot of my life through very difficult times. And I don't think they're equipped to handle them. While I think I still have the capability of doing it.

However, the assimilation process was not strong enough to close off completely the identity accommodation process, as can be seen in the respondent's ruminations over the direction his new position might take:

R: It's also possible that I will (a) be a great success and derive some satisfaction out of that or (b) a dismal failure and consequently make that loss to my ego and stack it up with the other losses of my ego that I already described as a result of this reorganization, and think very ill of myself. I don't think I will, but it's possible. I've experienced this before; it's been a long time . . .

Following this excerpt was a description of the events leading to the laborer's job the respondent lost almost 30 years ago, "a deep blow to my ego at the time." However, even at this point, the respondent wavered in his process of self-questioning to return to identity assimilation:

R: . . . Of course, it's not happening now, not at all. Many people react as you did: "Hey, that sounds like an exciting new opportunity!". . .

There was no such response on the part of the interviewer anywhere in the transcript except to refer to the respondent's new job as a "high-level position." Despite the respondent's last attempts here to bolster his identity through assimilation, he ends the description of the change in his work situation with the following admission: ". . . Yes, but, it wasn't my choice, I didn't go seek it." Here lies the truth about his competence that he simply cannot assimilate completely. Whatever his next position, the respondent's identity toward work will have been permanently altered, and possibly his identity regarding his family as well.

Family-to-Work Conflicts

In conflicts involving a negative effect of the individual's identity as a family member on the strength of the individual's work identity, a desire to maintain a strong emotional commitment to family leads to a reduction in the importance of intrinsic work factors. The result is a work identity based entirely on extrinsic considerations, in which the individual's sense of competence is not tied up in his or her work. In order to show that a change in work identity was secondary to a change in the individual's definition of his or her family position, it is necessary to rule out alternate explanations. One of these explanations that would be very plausible was described at the outset of this chapter. This is that the change in work identity could be the result of an assimilation process in which the individual was seeking an "excuse" for having a reduced involvement in work that would not reflect badly on his or her competence. The first example to be analyzed here could very well be explained in this manner.

The case in point is that of the clerical worker described in Chapter 7, who was discouraged about the lack of recognition she was receiving for her work. Her use of self-justification prohibited her from acknowledging that her own lack of ability was what caused her to be in a position that she regarded as underpaid and beneath her level. Although it is not possible to tell whether her work identity had at one time been defined in terms of intrinsic factors, she was clearly extrinsic in her current work orientation and negatively so, at that.

In contrast to the respondent's unhappy situation at work, she was greatly enjoying her relationship with her second husband, to whom she had been married only a few years. In her family interview, the respondent first brought up the discontent she was experiencing about how being at work 9 hours a day had detracted from her ability to devote time and energy to her husband:

Q: How does being a wife affect what you do in your everyday life?
R: It's kind of hard to say right now, because it's been the same dreary thing getting up in the morning early, getting to work, and coming home and doing the dishes.
Q: Sounds like a lot of work.
R: Well, being married isn't the work! Working outside is more or less the work.

Having established both the importance of her marriage and her inability to fulfill the demands of home and work, the respondent then proceeds in the Work Identity to describe a solution:

Q: Beyond putting the application in [for another job], what else do you think you might consider, or what else are you considering?
R: Staying home and taking care of the house. Quitting. Eventually.
Q: Which do you think you'd prefer?
R: Well, I think after all these years, I'd like to stay home for a little while.
Q: What is it about staying home that appeals to you?
R: Oh, I want to get my house done. There are things that just get pushed aside. Well, if you do them in one day. Little things I'd like to do. Fix the rooms up and get cleaned.

This plan of action of quitting work for the sake of her strong family identity and desire to commit more energy to her home now appears to represent her attempt to resolve a conflict in the direction of family to work. However, the plan also provides her with an excellent way to avoid confronting her failure in work to advance to a position that would signify her competence as a worker. If this strategy is regarded as an instance of identity assimilation involving self-justification, then the apparent conflict between the two spheres of activity dissipates. Instead, the respondent's family identity provides a viable way for her to rationalize her ineffectiveness in fulfilling her work identity.

The second case to be considered is a direct example of the family-to-work direction of identity conflict. This is a respondent who spoke freely and extensively of the incompatibility of her current family life and work situations. Though her work identity was for the most part an extrinsic one, even this level of involvement interfered with her strongly intrinsic family identity. This respondent's work situation was described in Chapter 7, where it was shown that the office in which she was secretary had grown from 2 to 5 people, all needing to have their work typed "in 15 minutes." Without a corresponding increase in secretarial staff, there had been an exponential growth of her workload. The expanding needs of her older daughter for attention and help with schoolwork and school activities, described in Chapter 5, had also become extremely demanding. This woman's situation had therefore reached a critical turning point:

Q: How important to you is the work that you're doing?
R: It started out being very important. But as I see the family life becoming more and more dominant, more and more overbearing, I just want to take off the time, that now I'm looking on work-wise as not being as important. When I took the job, and I was interviewed for the job, I stipulated in the interview I am a working mother. And I gotta get that up front. If the school calls and I gotta take my kids out of school because they're sick, I've got to go. I will compensate by coming in on a weekend, but I've got to let you know that I am a working mother. And this is a priority. Now, that's what I said up front. I was thinking I wanted this particular job because it was not demanding. It stopped at 5. And it had to stop at 5, because I couldn't allow it to come home with me. I had no free time to work at home. And in order for us to buy the house, I had to go to work. So I was trying to, when I decided to go back to work, trying to find the best of all three worlds. You know, myself, my family, and the work . . .
Q: What is happening with it right now?
R: Right now, it is getting to be very demanding. It's becoming demanding and my home life is becoming demanding. My husband's job is interfering. His job is becoming very demanding. So now, with all of this, rather than drop something in my family life, because that's important to me to see that they have as much as I can give them in that aspect, work is almost becoming a hassle. And I've said several times to myself "the heck with it. I've got to quit work. I can't handle it.". . . I'm finding that by the time that I get home, at 5:30, and by the time they go to bed, which is anywhere from 8, or 9, depending on the mood I'm in. If I'm in a lousy mood, it's 8. If I'm in a good mood, it's 9:00. That's becoming very pressured. That there isn't enough time between 5:30 to 8:00 to come home, to get supper, to get it down their throats, reasonably quickly, without them gagging on it, having no time really to sit down and by the time you get all that done, it's 7:30 . . . There's no time left in the day. I've run out of time. And it's frustrating. Because I'm constantly telling myself, "Now hurry, hurry, hurry." . . .

This very detailed description of the woman's feelings about her family and work is the very essence of the conflict model. In fact, it is an even more extreme version, because the respondent is on the verge of leaving her job altogether. Her goal was to return to work but on a part-time basis, perhaps in the administrative office of her children's school. At the present time, though, she was finding that her initial determination "to be a super-mom if it kills me" had to be abandoned.

If there is identity assimilation underlying this respondent's reaction to her situation, it may be in an exaggeration of the degree of conflict she is experiencing. She had returned to work after a number of years as a full-time homemaker. Her inability to handle the role of the "super-mom" may have represented such a serious threat to her sense of competence that the only way she could preserve it was by portraying the most impossible situation imaginable both at work and at home. Not being able to handle this situation would then be a reflection not on her identity, but upon the external circumstances. On the other hand, her account may have been very realistic. Given the strength of her family identity and her intense desire to maintain good relationships with her children, her desire to leave her job could have reflected the open realization that too much of her family identity was being sacrificed. This would have represented an accommodation of the super-mom identity to a work identity more compatible with her intrinsic involvement in her family.

The generality has now been established of the conflict model as it applies in both directions between family and work to time commitments, behavior and attitudes, and identity. It is now necessary to determine whether the same degree of generality applies to the compatibility model's assertion that work and family can be complementary if not mutually reinforcing areas of the adult's endeavors.

Compatibility Between Family and Work Identities

The burden of proof in establishing the validity of the compatibility or expansion model of family-work interactions is to show that involvement in one area serves to enhance involvement in the second. Although it is obvious that the individual does not have an unlimited amount of time and energy to devote to both, it is still possible for the individual to feel an unlimited desire to maintain two sets of commitments. Even though the hours of the day must always add up to 24, the person with the strong family identity may define the time spent outside of the family as a function of this involvement. Similarly, the adult with a strong identity as a worker may regard a family involvement positively because it will enhance his or her productivity at work. Another possibility is that the individual is able to meet the demands from both areas without undue strain by abandoning secondary commitments to other social activities, leisure interests, friends, or extended family members.

As the level of the individual's involvement in each area progresses from time commitments, to behaviors and attitudes, to identity, in may be assumed that the potential for identity processes to enter into the relationship will increase. For instance, the individual may use identity assimilation as a means of justifying a heavy involvement in work by saying that he or she is making a sacrifice for the sake of the family. However, it may be the individual's own identity as a competent worker that is the main beneficiary of his or her labors. Identity accommodation may occur when the worker recognizes that it is indeed important to have a strong work and a strong family identity, and then sets about finding ways to implement both.

Since the work-family relationship postulated by the compatibility model is a positive rather than an inverse one, it is possible for a weak identity in one area to generalize in a negative sense to a weak identity in the other. An individual who has little enthusiasm or interest in work may find the energy available for family involvements also diminishes due to a general loss of zest for living. Without a sense of purpose in work that is uninteresting and extrinsically unrewarding, the person may experience a general withdrawal that leads to a retreat from family and friends into the self. Having an identity as an incompetent worker may led the individual to avoid attachments that carry the risk of self-exposure in interpersonal areas as well. Indeed, it is just this sort of process that Erikson (1963) describes for the young adult whose weak sense of identity inhibits the establishment of an intimate relationship. It is also possible for the identity processes to operate in this sort of downward spiral of involvements in life. The individual who is neurotically convinced of his or her own lack of self-worth may interpret with suspicion overtures from friends or family members to try to establish close contact.

With this background regarding the types of work-family relationships to be sought, the analysis begins with compatibility at the level of time allocation.

TIME COMMITMENTS

The logical impossibility of adding hours to the day casts doubts on the feasibility of the "expansion" model as it applies to work-family relationships. No member of the sample gave a self-description as being in situations of feeling a lack of time constraints when both family and work were of importance, conversely, having too much time available in the day due to lack of interest in either area. In order to investigate the expansion model, the more conservative position must be taken that the two areas may be compatible at best.

Having made this assumption, evidence can now be examined that supports the idea that adults who have activities that are of equal importance can somehow find the time to satisfy the demands of both. One of the men who appeared to function according to this principle of compatibility was the school administrator described in Chapter 7, who worked late into the night many evenings, and gave up weekends and vacations when it was necessary to be available. Despite what seemed to be an overwhelming amount of work-time commitment, the respondent made the following claim in the Family Identity interview:

Q: How does your family relationship affect the way that you see yourself as a person?
R: . . . I perceive myself as a damn lucky person! That I don't have a lot of the stress and strains. I have a job where there's a hell of a lot of stress all day long. I go home and I look forward to going home. I've never known a day that I can remember that I didn't look forward to going home. Not because I loved what I did less, but because I loved what was ahead of me even more . . .

There was no perception of, or at least admission of perception of, any disparity between this respondent's time commitments to work and the enjoyment of and devotion to family. This response is reminiscent of the admonition to parents that it is not the "quantity" of time but the "quality" of time that one spends with children that is of importance to their development.

Another respondent, who was also highly involved with her work, fulfilled her joint commitments to her husband and 1-year-old daughter by spending lunch times at home and arriving home at 4:00 in the afternoon from her job, which she described as "full-time":

Q: What is your current employment status?
R: I'm employed.
Q: Do you work full-time or part-time?
R: I consider it full-time even though I come home about 4:00. That's full-time.

There is somewhat of a defensive tone to the respondent's description of her employment status, almost as if she is adding "So there!" to the end of her statement. She appears to recognize that this is not the conventional definition of "full-time" work, but it seems to be the only way she can fulfill her commitment to her infant daughter. Nevertheless, the respondent's dual sense of obligation to work and family carries through to her time commitments to work so that even when she is not at the office, she is devoting time to her job:

Q: What type of work do you do? You said you have a business.
R: ...My husband and I run a business. We have people coming into the house all the time. Sometimes I say I'm going to put up a "No vacancy" sign in the front walk!... So we work together. When we come home from work, you're still working, because you're still thinking, you're still doing, you know, you're still relating in that capacity.
...
Q: What effect on the rest of your life does your work have?
R: It is the rest of my life...

Having merged the two areas of work and family virtually into one, the respondent was able to fulfill both sets of time commitments without appearing to have detracted from either.

These two respondents provide examples of how time-consuming activities within the spheres of work and family life can coincide without creating undue stress or fatigue. If anything, both of these respondents gave the impression of having a considerably high degree of well-being, an impression that came through on the tape recorder as well as in person. One was described by the interviewer as having a relaxed appearance and seeming to be so happy with her life as to be in almost an enviable position. The other was described by the interviewer as appearing to be "congruent" in words and facial expressions, animated, and generally conveying a demeanor of self-respect.

These transcript excerpts also illustrate how the individual may rearrange his or her schedule in order to meet the demands of one set of commitments while still remaining involved mentally in the other. One respondent thought about work while at home, and the other thought about family while at work. Physical limitations on being only able to be one place at one time were not a constraint to their mental energies.

BEHAVIOR AND ATTITUDES

The test of the compatibility model in the area of behavior and attitudes would be to show that the actions and thoughts developed under one set of conditions benefit or at least do not interfere with the appropriateness of the individual's actions and thoughts in the other circumstances. Among the present sample, there were numerous cases in support of this model, extending from the direction of work to family as well as in the reverse. All of these examples were positive in the sense that the respondents appeared to have profited from their dual involvements. They had either learned something useful from one realm of behavior that they could apply to the other, or felt that they were happier because of the spread from involvement in one area to involvement in the other.

One type of carry-over from work to family that seemed to be especially beneficial was the phenomenon mentioned by several women who had taken outside work after having worked for years in the home. This reaction was described by one respondent in the following excerpt:

Q: What effect on the rest of your daily life does your work have?
R: I don't think it has any effect, really, except that it makes me more interesting. You know, I have something to say at dinner, and when everybody else has interesting things to talk about, I can add something to the conversation about a few things that happened at work. I've met some marvelous people in the work that I do.

This particular kind of effect, noted by former homemakers only, provides an interesting perspective on the complaints of homemakers described in Chapter 8 concerning the lack of regard they received in the home. As one of the other working women noted: "so day after day of being home and really, Ed would come home and have things to talk about and I would not have that much to offer, and I think you need to be outside your own four walls to realize what's going on." One interpretation that this statement suggests is that the sense of ennui that the homemakers reported themselves to have felt about their work may have carried over in a negative way to their family relationships.

Another type of interaction between behavior and attitudes across the areas of work and family is the transfer of mood from one area to the other. According to the conflict model, it is undesirable for a spread across these two areas in either direction to exist. It is inappropriate to let the feelings that one would use in the home be displayed on the job, whether those are positive or negative in quality. Conversely, what the worker feels on the job cannot be compatible with the feelings the individual should have toward family members. The opposite prediction is made by the compatibility model because work and family are regarded as mutually reinforcing each other. Moreover, unlike the conflict model, the compatibility model would predict that the transfer of feelings across areas may be helpful rather than harmful to the individual's effectivenss in both areas.

Consistent with the compatibility model, there were examples of direct transfers of mood in the direction of work to family. These were generally of the form shown in the following response taken from a Family Identity interview:

Q: Are there other reasons why your family is important to you?
R: Sort of relaxation when you're with them, can talk to them about anything, get a lot of gripes off your chest if you've got gripes. If you've had a hard time at work, often times I'll tell my wife about the rotten day I had at work and she'll listen and I feel better because I got it off my chest and well, she feels the same way too. And I think it's good to have somebody to talk to about it, get out frustrations. I don't think it should be done at a bar, you know.

The conflict model would predict that the respondent and his wife would be harmed in their relationship by his bringing home his problems from work. As can be seen from this statement, though, the respondent felt that both of them benefited from his having the opportunity to disclose to her his feelings.

Going in the opposite direction, the favorable effect on the individual's mood at work of feelings experienced in the home was described by another respondent:

Q: Does the relationship (with your wife) affect your daily life?
R: Yes, I'd say so. If you're not real happy with your homelife, you wouldn't be as content on your job or whatever you're working on. When your mind is at ease, you do things better, I believe.

What would happen if this man's feelings at home were negative and he carried his bad mood into work? The compatibility model would predict that, instead of suffering negative consequences because of his poor work attitudes, his mood state would be improved once he entered the work environment and began his work tasks. This "escape" into work from an unhappy situation at home was, in fact, exactly the feature of having outside work that former homemakers working full- or part-time found to be so enjoyable. Being in the work environment gave them stimulation and also helped them place their problems at home into perspective.

The mutually reinforcing effect of behaviors and attitudes at home on those at work was also observed to occur in a way that supported the compatibility model. One example in particular was striking in that it described a situation almost exactly like another respondent's illustrated as showing support for the conflict model:

Q: How does your involvement in the family affect the way you feel about yourself as a person?
R: . . . I'm an insurance salesman, and when I go out and sell insurance, I probably look at each prospect as a potential family and try to protect the family. That probably carries into my selling.

Contrast this reaction to that of the school administrator, who felt less effective with parents and staff due to the application of attitudes toward the family to that work situation. There is a fundamental difference reflected in the two adults' situations, with each having favorable implications for directly opposing models.

Up to this point, the compatibility model of work-family relationships has accounted equally well for the excerpts illustrating the nature of these relationships at the level of time allocations and at the level of behavior and attitudes. What remains to be seen is whether it will also be able to account for interactions between the identity of worker and the identity of family member.

IDENTITY

Compatibility between the individual's identity as a family member and as a worker would be said to exist when it is shown that the two identities enhance each other in a mutually reinforcing way. The type of enhancement that would consist of compatibility between identities is one that involves the individual's thoughts and feelings about his or her basic personal tendencies. When there is compatibility between these deep personal self-definitions, the individual feels a sense of integration or unity across the domains of everyday life. In addition, the identity processes of assimilation and accommodation are enlisted in the service of maintaining enhancements across areas of identity involvements. Identity assimilation would be used to minimize any potential conflicts, while accommodation would be used to make a change in one identity so that it is compatible with the other. The reason that the individual attempts to keep the two ares integrated, it is assumed, is that it is emotionally as well as practically more satisfying to feel that the two identities are complementary.

There were instances in which identity assimilation was used to minimize or offset recognition of potentially negative aspects of the work-family relationship. However, the majority of the cases involving identity compatibility were those in which the identity in one area created conditions leading to identity accommodation in the other area. These effects are positive in that they were interpreted by the respondents themselves as having had favorable consequences in the area of identity that changed.

Work-to-Family Compatibility

Identity accommodation in the area of family was found to result from changes in the individual's work identity in the cases of two women whose work gave them a new identity in the home. The effects of work on their identities went beyond the effects on attitudes and behaviors described for other respondents in similar situations. For the women described here, the effects of work were to provide a basis for self-definition that was not totally dependent on their identities in the family.

The first case is that of a woman who noted effects of going to work that included but went beyond the behaviors of having more things to talk about with her family. The effects she described were basic to her idea of the kind of person she was in relation to her family:

Q: Do you have any doubts or questions about being a wife?
R: Not really. My life has changed recently in the past year since I've started working. And I really thoroughly enjoy working. I would not just want to be home and just be a wife and mother. I would not be happy with that. But still, it all blends together. It makes a more rounded person out of me for having a job and, you know, going to work, and being more interesting.

Although this respondent described her family as "a part of my life that's being fulfilled," she required something more in order to be fulfilled as a person:

Q: What is important to you about your work?
R: Umm, I guess it's the one thing that's really just mine. It has nothing to do with Ron, or the children, something that I can do and I get the credit for it. I enjoy being with other people and my children are grown up and they're gone for the most part, and it would be lonely being home and I just enjoy having something worthwhile to do.

There is some extrinsic work motivation represented in this statement, as indicated by the respondent's desire to go to work to be "with other people" to avoid being "lonely." However, the basic thrust of her response is intrinsic in meaning. Having something only she gets "credit" for gave her a sense of competence that she would not otherwise be able to find. This sense of competence contributed to her identity as an individual, and allowed her to feel more fulfilled as a person. She was then able to feel more gratified in her family situation because she could enjoy her family relationships without fear of submerging her identity. It is also possible that without having to "defend" herself with identity assimilation against the depreciation of her role in the family described by the full-time homemakers, she was experiencing the satisfaction associated with a state of identity equilbrium.

For the next respondent, work provided a similar basis for an alternate identity as a person outside the context of the family:

Q: Why is it important to you to be able to depend on yourself?

R: ... It's a whole other area that I share with people other than home, other than sharing ideas with people at home. I mean, there's things that I talk about with people at work, technical problems, or just things that happen that we talk about, that's something that I just had, I just share with other people.

This response in and of itself suggests the effects of her work on identity but does not necessarily reflect on the respondent's family identity. In another statement, a response given in the context of the Family Identity interview, this connection becomes clearer. The interviewer at this point was asking follow-up questions concerning the respondent's statement that she was presently trying to decide whether to work fewer hours so she could spend more time with her family:

Q: What are you doing to try to work this out for yourself?

R: ... I'll always work. I'll always be in a position to work outside the home. Also, because of the security it gives me. I need to know I can look after myself and my daughter if I need to. There was a time in my life when I did. And so I like some, that will always be a portion of the "pie," just so I know that it is there if I need it.

The way that the respondent's work contributed specifically to her family identity, then, was that it allowed her to feel more secure. This is the respondent who was described in Chapter 7 as one who regarded her salary to be an important feature of her work because of the contribution that earning a salary made to her sense of competence. In addition, as can be seen from the above statement, earning a salary gave her a feeling of security within the context of her family. Through her financial autonomy, she probably derived secondary benefits of a practical nature, such as greater power in the family's economic decisions. This financial power may in and of itself have represented an important symbol of her status in the family. However, the effects went beyond these benefits to a deeper level of self-definition. By working, the respondent was able to define for herself an identity as a family member whose economic well-being was not tied up totally in the fate of her husband's earning power.

The effects of work on family identity were, for both of these respondents, not entirely direct ones in the sense that some specific feature of their work identities carried over into the family sphere. Instead, they both described situations in which they were able to gain a work identity that was based on experiences and rewards derived from outside of the family setting. Having this work identity allowed them to achieve a position in the family that was closer to their ideal family identity and so made them feel better about themselves as family members.

Family-to-Work Compatibility

One of the primary effects on work identity of an individual's family identity is the definition of work as a means of ensuring the economic well-being of the family. The above cases showed how having an identity as a worker could enhance the individual's satisfaction in the family at least partly through an economic route. When the effects are reversed, it is the individual's work identity that is affected by assuming the practical and emotional responsibilities of caring for a family. There were seven respondents who specifically mentioned that the importance of work was to earn money for their family. For these individuals, it may be assumed that their desire to make money by working was not simply extrinsic in the usual sense of working toward monetary rewards. Instead, the money earned from work allowed them to fulfill the very intrinsic desire of providing as best as they could for their family's well-being.

A variation on this influence of the family on work was the case of a respondent who was working in the family business. This respondent's sense of dedication to the family kept him in a work situation that at times was inconvenient if not frustrating:

Q: What's your current employment status?
R: ... it sometimes gets to be a hassle because you see your family all day long and then when you get out of work they tell you "Oh, come on over," you know. It's like you're working with your boss and then after work they want you to come over, that gets to be a little bit of a grind working with your family. But, other than that, I feel like, 'cause my father's getting older and I let him take it easy a little bit and I'll work a little harder. 'Cause to me, like the family's the most important thing, the family unit.

Despite the respondent's annoyance with some of the irritations of working with his family, his identity as a good son who helps his father served to maintain his identity as a worker in the family business. In addition, his work identity was truly affected by his family commitments, in that the respondent derived feelings of competence from his ability to complete his work tasks effectively. The satisfactions he derived from his work included seeing the results of his efforts and having a sense of autonomy. These satisfactions might have been gained in another type of work, but the respondent regarded the particular type of work that he was doing as being consistent with his skills and interests.

There is also an element of identity "foreclosure" (Marcia, 1966) to the respondent's desire to work for his family. The respondent's current work status had its origins in his early adolescent years. He had not questioned the wisdom of going to work for his father either before or since that time:

R: ... and ah, geez, I've been working there since I was a freshman in high school. I used to go in after school and I always liked it. I always wanted to go into it 'cause I never wanted to go to school after high school. I wanted to go into the family business...

This statement illustrates the classic "foreclosed" identity pattern of arriving at a work commitment early in life and never going through an actual identity "crisis" or period of exploration. In terms of the adult identity model, it might be said that the respondent was using the defensive rigidity form of identity assimilation. by not looking at any alternatives, the respondent was protecting his identity from any threats to which such an evaluation process might lead.

The respondent also showed signs of identity assimilation in the form of his rationalization for why he was employed in the family business. By working for his father, not only was the respondent able to verify how devoted a son he was, but he also gained some practical advantages. The family business allowed him to obtain a work identity without going through the painful process of finding a niche for himself in the working world. The family business also provided the respondent with a ready means of obtaining a job that had the possibility for advancement: "my father's always been, he's always been the boss and . . . now I'm starting to be the boss and I like it." However, it appeared that identity assimilation prevented the respondent from acknowledging that these advantages were in any way connected with his desire to help the family. It would detract from the respondent's identity as a good son to admit that working for his father satisfied the respondent's own personal interests. The respondent's desire to regard his family identity in a certain way interfered with his accurate perception of his work motivations in such a way as to constitute the self-justification form of identity assimilation.

In a third kind of family-to-work effect on identity, the respondent described himself as better able to work because of his relationship with his wife:

Q: How does the relationship affect what you do in your everyday life?
R: Well, . . . when I go to work it helps me concentrate on what I'm doing at work as opposed to concentrating on the desire to develop a close relationship with another person because I already have that relationship and don't have any great desire to go out and develop another one.

Although this statement may have the overtones of an effect on behavior and attitudes, the effect of this respondent's marriage on his ability to work seems to be at a deeper level. In the following statement, he provides a more general description of the implications that his identity as a partner in a close relationship has for the other areas of his identity:

Q: Could you tell me something about this relationship . . . why do you feel it's so important?
R: It seems to be very important as far as security purposes. Actually, the reason I would give it the greatest importance is because it is important in allowing me to be successful in every other aspect, giving me some stable base from which to to work . . .

The importance of this respondent's identity as an intimate partner, then, is in its providing a basic sense of self-definition as a person who is loved:

Q: Can you describe any effect it may have on the way you feel about yourself as a person?

R: Well, it would by and large be a very positive effect in the sense that it makes me feel wanted and needed by one person, which is very gratifying to me...

It is interesting that the quality of security that he derives from his marital relationship is precisely that feature of identity that the two women respondents described earlier were trying to overcome. Instead, they regarded as desirable a family identity based upon their own independence. The issue, for this respondent, actually did parallel the women's concerns somewhat. His case has been excerpted in Chapter 4, where it was shown that his dependence on his wife was something he was beginning to question.

In any event, having his needs for security met, the respondent was then able to focus his energies on his work, an area in which his sense of identity was far from resolved. The respondent had deep self-doubts that he expressed about his ability to be successful in his work as a graduate student:

Q: ...You also mentioned that there has been a change in your attitude about your own abilities?
R: I think there came a point in my first year that I had to come to terms with the fact that there were people better than I was. Even when I work hard, they were still better than I was. I don't think that's easy to come to terms with when you have some success in the past...

In addition to doubting his own competence, the respondent was also beginning to doubt the value of his chosen profession:

Q: How does being a student in political science affect the way you feel about yourself as a person?
R: I think there's a really deep question which I'm not sure I could answer rather well because political science is a field of endeavor that attempts to strip away meaning from people's lives...If I were to compare myself before and after taking political science, I would have to say I don't have as picturesque an image of my personality as when I started studying.

This respondent's situation provides an excellent illustration of how a favorable identity in one area can compensate for failures or difficulties in another. Without the respondent's sense of security in his relationship, his conflict over his work in graduate school would probably be greatly magnified. As it is, his identity as a partner provides him with some resolve to continue in his present course of studies rather than give up in defeat and change career orientations. In his words, "we have been married 5 years and I have been in school 5 years"; "I don't think she would be too thrilled with a change."

In contrast, the next case provides a dramatic illustration of the serious difficulties faced by an individual whose family identity provides no "secure base" to counter insecurities experienced as a result of failure at work. The respondent is one whose situations in the family and at work were described separately in Chapters 3 and 7. She had severe doubts about the quality of communication she had with her husband, but after a reconciliation following a brief separation felt that she "had to have him in her life." At the same time, her work situation was going very badly: "it's not the kind of situation that's conducive to self-confidence, which I think I could use a little more of."

The respondent's method of resolving her problems both in her family and at work was to use identity assimilation. With regard to her husband, she used defensive rigidity to minimize the seriousness of her concern: "it's probably unusual that I brought it up, it just happens to be this particular week, I haven't let that question seem important for quite a while . . . ." In her work, the analysis in Chapter 7 suggested that she used self-justification to attribute her apparent failure to her own lack of interest rather than to any incompetence on her part. When the two interviews are directly compared, it can be seen that, in addition, the same reason was given for her present course of nonaction. The first statement refers to her description of her perceived constraints in the area of family:

R: . . . I'm not going to approach the question in any serious way, but that's only, my plans are to work out other factors in my life, and other stresses that we have as a family, and I feel that it's possible, that my negative feelings, there may be some changes that will happen. My husband's work and his attitude about himself, for example, is an important factor. And that he's currently planning to change employment fields and this is something he's been working on for a long time, so it could make a big change. How and when he goes about it is important to me.

In the Work interview, the respondent describes herself as in a similar state of limbo:

R: I'm just biding my time right now until we're more secure economically as a family. My husband has not quite settled in his career, and the amount of time and energy required from my young children. I decided that that has to be a priority now.

One interpretation of these statements is that the respondent's identity assimilations in both areas complemented each other. Her husband's career instability could be used by the respondent as an excuse to avoid confronting her own questions about her identity in each of the two areas. A second interpretation is that it was the insufficiency of the respondent's identity as a spouse as compensation for her problems at work that was the underlying basis for her use of identity assimilation in both areas. Had her husband been able to reinforce the respondent's identity as a wife, she would have had no reason to use identity assimilation in the area of family identity. At the same time, she would have felt confident enough, like the political science student, to use identity accommodation to confront her weak identity as a competent worker. A third interpretation is that the respondent's weak identity as a worker lay behind her inability to confront directly her family problems.

These possible interpretations, and any others that may be ventured, are impossible to rule out without the statements of both the respondent and her husband to compare, and more information about the respondent's and her husband's work situation. All of these interpretations are consistent, though, in suggesting that the basic problem of this respondent was not one of incompatibility between the areas of home and work. If anything, the respondent's perception that her problems in both areas had a common basis is support for the assumption of the compatibility model that work and family are mutually reinforcing areas of identity.

The Conflict and Compatibility Models: Implications for Identity

It is now possible to evaluate the relative merits of the conflict and compatibility models, having proceeded systematically through all possible combinations of work-family relationships in all three realms of possible effects. What emerges clearly from this analysis is the conclusion that both models are equally capable of explaining observations from the present set of interviews. This is not a satisfying conclusion from the standpoint of trying to narrow down two competing theoretical explanations to one. However, the conclusion is not at all disturbing, in retrospect, from the standpoint of understanding identity.

The reason that both models are adequate in explaining different cases is that there is no inherent relationship between the adult's work and family identities. How the two identities are related depends on the importance and meaning they are given in the context of the individual's total identity as a person. If an individual regards herself as a worker who wants to achieve career success at all costs, involvements in the family domain will be regarded as prohibiting. Similarly, if an individual regards himself as a "family man," it will be difficult for him to find satisfaction in a time-consuming job. He will regard as an intrusion on his personal life any attempts by his employer to be forced to put in more effort on the job. However, if the person regards both areas of life as important to his or her overall identity, then compensations will be sought across areas to resolve potential conflicts. These compensations may be no more complicated than using one's imagination to think about one area of activity while engaging in the other. The individual's imagination may also be applied with more practical results, by designing creative solutions to potential work-family incompatibilities.

Identity processes may also become involved in the work-family relationship when it impinges upon the individual's separate and integrated identities as a worker and as a family member. The importance of one area may be minimized through identity assimilation in order to achieve greater compatibility between them, if both areas are important within the context of the individual's integrated identity. Conversely, the appearance of conflict may be created through identity assimilation. The individual may give the impression that the importance of one area has blocked the achievement of success in the other. This artificial conflict provides an "excuse" that the individual can use to maintain a sense of competence in the area of potential uncertainty. The alternate process of identity accommodation may serve as a route to compatibility if the individual becomes aware of new solutions to long-standing problems that had stood in the way of integrating work and family identities. However, it is also possible that the individual discovers incompatibilities when a newly emerging identity has the potential to offset the importance of the other area.

Demonstration of the role played by identity and the identity processes in determining the nature of the work-family relationship strengthens the proposition that identity is a pervasive force in adulthood. Not only does identity serve to define the individual within the major realms of the adult's life, but it also can serve as an integrating force among these. This integration is accomplished via interconnections that are organized around a set of implicit principles of what is important in life. The present chapter has explored some of these implicit principles as they apply to the two main categories of the adult's productive and emotional enterprises. In the next chapter the results of the individual's attempts to make explicit the principles that give life its overall sense of purpose will be examined.

10
Purpose in Life

When asked the question "What is the most important principle you live your life by?", the 94 respondents in the sample provided answers that revealed as much about their identities as it did about their value systems. Statements such as "my values are my life . . . the rules of the body, the rules of the mind" and "the key to everything else" revealed the potential for a sense of values to be a dominant feature of adult identity.

The statements of major values or principles also reflected the overall integration of the respondents' identities, the integration that determined which areas of their life dominated their overall sense of who they were as persons. For those individuals whose identities were dominated by their position within the family, the principles that they described reflected orientations toward doing things with and for their family members. For those individuals whose identities were dominated by their views of themselves as competent workers, the values of hard work and competence emerged.

Other features of the identities of the respondents related to the identity processes were also revealed in the way the respondents described the criteria they had for evaluating themselves as "good" persons who followed their values. One of these was the individual's tendency to view the world and the self from either an assimilative or an accommodative perspective. Those people whose principles originated from the view of themselves they had "always" held represented the extreme end of the assimilative perspective. In contrast, individuals who felt that it was important to be flexible and "keep up with the times" had a generally accommodative approach to their lives and their identities.

The questions concerning values served another important function. They provided data that clearly refuted the existence of sex differences in basic life orientations. Contrary to the claims of feminist writers (e.g., Gilligan, 1982), both men and women described the important to their identities of being assertive, independent, and competitive. Even more significant was the common tendency of men and women to describe as important the relationships that they had with other people and the responsibility they owed to their loved ones. The portrait of men that Gilligan and others have painted does not include this feature of their value systems. However, the present sample of a cross-section of adult men clearly saw themselves as valuing love, friendship, helpfulness, and selflessness.

By the same token, women were just as likely as men to view other people in the "male" terms of equity and reciprocity. Perhaps there were differences in the way that men and women expressed these tendencies in their role enactments. Their underlying identities, though, were oriented toward the same basic principles.

In contrast to the distinction between "male" and "female" orientations, the distinction offered by Rokeach (1973) may have much greater explanatory utility. Rokeach described two major dimensions of values: (1) personal or social and (2) terminal or instrumental. Along the personal-social dimension range the values that apply to the individual versus the values that apply to society at large. A personal value would be, for example, happiness. A social value would be world peace. The terminal-instrumental dimension comes very close to the extrinsic-intrinsic dimension used here in earlier chapters to distinguish between ends and means. A terminal value would be accomplishment, while an instrumental value would be intelligence. Rokeach reported findings that supported his position that the two dimensions of values accounted for a great deal of the variation in human belief systems.

The present investigation was not intended to serve as a definitive test of Rokeach's theory, but the theory was nevertheless a useful one for interpreting variations among the adults in the sample in how they described their principles in life. The values described in this chapter were those that would be regarded as more central to the individual's identity because they are "personal-instrumental." These were the values described with the greatest frequency within the sample that fit the criteria of the personal-instrumental category. Their distribution is shown in Table C.3 of Appendix C.

The reason that personal-instrumental values were regarded as the most central to identity relates to the definitions of "personal" and "instrumental." Personal rather than social values would seem to have greater applicability to how the individual evaluates his or her identity as a principled individual. While it is difficult for the average adult to accomplish or realize goals for improving society as a whole, it is within the realm of possibility for any individual to fulfill the values that apply directly to his or her own life. The assumption that instrumental values are more central than terminal ones is based on the parallel between the terminal-instrumental and extrinsic-intrinsic dimensions. Just as intrinsic factors in work and family are more central to the individual's unique identity as a worker and family member, the instrumental values should promote greater involvement of the individual's identity in fulfillment of values.

Honesty—A Word Often Heard

Although Billy Joel's song claims that "honesty is hardly ever heard,"[2] it was a theme given frequent reference by the respondents in the sample (18 women and 18 men). In fact, Rokeach (1973) reported that the personal-instrumental value

---

[2]"Honesty" by Billy Joel. Copyright © 1978 by April Music, Inc.

of honesty was regarded by people of all ages in a nationwide survey as the most important principle in life. In the present study, honesty was used to refer to the value of not stealing, cheating, or lying. The following excerpt illustrates this definition of honesty as used by a respondent who frankly admitted to some of her weakness in this regard:

R: . . . I've never robbed a bank even though I've thought about it, I guess everybody has. You know, how would I get away with it, could I do it, how much money they'd get away with, and what would they do with the money. I have thought about that a lot of times, but I never would do it. I don't like cheating. I never have. I have cheated, but I've never liked even that. When I've done it, I've felt bad . . . I never did it in college, but I did do it in high school at times when I was exhausted trying to study and I could not do it and so . . . Well, I guess honesty is number 1.

This respondent's candor was tempered somewhat by her tendency toward identity assimilation, through which she projected dishonest motives onto others (switching from "I" to "they") and used self-justification regarding herself (being tired as an excuse for cheating). As will be seen in a number of cases, there is usually much stronger evidence of identity assimilation when honesty is defined as not engaging in illegal or immoral practices.

At a deeper level, one's identity as an honest person may include a broad range of attributes, some of which are very central to the individual's total identity as a person. The importance of honesty, when examined at that level, is what having an identity as someone with that value implies about the person's overall sense of purpose in life. What does it say about an individual's identity if that individual values honesty? Is a person who values honesty more likely to use identity accommodation to gain a "realistic" and "honest" view of the self and experiences? This next respondent provided an answer to this question, based on her own broad definition of what it meant to be honest:

Q: Could you describe for me your major values? The principles you try to live life for?
R: Honesty, number 1. Making commitments is a big thing for me, too. It doesn't matter what the commitment is, but just to have a direction in my life would mean just to make a commitment to something, whatever seems right at the moment and follow through.
Q: How strongly do you feel about these?
R: Honesty, number 1, that's why I said it first and I should explain that a little further. I don't mean don't ever tell a lie. I guess looking at the world honestly and taking things as they are, and dealing with them, or using them, or whatever. Being realistic would be the better definition. I don't have a code of rules I live by. It's more of a feeling, I guess.
Q: So, instead of honesty, you mean being realistic?
R: Being honest about what is real and what isn't. What I can do things about and what I can't.
Q: The second one was making a commitment.
R: They all tie together.
Q: Could you connect those together for me?
R: I think that if I'm being realistic about life then I could form a direction from that, and

then make a commitment to whatever my goal is in that direction. I think they go hand in hand, but they are not the same thing.

. . .

Q: How do your values affect the way you feel about yourself?

R: Of course, if I could stick with those values, I'll feel great about myself. They are part of me, they aren't some thing I could judge separately. . . . I think they make me evaluate and make sure that I am doing what I think is the right thing at the right time . . .

Q: Do you ever consider having a different set of values?

R: No.

This respondent's definition of honesty in relation to her identity was exceptional in its depth of analysis and breadth in defining "honesty" as giving her a life purpose. Her response also illustrates the potential for "honesty" to translate into identity accommodation as a means of interpreting one's experiences in a realistic fashion. With this set of values, there is no reason for her to change, since identity accommodation will be a continuously self-correcting mechanism.

For the rest of the respondents who described honesty as important, though, the term had a much more concrete set of referents within the contexts of family and work. Their self-evaluations also generated considerably more ambivalence, as evident in the predominance of respondents who seemed to be using identity assimilation.

HONESTY IN FAMILY AND WORK

The "Good Parent" and the "Good Child"

The importance of honesty as a personal value translated into honesty as a value to teach one's children for respondents with a strong family identity. By their actions as well as their words, these parents hoped to communicate to their children the need to tell the truth and not to steal or cheat. As one parent observed:

R: . . . you've got to set values because if you don't have values, your kids aren't going to have values. . . If in one breath I'm telling my children value-wise "don't steal," then I take them into a store and I slide something under my arm, then I'm not teaching them very well. . .

The decision not to steal was a fairly easy one for this women to make since it would clearly be a violation of the value of honesty. However, the correct way to model the value of honesty for the sake of teaching one's children is not always so clearly apparent:

R: . . . I believe in a lot of honesty and I try to teach my little girl that being honest, you know how important it is, it bothers me when she's getting to an age now where last week when she said "Does the Easter bunny bring the candy or do you and Mommy?" And I looked at her and I wanted to be honest, and I said "Well, I don't." And this is true because her mother does . . .

Honesty as a value important to fulfill in one's marital relationship was only mentioned specifically by 5 respondents, and only as a passing statement by 3 of them, as in the following statement: "I try to be honest with my spouse . . . to keep an open relationship." It is somewhat surprising that honesty was not mentioned more frequently in this context, since maintaining open lines of communication was such a prominent feature of identity as a spouse. There were, however, 2 respondents who described the disastrous consequences to their marriages of not being honest. One of these respondents was considering a separation from his wife, and the other was divorced from her husband. The divorced women, in her lengthy description of her ex-husband's lack of honesty, showed how badly a relationship could deteriorate when it lacked honesty. What is interesting about her statement in addition to its bitter content as the way it reflected the respondent's own use of identity assimilation:

Q: What about the value of honesty, what is especially important about that?
R: It's personal honesty. Honesty about your identity, being willing to call a spade a spade, and not trying to create untrue expressions of yourself or any aspect of your life.
Q: You seem to have some anger around that.
R: Oh, very definitely. My husband was, without a doubt, the personification of a phony and it had made his life miserable. He always tried to be something that he isn't and it isn't that he had anything to hide, in my opinion, particularly . . . You know you can apologize for being what you are, but you are. Be honest about it.
Q: What is exactly important about it?
R: You can't have an honest relationship with somebody if you aren't honest about who you are. He went through life talking about the noble institution of matrimony and when I left him he kept saying "I believe in marriage." Well, he did believe in marriage so long as he put it his way. As long as he did whatever he wanted to do all that married life. His idea of marriage was a label and not a relationship. Very curious. Like he believed in religion too, with a capital "R". But I think he was one of the most unreligious people I've ever known.

Up to this point in the respondent's description, there is every reason to believe that her ex-husband's lack of honesty was a serious detriment to their marriage. The next interchange throws this conclusion into serious doubt:

Q: How do your values affect the way you feel about yourself?
R: I'm practically a Girl Scout. I believe in loyalty, honesty. I feel good about myself because I think my values are the important ones. But doesn't everybody?

Here, the respondent reveals in virtually its most pure form the use of self-justification. Her assimilative stance regarding her own values is what casts aspersions on the description of her ex-husband's lack of honesty. The other respondent who regarded his marital problems as due to his placing "so much emphasis on honesty" showed a similar use of self-justification. Whether or not these respondents were accurate, though, their perception that their spouses were being dishonest generated a considerable intensity of feeling. It may be that honesty is a quality taken for granted in one's spouse, and it is only when it is not perceived to be present that it provokes a reaction.

By regarding honesty in terms of the individual's identity as a parent and spouse, it is possible to see how this value is implemented on an everyday basis within the context of the home. Turning around the adult's family identity from parent to child provides a compelling explanation to account for the importance of this value. The word "upbringing" was used by a large proportion of the sample (19 women and 24 men) to describe the origin of their values. Many of these respondents, who regarded their upbringing as having been an important influence on their present values, had described honesty as an important value (8 women and 11 men). Another large group (7 women and 7 men) who described themselves as "religious" persons had also regarded their upbringing as being an important influence on their values. Although not singled out specifically, honesty seemed to be part of the value systems of the respondents who regarded themselves as "good Christians" or as "following the Bible":

R: . . . I guess I go by the basic Christian values . . . I don't cheat. I don't steal. I try to be honest with people . . .

The connection between honesty and upbringing can be seen in the following excerpt:

Q: Why is honesty so important to you?
R: I was caught lying when I was younger, it was before I was a teenager. I was really stupid. Something with my father. He told me to go get his slippers, and I couldn't find his slippers. They were in my room and I couldn't find them and there they were, so I hid them, but he knew where they were. So, when he came in to look for them they weren't where he knew they were. And he said "You moved them," and I said "No, I didn't." He said "Yes, you did; you're lying." I said "No, I'm not," and he said "Yes you are and anything less is a lie." And after that I got a spanking and I got a punishment and a lecture, you know, about honesty and lying. That always stuck with me so as I was growing up, and became a smarty teenager, I never lied to my folks. If they wanted to know where I went, I told them. If I was sneaking out on them or something like that and they didn't know it and they didn't ask, I didn't volunteer the information. But had they asked, they'd gotten the right answer. But I'll never forget that. I don't know, that left such an impression that he thought so poorly of me because I had lied, over such a stupid thing and I knew it was a stupid thing, that I said I would never lie again. And honesty just falls right in with it.

This respondent's detailed account of this incident suggests that her present value had its origins in her attempts to maintain an identity as a "good daughter" in relation to her father. In order to maintain this identity, though, it was necessary for her to use the self-justification form of identity assimilation by devising a system of fine distinctions about what constituted a lie. This system allowed her simultaneously to feel virtuous and have a good time with her friends.

For another respondent, the enforcing by his father of the value of honesty was carried out in a more painful manner:

Q: Do you ever considering having a different set of values?
R: No, not at all . . . That's the way I was brought up. My parents instilled it in me when I was a kid. If you want it, you have to work for it and you have to do it honestly. A couple of times when I was a kid I got belted, a couple of good times.

The tendency to carry directly into their adult identities the values of their parents represents the defensive rigidity form of identity assimilation, and it was one of the more common forms of identity assimilation observed in the sample with regard to values. Those individuals who traced their values to childhood sources were living out as adults the identities as "good children" they had tried to maintain in relationship to their parents. One respondent stated this directly:

Q: Do you have any idea where this value originated? When it developed?
R: I'm sure I do. My mother was a very strong person in my life much more than my dad. And sis also beat this into me, to be honest and not tell a lie. I'd try of course to tell little white ones which everybody does, and it shows right on my face. I can't get away with it. But she was adamant about that! I was a good daughter and followed that along pretty much.

The values of individuals such as this respondent, who regarded themselves as having been strongly influenced by their upbringing, were only partly a reflection of their principles or purpose in life. Instead, the process represented by this self-description was a demonstration of the potential for a continuing impact on the adult of an identity established in interactions with one's parents. So dominant was the influence of her mother on this particular respondent that she described herself as "automatically" being honest in her everyday life, and having not a single doubt or question or even an idea of what she would challenge about this value.

The tendency toward this particular type of defensive rigidity was observed with regard to values other than honesty. However, it is in relation to honesty that the connection between the "good" child and the "good" adult is clearest. While abstract values such as "peace" and "justice" require the development of higher order thinking processes, even a 3-year-old child can discern at a primitive level the difference between the "good" and "bad" poles of the honesty continuum. As parents use this distinction to establish codes of behavior, the child learns that the route to parental approval is to follow their rules. The alternative may be severe punishment, as suggested in this respondent's description of his own attitudes as a parent toward honesty:

Q: How strongly do you feel about the value of honesty?
R: I feel very strongly. If I catch any of our children not telling the truth, I tell them if you do something wrong, chances are you will get punished and if I found out that you did something wrong and lied about it, you are a lot worse off. I'm very strong on truth and trust.

In following rules such as those described by this parent, the child not only can gain the approval of the parent, but also may gain an identity as a "good" child. Having obtained this identity at such an early and vulnerable point in development, the desire to protect it is strong indeed. To engage in any serious contemplation of violating this value would constitute such a powerful thrust that the tendency toward identity assimilation remains predominant for many adults.

An Honest Day's Work

The value of honesty was also expressed in regard to the individual's identity as a worker. There were differences among the respondents in how they defined an honest worker, but for the most part, the honest worker was regarded as one who carried his or her own code of ethics into the business world.

The simplest and most direct connection between work identity and identity as an honest person was expressed by a respondent who regarded himself as an honest worker because he abided by the laborer's code of ethics:

R: . . . In working you believe in giving a day's work for a day's pay. You don't believe in just goofing off all day and go in to collect your pay. I like to work a day's work for a day's pay . . . You try to live as honest as you can.

For this respondent, it would just be as dishonest to "steal" time from an employer by not performing his work tasks as if he were to engage in theft of property. There was nothing specific about his work, though, that demanded or inspired reliance upon his identity as an honest person. The following excerpt illustrates how the respondent's identity as an honest person translated more directly into his particular work in real estate:

Q: Why is honesty so important to you?
R: . . . Nowadays in business, everybody lies, everybody steals, everybody does this, everybody does that. I don't think it's totally necessary. You can get ahead farther and faster sometimes if you want to do it that way, but when I do something and I get there, I want to know that I did it and I did it right. . . I never have in real estate sold houses to people without, uh, in fact, I've talked people out of buying houses because I didn't think that the house was worth the investment, the money they're asking for, or there's problems with the houses and I'll explain it to them so when they buy the house, they buy it with their eyes wide open and they can't come back and say you didn't tell me this. If I was aware of it, you were aware of it and I advise people, you know I advise, it's my opinion. You take it the way you want to take it, but if you ask for it, you'll get it . . . I'm very strong on my principles.

There is an element of self-justification to this statement, and also defensive rigidity in the respondent's earlier admission that his value of honesty is a product of his upbringing. Nevertheless, the important feature of this statement is that the respondent perceives himself as someone whose honesty in his work is a direct outgrowth of his identity as an honest person.

For another respondent, it was the incorporation of her work into her identity that she regarded as having influenced her value of honesty:

Q: What kinds of values and principles do you lead your life by?
R: It's tough. It's the schoolteacher in me, undoubtedly . . . I like to expect as much honesty as you can give. I don't expect total honesty from everybody in every situation, but as upfront as you can be.

Another interesting feature of this approach to the value of honesty was that she regarded it as important for social reasons:

Q: Why is honesty important to you?

R: If people are honest... how could you generate any huge problems? You'd go along fine if you're thinking of a big group of people.

The more common tendency of the respondents was to regard honesty as a personal value that was important in the individual's own life, but not necessarily for the benefit of society. It is possible that being a schoolteacher not only led her to value honesty as a standard for herself but also as a way to keep peace among the "big group" of people in her own classroom.

The way that this respondent actually defined her own identity as an honest person shows an intriguing combination of identity accommodation and assimilation in that she is willing to admit to not being perfect, but does not use this awareness to stimulate any reflections upon her own identity:

Q: How would you carry out your value of honesty in everyday life?. . .

R: . . . everyday little honesty, I'm always amused; you sit around the teacher's room or at home in the kitchen, and we're always griping about something, and that kind of comes under an honesty idea where they all do it and I join right in myself, too. If you're discussing a principal, you don't like this particular person, you don't like his way of doing things, and you say "Boy! I would tell him this and I would tell him that," and you know full well that you would never say that, which I suppose has something to do with honesty. I don't think, I'm not honest to a fault. If I pick up a pencil and walk off with it, I don't get all upset and bent out of shape and say I have to return this pencil. I don't even think about these things, even though I know they add up.

Her admission of her own hypocrisies and unintentional "lifting" indicates that the respondent does have an appreciation of her failure to live up completely to her value of honesty and so is using identity accommodation. However, her identity regarding her values nevertheless was based at least partly on defensive rigidity and lack of insight into her own identity, as can be seen in the following series of questions:

Q: Do you ever question or wonder about your values?

R: No, I've never wondered about them. I should have had things to wonder about a week before you came. I'm not a "find myself" person. I don't do a lot of introspection.

Q: Is there anything that keeps you from considering alternative values?

R: I'm satisfied. They seem to work. I'm secure with it. I don't see any reason to change for any particular reason. . . there could be a possibility of change, but otherwise this is a part of me since I was little even without thinking about it.

Although the respondent is aware of her own failure to live completely up to her image of what a totally honest person would be, she is not particularly eager to examine the implications of this mismatch between such an identity and her behavior. Instead, she seems willing to redefine her identity as someone who is not "honest to a fault," and then to settle for the security of having her values be consistent with her behavior for at least most of the time.

This respondent regarded her identity as an honest person as reflecting her identity as a schoolteacher, but she did not specifically state that she had accommodated her identity regarding honesty to be consistent with her job. Such a statement was made by a respondent whose work as a manager demanded of him that he exercise the value of honesty:

Q: What is important to you about the value of honesty?
R: It reflects more in fairness; trying to be honest in your own mind about being fair to people. If you're going to do it once, you're going to do it all the time. It is a thing I practice in my job. I have to be even-handed in discipline records. The law watches you more now . . .

The value of honesty is somewhat blurred, for this respondent, with another value of his, which is "fair play." Apart from this issue of definition, it is apparent from his statement that the respondent regards the need to practice this value or values in his job as a change in his experiences to which his identity has had to accommodate. His values also affected his attitudes and behavior toward other people in the work setting:

Q: How about outside of work? How does honesty affect your view of yourself?
R: In dealing with the public, expecting people I deal with to operate the same way. Whether it's a contractor who does work for me, or it's at the store.

The respondent did not really answer the question that was put to him, but actually gave an illustration of how he was affected at work by his value of honesty. His statement demonstrates how an individual's identity can influence the way that experiences are perceived. In the case of this respondent, his expectation that people would be honest with him caused him to use honesty as a criterion for evaluating how they really did interact with him. The next respondent described the irritation and annoyance that he felt when other people failed to live up to his own expectations of honesty:

R: . . . I place honesty very high, and I just get upset when people lie to me or let's say, let's relate to work, which is very easy. If you award a contract to the sub-contractor with certain terms and specifications spelled out very clearly, and the sub-contractor tries to cheat, so to speak, substitute with unequal materials or workmanship, that really upsets me very much, and I try to treat people honestly and fairly and be treated the same way.

This respondent's expressed disappointment with his colleagues at work has mixed in with it what appears to be a heavy dose of self-justification. It is his sub-contractors, not himself, who behave dishonestly. His perception of dishonesty in other causes him to reinforce his own identity as an honest worker, which in turn raises his standards even higher in judging others.

Identity assimilation can be used in the service not only of maintaining one's identity as an honest person, but also to protect threats to the individual's work identity as a competent person. The next respondent, a full-time homemaker, converted her perceptions of the dishonesty of employers into self-justification of her own competence:

Q: What kinds of things do you particularly focus on when you think about honesty?

R: ...I think of, it goes back to career again,...I have lost out on several jobs because it wasn't myself that wasn't being honest but it was other people that were not being honest with me and telling me that I could have a particular job and then later on they come back and say "Well, I'm sorry but you can't have it." Um, in connections, if you don't know somebody, you can't have a job. Really, I think so. I've been quite upset a number of times because people haven't been honest with me because of that...Um, it's just that I've had people more or less kind of double-cross me...in respect to getting a couple of jobs that I was offered, it was a couple of weeks later I'd find out that I couldn't have it because of somebody else. The boss's wife was getting the job instead of myself which I just didn't think was fair, and that, I think, ties in with honesty.

Who can say whether this respondent was not describing an accurate situation? It is very possible that she actually received offers that were then rescinded. However, it does have an air of implausibility for such an event to have happened twice in almost identical circumstances. Instead, it seems just as likely that the respondent defined as an "offer" some vague statement or indication from a prospective employer that she had a possibility of being offered a job. For her to attribute her lack of job-hunting success to these "double-cross"ers instead of herself would obviously serve to protect her identity as someone who could be a competent worker. In addition, it would also give her a good excuse not to follow through on what were ambivalent intentions to seek outside employment rather than be "happy" making her family "happy."

This respondent's dilemma illustrates a paradoxical aspect of identity assimilation when it is used to protect an identity as an honest person. This woman has, in a sense, inadvertently "lied" about her situation in order to protect her work identity. However, she would find it just as difficult to admit to being dishonest as she apparently found it difficult to admit to being unsuitable for a job. As a result, the individual must be doubly dishonest about herself. Although two wrongs add up to a "right," in that she can sustain a favorable identity about herself, there will ultimately be a price she must pay in the disequilibrium within which she is functioning.

The problem of the rejected employee or potential employee that is illustrated in this excerpt complements the problem faced by the supervisor or employer who must be the bearer of bad tidings to such an individual. If the value of honesty is clearly uppermost in the employer's identity, he or she can dispense of employees who do not meet this criterion without giving the matter much thought:

R: Honesty is [essential] as far as my position as a manager...If a person lies or cheats or something, I just write them off...I think if a person lies or cheats or steals, we just have no use for them. If a person lies to you once you can never trust them again. That's the way I feel.

If the individual has an identity as both a fair and an honest person, though, it is much more difficult to decide on a course of action with employees who fall short of the mark. In Chapter 7 the problem of the personnel director who wished to maintain his identity as a "fair" person was described. This same respondent was found to value honesty as well, and as a result he faced considerable ambivalence regarding which value he was more obligated to fulfill. There are many instances like this, in family as well as work situations, in which it is impossible to maintain an identity as an honest person if one also wishes to maintain an identity as a considerate person. In the next section cases in which the value of honesty comes into direct opposition with the value of consideration of others are highlighted.

To Thine Own Self Be True

One of the most familiar quotations from William Shakespeare comes from a speech of Hamlet's:

This above all: to thine own self be true,
And it must follow, as the night the day,
Thou canst not then be false to any man.

In less poetic terms, members of the present sample expressed the corollary of this sentiment:

R: . . . If you can't be honest with somebody else, you can't be honest with yourself. . .

Having a sense of "self-respect" was what another respondent found to be the result of being honest with other people. The price for being honest, though, is that of hurting someone else's feelings:

R: . . . I'm going to tell the truth even if it hurts, and people know that, and if they don't know that, that's their problem.

For some individuals, though, the value of being completely honest in one's interpersonal relationships was not so unilaterally positive. The statement below is from a part-time homemaker who is speaking about "being taken advantage of" by her children:

R: . . . I wish I could say "no more" of certain things. Just as an example, if anybody is going anywhere, it isn't even a question of who is going to drive, they automatically assume I will. And sometimes I feel resentful. That's what I mean.
Q: But how is that tied with your values of honesty and integrity?
R: That's when I wish I could be more honest. . .

The resentment that the respondent reported feeling was anger directed at herself for not telling her children about her own feelings in the situation. It may be speculated that her reason for not being more "honest" was that to do so would have conflicted with her identity as a mother. She described her family as "everything," and her role as a mother as something she would not want to change, although she admitted to having "lots of days when you think you should have stayed single and become a nun." However, to follow through on her self-doubts would have meant leaving too large a gap in her total identity as a person. Honesty had to suffer at the expense of the identity as a loving mother.

In the case of this woman, her identity as a mother was so strong that the conflict with her identity as an honest person was resolved without much apparent difficulty. When the alternative to one's identity as an honest person is based on another value having the same importance, the conflict may be more severe. This was evident in the following excerpt:

Q: How does this value of honesty affect the way you see yourself?

R: Sometimes it's good, and sometimes it's not so good. Sometimes people aren't looking for an honest answer, and there am I giving it, and I may have offended. Sometimes I don't know how to put it in its right perspective. I could see myself as being a little cold that way, and really, when somebody asks you something, you should try to read into it if they're really looking for a real honest answer or sort of a compromise.

Q: So, I think you're saying that being honest sometimes makes you feel cold.

R: I mean, there's the honesty when you won't steal out of the cash register, and there's the honesty when your best friend says "Do you like my new hairdo, isn't it just great?" Uhh, you know, those are two different types. I would be the one who would say "Yuk" and I'd hurt the person's feelings.

. . .

Q: What might you do differently if you didn't have this value?

R: I don't know. I don't know what I would do differently. I wouldn't be as honest, I guess. The opposite. I don't know how. I'm not saying that everybody I know isn't the same way. I don't know what I would do differently.

This respondent's means of resolving her conflict between honesty and compassion was to favor compassion, although she does not really seem convinced that she would behave differently than she does at present. One means that she uses to convince herself that being less honest with other people would not really be such a violation of her identity as an honest person is to delineate subtle lines of demarcation between honesty and dishonesty. It is dishonest to steal, but not to distort the "true" answer to a friend's question. A similar sort of fine-tuned distinction was evident in the next respondent's statement:

R: . . . I try to be totally honest with people up to the point, if I'm talking to a stranger, I'm totally honest with that person up to the point of hurting their feelings and I have to, because how do you know when you are going to hurt someone's feelings except obviously they get all upset. If you don't know the person what do you care, anyway? With my friends, I may make a suggestion and I know that we've talked about that, so I know I can do it . . .

Here, the respondent distinguishes between whose feeling she would care about hurting, and whose feelings she would not care about hurting by being honest. Another method of handling this dilemma is to regard as a learning experience encounters with people in which values and consideration are pitted against one another:

Q: Do you ever have any doubts or questions about your values?

R: Sometimes. Yes.

Q: Could you tell me something about what they are?

R: My doubts?

Q: Um hum.

R: When I think I'm being honest and upright, and relating to a person the way I think I'm coming across, and I'm not. Then I try to question how I came across and what I've done wrong. I guess somebody gets upset with you and that's not really what you meant. You know, it's like, how did I come across, that that person was upset? I must have come across differently, and maybe I should have approached the subject differently, or maybe I shouldn't have approached the subject at all, and I try to relate from that point.

Q: Have you been doubting the value of honesty or being forthright?

R: No, I'm just questioning the approach.

Q: Whether you're carrying it off as well?

R: As well as I thought I could; just like everybody's needs are different. It's like, if I said something to you now, and something to you in 10 minutes, my tone of voice, your mental attitude, whatever, could change the full meaning of it and that's the type of thing, being able to read a person before you speak to them.

This respondent's solution to the conflict was to change herself rather than to change her definition of what was honest and what was dishonest. In trying out new behaviors, and evaluating the results, she was engaging in a form of self-evaluation that approaches the evaluating alternatives form of identity accommodation. She was not examining alternatives to her dual and potentially conflicting values of honesty and not being overly critical of people. Instead, the respondent was examining alternatives to her identity as a person who was perceived favorably by those with whom she interacted. Experiences that disconfirmed this identity were used as the basis for trying to find a combination of values that would allow the respondent to obtain a closer match between her identity and future interactions with other people.

From the cases presented here, it can be seen that there is not a straightforward relationship between being honest with others and honest with oneself if the individual also places a value on being considerate in interpersonal relations. The inherent conflict between these values was so strong that the respondents who observed such a combination within their own identities were among the most self-doubting of the sample. The straightforward concern with either honesty or consideration alone leads to fewer doubts about one's values. People who regard themselves as honest or considerate may still have doubts about how well they carry out their value in practice. However, they are spared the burden of indecision and ambivalence regarding what their identity should be.

Having examined honesty as a value, and honesty as it may interfere with consideration for the feelings of others, the identities of people who valued only consideration for others can now be explored. Like honesty, consideration of other people was a widely endorsed value. Also, like honesty, consideration was a value that was heavily bound to the contexts of work and family.

Values in Interpersonal Relationships

Having good interpersonal relationships in which the feelings of other people were the primary target of concern was the only value or at least a primary one of 19 women and 26 men. An additional group of 16 women and 7 men regarded having good family relationships in particular to be a primary value. This group of respondents included only those who saw no potential conflict between being honest and being considerate. Even the 8 women and 7 men who had also mentioned honesty as being important did not give any reasons for a problem to exist in being both honest and considerate. Their unambivalent endorsement of relationship values was due either to a clear preference for one or the other or because they were not aware of any incompatibility between the two. The individuals whose identities were based on the values of consideration and kindness saw these values not only as a central feature of their relationships with others, but also as a central feature of their own regard for themselves.

THE GOLDEN RULE

"Do unto others as you would have them do unto you." Although people who abide consistently by this value are regarded as paragons of virtue, their behavior can be interpreted in another, less flattering, manner. Those who behave kindly and considerately toward others may stand to gain some real, practical benefits as a result of their actions. If they deliberately set out with this intention in mind, their kindness may be seen as a form of manipulation. Even without such diabolical premeditation, the individual may interpret the Golden Rule with regard to the cost-benefit ratios attached to being kind and generous in actions and attitudes. The individual who takes this stance has a value based on the principles of exchange in the marketplace rather than a value based on empathy for the needs and feeling of others. Because of its emphasis on results that accrue to the self, the exchange interpretation of the Golden Rule may be regarded as extrinsic rather than intrinsic. As it turns out, this version of the Golden Rule is particularly evident in the context of work, where financial considerations are of such singular importance.

Out of the total of 13 respondents (4 women and 9 men) who regarded the Golden Rule to be a primary value, 8 (1 woman and 7 men) expressed an exchange interpretations in their statements. This particular version of the Golden Rule took several forms, but all respondents shared the same desire to protect their own self-interests by "doing unto others." The self-interests that they wished to protect, moreover, were those that related to their work.

The first form that this materialistic interpretation took was to reword the Golden Rule into negative or defensive terms:

R: I believe very deeply in the Golden Rule, do unto others, or sometimes as it's stated, do not unto others that which you would not have them do unto you . . .

This respondent recently had something done "unto" him; he is the executive described in Chapter 9 whose identity as a competent worker had suffered greatly as a result of the radical reorganization of his place of employment. Perhaps reflecting the bitterness associated with this experience towards his company, the respondent continued the description of his values as follows:

R: . . . I believe in that. I also find myself wanting to get even. It probably has to do with a sense of honor . . .

By "sense of honor," the respondent seems to be making an oblique reference to what he had earlier described as a "loss to my ego" resulting from the unkind treatment he had received. Another respondent shared this sense of bitterness toward his place of employment regarding his position within the organization. He expressed a slightly different variation of the "negative" Golden Rule:

R: ... Leaving the other guy alone. Don't know if it's the simple case of the Golden Rule, or what you want to call it. Live and let live.

Part of this respondent's bitterness was directed at one of his sons, who the respondent regarded as being "selfish, self-centered, and egotistical; . . . somewhere out there the world owes him a living." However, some of this motivation attributed to the son appeared to be shared by the father, although the father regarded the son as being "diametrically opposed to me in about everything." The respondent harkened back to his Work Identity interview, in which identity assimilation was used to protect his sense of competence, by claiming pride in not having played "the game" of his bosses in order to get ahead:

Q: How do your values affect the way you see yourself?
R: I feel that I can look myself in the mirror. I may say "dummy" but I can stare back and not be ashamed. Maybe I haven't been as successful as I'd like to be. But like Frank Sinatra said, "I did it my way." Even if it wasn't right.

Despite his protests to the contrary, the phrase "my way" does express a certain degree of egotism, the quality he abhorred in his son. The respondent also was greatly concerned about any of his children "getting in trouble with the law." However, this concern seems to be more one that he has about himself rather than about his children. As a youngster, the respondent had been a member of "one of the toughest gangs in the area," and had been "knifed a few times." In this next sequence of questions and answers, the respondent reveals quite clearly that now, as an adult, his concerns about his children represent his own fantasies about breaking the law:

Q: Are there things you would do otherwise if it weren't for these values?
R: Oh, probably would be in some kind of shady deal somewhere or other. I never felt the risk was worth it.
Q: Do you ever consider having a different set of values?
R: Yeah. (laughs) When I pick up the paper and see these guys embezzle half a million and they get 3 years probation or something.
Q: Have you actively thought about changing your values?
R: No.
Q: Why? What keeps you from doing it?
R: The main thing that keeps me from doing it, well, if I was in a valley and money was really tight. If I was in a bummer and someone came to me with the right opportunity. I guess human nature what it is, you'd have to give it more thought than normally.
Q: Which way would you swing?
R: (Laughs) I guess I wouldn't.

The respondent's emphatic assertions that he would not change his values conflict greatly with his apparent fascination over making money illegally. This use of the projection form of identity assimilation makes it possible for the respondent to preserve his identity as a good person who abides by his version of the Golden Rule.

The connection with work identity in this respondent's statements about his values seems much weaker in this set of questions than in the "my way" response. The only possible link is that the respondent's occasional flights into thoughts of becoming an embezzler represent his desire to make more money and take a stab at his company in the same blow. It also appears that the Golden Rule has become translated, at this point, into the value of honesty. The respondent appears to equate the two by regarding the Golden Rule as a basis for not infringing on the rights or property of others.

The next form of the extrinsic interpretation of the Golden Rule represents a considerably more straightforward concern with material rewards. This is the statement of the respondent who was described in Chapter 9 as very eager to become financially independent in order to promote his "creative" interests. In the course of the Work Identity interview, the respondent had made vague references to establishing contacts with people who could be of use to him in achieving his career goals. Knowing this about his work identity helps to interpret what he means in his statement of the Golden Rule:

R: That main one, do unto others, trying to reap what you sow. I try to sow a positive seed. I have a strong belief that all the seeds I've planted will eventually blossom.

Another respondent expressed a similar "investment" sort of attitude in his statement of values, but it was oriented toward his parents and friends:

Q: Could you describe for me your major values, the principles you try to live life for?
R: It comes right down to if I can help somebody, I'm going to help them. Someday I may need it. It's like with my family, I don't have to help them, but when I grew up I had everything I could possibly want and now that it's gone, why shouldn't I return it?. . . If friends need money, they've got it. Some day I may need it . . . If you don't give it, you are not going to get it.

The latter part of this response provides the lead-in to an analysis of the relationship between the respondent's identity in work and identity with regard to values. In his Work Identity interview, he described an earnest desire to start his own business: "I will never sit behind a desk 9 to 5 again." It turns out that the most likely route toward this goal involves having his "friend" make him a partner. It is not unreasonable to suspect that this may be the same friend referred to in the above excerpt.

How can these individuals, who espouse the extrinsic form of the Golden Rule, maintain favorable identities regarding their values? With values so transparently materialistic, it would seem that they would find it difficult to justify such an extreme perversion of the Golden Rule. This respondent described his identity regarding his values in terms that suggest an answer to this question:

Q: Does this value affect the way that you feel about yourself?
R: I feel pretty good about myself. I don't think I'm a nasty person.

This statement seems to reflect the use of identity assimilation in the form of self-justification. In this way, the respondent can avoid thinking about the discrepancy between his manipulative behaviors and his identity as a person who follows one of Western society's most hallowed principles. However, the respondent also had adopted the more intrinsic version of the Golden Rule in regard to another aspect of his work identity as a bartender:

Q: How does belief in your value affect what you do in everyday life, in your decision making, interactions with friends, and so on?

R: I have to put myself in their shoes once in a while. Sometimes I don't always agree with what they want to do or what they're thinking, or what they are doing. They get my viewpoint, it comes across pretty strong. You're basically a philosopher when you're behind the bar. They always come to you with their problems.

There is a definite interaction between an intrinsic feature of the respondent's work and the intrinsic interpretation of the Golden Rule based on principles of empathy rather than exchange. This interaction appears to involve a form of identity accommodation through which the respondent has changed his own identity regarding his values as a function of his work identity as a person who works with people.

The blending of intrinsic and extrinsic definitions of the Golden Rule regarding work was based on a different set of considerations by another respondent, who worked in the building trade. His version of the Golden Rule was definitely based on the intrinsic considerations of maintaining good relationships:

R: ... The primary values, fair play, treat everyone equal, and try to get along with everybody on the job, your friends and neighbors... I think it's the Golden Rule, or whatever you want to call it.

This respondent's experiences of being fair on the job influenced his identity as a person who professed the value of the Golden Rule: "It's given me a whole new different attitude on life." The extrinsic part of his value, though, remained implicit in his statements. By being fair with his competitors and "friends" alike, he could make his own position at work much more favorable as he acquired a good reputation in the business.

It is possible that because of the extrinsic meaning always attached to work and work-related interactions with people, there can be no intrinsic version of the Golden Rule that applies in this context. Similarly, because an adult's work identity can never be completely intrinsic, it is doubtful that any relationships between work identity and belief in the Golden Rule can be based on purely intrinsic considerations. Should an individual appear to have an intrinsic definition of the Golden Rule as applied to work, it probably involves at least some identity assimilation as a means of maintaining a favorable (i.e., non-materialistic) identity regarding values.

The intrinsic interpretation of the Golden Rule is that it is important to empathize with the other person's position because only then can one behave in a truly kind and helpful manner. There is no other benefit associated with kindness than the knowledge that the individual is being considerate of someone else's feelings. This knowledge can then feed into an identity as a person who believes in humanitarian values, an identity that will almost invariably be favorably interpreted. The Golden Rule, in its intrinsic form, was succinctly stated in the following excerpt:

R: My main value would be to be the best person that you can be, to be kind and a thoughtful person. Treat people how you would want them to treat you, I think, and be kind.

The origin of her value was described by this respondent as emerging within the context of her family:

Q: Do you have any idea how this value developed?
R: I don't know, through the years bringing up children, I think you try to keep your children, learn from experience and how their parents are. It's just natural to try and be that type of person.

This statement is consistent with the expectation that, compared to work, there is a much more solid basis for a relationship between the Golden Rule as interpreted intrinsically and the individual's experiences in the family. The family identities of the adults in the sample, even when appearing to have a strong extrinsic basis, were shown in Chapters 3 and 4 to be ultimately tied in with intrinsic factors. Therefore, the adult's identity as one who treats others considerately should be strongly related to family identity. However, this respondent was the only one in the sample who specifically related her identity regarding the Golden Rule to her family identity. It is possible that the quid pro quo nature of the Golden Rule, even in its intrinsic form, is inherently so laden with the idea of exchange that it is not generally seen as relevant to family identity. To find the value that is associated with family identity, it is necessary to define relationship values in broader terms that involve a different form of reciprocity based strictly on feelings. Such relationship values characterized not only the family, but also a general category of interpersonal involvements. These more general values of love, kindness, consideration, and forgiveness form a group that share the quality of charity toward others, or "love thy neighbor."

LOVE THY NEIGHBOR

The traditional injunction from Jesus Christ to "love thy neighbor as thyself" aptly covers a range of relationship values that were mentioned with considerable frequency among the respondents (7 women and 9 men), in both secular and nonsecular terms. The following statement is a fairly accurate representation of this value:

R: I suppose it's trying to get along with other people, to overlook their faults and hope they overlook yours, consideration for someone else, someone else's feelings, likes or dislikes. It makes it much easier to get along with everybody. Regard someone else's feelings.

Another respondent expressed some of these same ideas but with considerably more detail and animation:

R: . . . it all comes down to love thy neighbor, right? I find myself sometimes, just at work today, and being Christian, I think of this all the time. You can smile at somebody and say "Hi, how are you doing?" but if in your heart you're cursing that person, you might as well not even say hello to them because you are a hypocrite. Like at work, I was thinking "Oh, that dummy, look what he's doing," but then I stopped dead in my tracks and I said "Well, I was criticizing him for what I do sometimes, I'm no better than he is, so shut up," you know, so I stopped thinking that, okay? Most of the faults that we see other people have are our faults and we are criticizing ourselves. I see so many people that don't get along with each other. You know, honest relationships, that's what living is, relationships with one another, right? You have to forgive people . . .

Q: So, how important to you is the value of consideration?

R: Numero uno. Number 1 all the time, 100%. I can't stress that enough, I get so excited when I talk about that.

Part of the respondent's animation may have been accounted for not by the situation at work he referred to, but by his frustration with a flawed marital relationship:

R: . . . And that tells me, she says she loves me, right? Well, like the good Lord said, and we're both Christians, how can a Christian think sometimes the way they do? They're supposed to be Christians. You're not going to heaven just because you believe in the Lord. It's what you do that counts.

This remark was made in the middle of a long commentary about what he perceived to be his wife's overcompulsiveness (described in Chapter 3). It is this quality in her, as well as what he regards as her strong temper, that he is so unhappy with in his marriage. There is, then, a glaring incongruity between his lack of patience or forgiveness toward his wife, as shown in the Family interview, and his identity as a Christian, as shown in the Values interview. It can only be accounted for by his use of identity assimilation regarding his identity as a husband, and his inability to admit to flaws in his own behavior in his interactions with his wife.

Another man described his value of charity as a part of his identity that developed over time rather than as an immutable belief carried with him from his religion or his upbringing:

Q: Could you describe for me your major values and principles you try to live life for?

R: Well, that's a pretty good question. I guess everybody looks at that, what your life really is for, and it's something I've thought about a lot . . . I guess the principle that I try to live for is just being, try and be as good to everybody as you can . . . Just try and be able to relate to everybody, I guess would be a principle in life, because you can learn a lot about life through other people and there's nobody that has experiences like you've had . . .

Q: How strongly do you feel about this value?

R: I feel very strongly because I'm sure I have enemies. Who doesn't? I try and have everybody like me if it's at all possible. If somebody does me wrong or I do somebody wrong I always try to forgive and forget. It's not going to do you any good to hold grudges or anything, so you might as well learn to live with everybody.

Q: How do you suppose you developed this particular value?

R: I guess it comes with age. I don't know . . . Not that I'm a whole lot different than I was
before, but maybe a little wiser I guess . . .

Q: So you think you developed it as an adult then?

R: Yeah, I guess so. I never tried to put anybody over or anything and I always try to be
likeable, but not everybody's going to like me. I guess it developed more as I became
older.

This respondent's attitude toward the value of charity was unusual in that he
described a process of identity accommodation through which he arrived at his
identity, and also was able to evaluate this identity at the present time for flaws
in the way he implemented it, or how other people regarded him.

In general, as in the case of honesty, the value of charity tended to draw out
assimilative reactions on the part of respondents who described themselves as
having this identity. The most common form of identity assimilation was self-
justification, seen in the case of the respondent just described. Other statements
exemplifying self-justification involved making comparisons of oneself with a
more generalized group of "other" people who did not follow this value:

R: . . . I look back now and I'm glad that I had those values because I think those values
have changed just from my generation to the next . . . I've gone in the schools and I see
that the discipline is not there, the respect between the teacher and the student. It
bothers me because it was there when I was going and it isn't now. Just that part right
there, I can see the difference in the values. Kids nowadays are different from us.

This respondent, at the age of only 34 years, already perceived a generation gap
between herself and her teenage children's cohort. In addition to her rigidity
about the "old days" being better than the present, there is also a considerable
degree of self-justification. Simple arithmetic shows that this respondent's generation was the youth of the 1960s. The behaviors of young people from her generation were hardly considered to be as respectful of others, including teachers, as
the respondent claimed.

An interesting counterpoint to this respondent's perspective is provided by a
53-year-old woman lamenting on the general lack of caring displayed by "society
in general":

Q: What about these values is important to you?

R: Well, I don't think there's enough right now, and I think we have to bring some of this
back. To me, society is the "me" generation of the late 60s and 70s and has to be
turned around. It can't all depend on what one individual wants; it's got to be good for
everbody.

And, reflecting her own use of self-justification, the respondent described herself
in the following terms:

Q: How do the values that you hold affect the decision that you make?

R: I try to be fair. I try to understand feelings and the situation at hand. I try to devote
my time so that I can do some of the things that might help other people when they're
in difficult situations.

Although she admits to not being the "perfect person," the respondent neverthe-less appears to hold her own values in considerably higher regard than those of other "citizens of this country." In addition, her attitude toward change reflects the defensive rigidity form of identity assimilation:

Q: What might you do differently if you didn't have these values?
R: They're so much a part of me, I have no idea. That's just the way I am. I don't know what I'd do otherwise.

Identity assimilation as a means of projecting a positive image of one's identity with regard to values may be applied to one's children, if they are seen as an extension of the individual's own identity. The following respondent shows this particular transformation of self-justification:

Q: How strongly do you feel about this value?
R: I feel it is very important, very important, because I think it's probably one of the things I'm a little bit disturbed with young people today is the fact that they're, my chil-dren are not,...the young people today are more willing to accept than to give. And this bothers me. It really does. And I think, I don't know whether I'm trying too hard, but I really feel nobody can ever give too much of themselves. I really don't.

In addition to self-justification about her own children, this respondent presents a glowing picture of how she herself has maintained a flawless identity as a help-ful person:

Q: Do you have any idea when that value became important to you, or how you devel-oped it?
R: No, I really don't, because I have always had that feeling for a long time. From the time I was in high school, I would always take in stray cats and dogs and try to help other children. I used to babysit for neighbors next door. As I mentioned before, I love people.
Q: How do your values affect the way you feel about yourself?
R: Well, that's a good question, because sometimes I think I get wrapped up in other peo-ple and sometimes forget about myself, which my spouse has pointed out to me differ-ent times. Every once in a while I have to stop and take a little time and think "Okay, this is time to think about myself."

The respondent's self-portrayal is as a person who is so completely living up to her value of helping others that it leaves her little opportunity to think about herself. It is possible that she really does question this value, as indicated by her last statement. In a later explication of this statement, though, she reveals that the concern is not so much over her values as it is over the fact that she has been overeating:

R: A good example of that is right at the present time, I have been baking and cooking and what not, handing out food to different people, and while I'm doing that I'm eating myself, and yet deep down I am so mad at myself because I gained so much weight that I'm very unhappy with myself...I'm involved in so many things up at church, and everytime we go to a meeting somebody has goodies...I always have to try every-thing out.

The questions that the respondent has are serious, to be sure, but they are not questions about values per se. This respondent, and the two that preceded her, remain examples of the various forms that identity assimilation can take in order to help an individual maintain a favorable identity as a person who implements his or her values. These three cases, moreover, are all from women who are each devoting themselves primarily to their families. Even though two of them work part-time, they regard this work as important in order to help their families and they define their identities primarily as mothers and homemakers. The value of selflessness expressed by these respondents, and their defensive attitude toward this value, is consistent with the approach taken by the full-time homemakers in the sample regarding their work identities. The identities regarding values of the respondents summarized here help to reinforce their identities as people who regard devotion to others as their primary work.

It is when the individual's identity regarding values begins to coalesce with the identity in the family that the value "Love thy neighbor" becomes translated into a value that is expressed specifically toward family members. This form of the value of charity is examined next.

CARING FOR FAMILY

The potential for importance of the family to dominate the individual's identity is realized in people for whom the value of caring for the family is the primary goal in life. The respondents who chose this value for themselves were ones in whom there was a total melding of a sense of individual purpose in life with the desire to ensure the well-being of the family. This fusion of the family with the individual's identity is apparent in the following excerpt:

Q: Could you describe for me your major values and principles that you try to live life for?
R: Well, right now, when I was a kid I was living for myself and right now I'm living for my family . . . I'm living my life to give my family a home, give my family a good place to live, a good church to go to, and it's really a simple life. I like to see them have a good time once in a while and I like to be with them. I like to stay home. I don't like to go out at night with other people all the time like I see some people doing. I come straight home from work. I don't stop at a bar.

It seems that the individual with this value derives not only purpose in life but a feeling of pleasure from implementing this value. In the next excerpt from another respondent whose primary value is caring for family, this can be clearly seen:

R: . . . I feel that if I'm happy first with my wife and our future kids, that's number one. That's the most valuable thing that I could have.
Q: What to you is especially important about that?
R: That I would be happy with that. That would, as far as my existence goes, would be my whole life. That would keep me happy no matter what. I wouldn't want anything more.

The value of caring for family members is not, then, a totally selfless one. The individual who holds this value is similar to those respondents whose family identity was based on a sense of personal gratification. In addition, by placing personal gratification contingent upon the presence of other people and their appearance of happiness and well-being, the individual's self-evaluation becomes dependent upon their fate. It then becomes relatively simple to enlist the identity assimilation process. When loved ones fail to prosper, the individual can claim it to be due to their weakness, and when they succeed the individual can bask in their reflected glory. There is a price to be paid, however, for this sense of comfort and the protection provided by identity assimilation. Identity accommodation becomes a much more difficult process to invoke when the individual's identity is based on valuing the family. To admit to failure involves not only the awareness of one's own weakness, but also the pain of knowing that someone who is loved has suffered a setback.

The potential for this kind of identity to lead to a state of disequilibrium because of the difficulty of using identity accommodation is evidenced in the case of the next respondent. Her particular version of the value of caring for her family was focused on the children receiving a good education and being able to "do well in life." It appeared, however, that this value was not being completely fulfilled:

Q: How strongly do you feel about that value?
R: It's very important. I hope my son does well. Right now he's not the greatest student in the world, but he still may do well in the future.

Her values regarding her children's education were based on a desire to see them not have to "struggle" as she did when she was young. There are, then, these two pieces of evidence regarding her values. One is that she wants very badly for her children to have a better life than she did, and the second is that her son is not doing well enough in school to provide her with a guarantee that this will happen. This disparity between her identity and her experience is so difficult for her to reconcile through identity accommodation that she uses identity assimilation to avoid confronting the issue. The following exchange was one of the more dramatic instances of defensive rigidity encountered in all of the interviews:

Q: How do your values affect the way you feel about yourself?
R: If they do well, I feel good, it makes me feel good, I mean better. These questions are tricky.
Q: That's okay. It's not what you expected?
R: Right. I like to give simple answers.
Q: What kinds of things do you do especially because of your values?
R: I don't know what you mean.
Q: Does the belief in the value you have in regards to your children and their education, their ultimate success, cause you to do anything you would not do otherwise?
R: I can't answer that. I really can't. I don't know what to say.
Q: Let me try another one. How does the belief in your values affect what you do in your everyday life?
R: You've caught me on a bad day. I've got a headache. I've been taking Tylenol and I've been taking it for 4 days straight. Let's see. Just say that one more time and I'll really concentrate. I'm wasting all your tape here.
Q: Don't worry about it.

R: I'm embarrassed because I can't answer. I'm an educated schoolteacher and I don't know how to answer your question.

Q: They are hard questions. People don't think of them every day, so that's fine. Don't worry about it. How does belief in your value, and we were talking specifically about the value of your children's education and their ultimate success, affect what you do in your everyday life?

R: This is it. I work hard. I work very hard so that I can keep my job so they can do well in school and not have to struggle like I did, I guess.

Q: That's fine. Do you ever consider having a different set of values?

R: No way.

Q: Do you have any doubts or questions about your values?

R: No, because I've lived this way all my life. I've just always been a hard worker and I expect my kids some day to be just as much of a hard worker and to succeed. I guess that's all.

The respondent's almost desperate attempts to avoid answering the question about the effect of her values on her everyday life seem to reflect the anxiety created by admitting that her son is not a good student. In the latter part of her response, she finally answers the question with self-justification about how hard she works. Just prior to that, though, her remark about being an "educated schoolteacher" suggests another reason for the difficulty she faces in admitting her son's failures to achieve. It is inconsistent with her own identity as not only someone who is educated, but as someone who *teaches* others, to confront the realization of her son's lack of interest in his own education process. This interpretation receives support from one of the respondent's first statements in the Values Identity interview:

R: . . . I think being a schoolteacher, it's very important, and I always did well in school and I want my kids to do well also, because it's very important. My job is very important to me and I intend to teach until they throw me out or until I get too old to move or not do a good job for my kids.

It was not only that the respondent had a job teaching others, but that she herself had been a good student, that made her disappointment with her son more poignant. In addition, her job itself was a major component of her identity for the intrinsic reason of being able to "help" others and because of the recognition that she received from her students: "They're happy, I'm happy, the principal's happy. And that makes me feel good, knowing that I'm doing a good job. It gives me a better self-image of myself."

The next respondent, whose values regarding her children's education were almost identical, was able to use identity accommodation to admit that her plans regarding her children were not working out as she had hoped:

Q: What is important about that to you?

R: I don't know why, but it is important. I wanted all the kids to go to college because I didn't go. My spouse had a little, I didn't have any. Their education was very important. I don't know whether it was because I wanted them to succeed a little bit sooner than what we did and not take 15 to 20 years before seeing the end of the rainbow. I don't know why. They're like your product and you want to see them have something better and quicker than I did. As it turned out, my oldest son disappointed me a little bit because he had a year of college and didn't like it. I was really down.

However, her son's behavior after that unsatisfactory year at college caused her to question her values regarding his education:

Q: It sounds like you tie together their education with their future success.
R: Right. And that may not be right either because I can see our son already having some success at 23.

Despite the signs that her values about education may not have been right, though, the respondent still admits, in answer to the next question, to having self-doubts about how she implemented her values:

Q: How do your values affect the way you feel about yourself?
R: . . . it isn't all materializing the way I want it to. Then I don't feel that I did my job right. That my husband and I lacked some kind of guidance to the kids. We should have put a little more pressure. I feel a little bit guilty.

In response to a later question, though, she expresses the opposite self-doubt:

Q: Do you think you might have any doubts in the future?
R: Probably. There are times now that I have doubts or questions when I sometimes see the by-product of myself in the children. That I've either done too much for them or have been overprotective . . . I see other kids turning out okay even though they didn't necessarily have a parent home doing all the things I did . . .

Her subsequent recognition that it is "too late" to do anything to resolve these questions may reflect identity assimilation, but it also reflects the reality that her children really are grown and she cannot reverse the clock to try things out differently. However, she did acknowledge that her values are "not necessarily right for everyone" and so at least has a nondefensive approach to her identity in this area.

    Why should one respondent be so defensive and the other so open about such a similar discrepancy between values and the behavior of children in not obtaining a college education? The first respondent was seen to have invested a great deal of her own identity regarding herself as a mother and as a teacher into her child's success. The second respondent's investment in her children was based on an identity only in the area of family. In addition, the second respondent did not have the same vested interest in having her children be well educated because she did not define herself as a well-educated person. When asked about the origins of her value, she admitted that "I always had that feeling of inferiority to college peers." In a way, she had less to lose by having a son who did not complete college, because it was less of a contradiction with her own experience. It would have helped her to compensate for her lack of education to have a college-educated son, but his failure to do so would not fly so directly in the face of a value she had worked to fulfill for herself.

    By contrasting these two respondents, a strong case can be made for the interpretation that individuals who regard as primary the care of their family, and in particular the success of their children, have a high investment of their own identities in the outcome of their children's efforts. This high investment can interfere with but not prevent the individual from using identity accommodation. When the child's success or failure reflect directly on another important feature of the parent's own identity in addition, identity accommodation can become almost impossible to engage in without extreme anguish at times of the children's failure. The coalescing of the work and family identity into one set of values, as seen in the first respondent, means an almost complete blending of his or her own identity with that of the child. The potential for identity accommodation to take place may increase as such an individual achieves a way of disentangling this combination of identities from one another. The separation of these identities may occur as the parent shifts attention to another child in the family, becomes less invested in the work identity, or finds a way to reduce identification with the child in question. Such a process may occur even when the child is successful in achieving the parent's goals, but it is more likely to take place when the child's failure creates a disequilibrium between identity and experiences.

In general, identity assimilation was much more prevalent in the respondent's descriptions of their values regarding their families than was identity accommodation. In addition to the examples already cited, there were several more cases of defensive rigidity and self-justification as well as some prime examples of lack of insight. For instance, the lack of insight form of identity assimilation was represented in the following excerpt:

R: I suppose it's the old corny bring up your children to be decent and honest, and be a good wife. I don't even think about these things. I just do them and don't think much about them if they're goals or not.

This kind of automaticity may emerge either from a very shallow sense of identity or from one that is so deeply engrained that no thought is required to carry it out. That the latter is the case is suggested by the defensive rigidity that generally accompanied such an identity, and statements to the effect that this is what the respondent had "always" wanted to do.

The predominance of identity assimilation in the case of an identity in the area of values that blends with family identity suggests that this kind of value penetrates deeply into the individual's total identity as a person. The penetration is even more complete when the identities in family, work, and values are all oriented around the same themes. To question the value of caring for children poses the potential for threatening the individual's entire basis for existence. It is therefore natural that identity assimilation is used to protect the individual from this threat. This identity process also gives meaning to the daily activities at work and at home that follow as a consequence from an identity as someone whose life is based on the value of caring for the family.

Values: Summing Up

Having explored the two basic values expressed by the adults in the sample, it is now time to reflect on some conclusions about values and identity. In the first place, it is apparent that the values of the adult are highly intertwined with beliefs regarding what is important in work and in the family. How the individual judges whether he or she is fulfilling life's purpose is therefore frequently based on performance in these sectors of the adult's identity. Values are rarely experienced as vague or abstract goals in life; instead, they are tightly bound to the views that adults have about their competence as workers and their ability to raise their children in a loving and supportive environment.

The second conclusion is that men and women are equally likely to derive a sense of basic purpose in life from fulfillment in the realm of family relationships. Although men were found more frequently than women to have the materialistic ideology of the Golden Rule, this tendency did not detract from the possibility for a man to have his identity heavily invested in the well-being of his family. This finding parallels the observations in Chapters 3 and 4 regarding a lack of sex differences in family identity. With regard to values, it appears that although men may think more in terms of the exchange mentality of the marketplace, they do not think any less in terms of the generativity principle of the home.

Finally, because of the strong implications that failure to achieve a purpose in life would have, there is a striking tendency for individuals to defend their identities with identity assimilation regarding their values. The examples analyzed in this chapter illustrate amply just how prevalent is the identity assimilation process. These examples were not intended to show the respondents to be hypocrites or liars. It is unlikely that the respondents would regard themselves in this cynical way, and to apply the label of hypocrite to them is to miss the point. The point is that the respondents believe themselves to be following a purpose in life that is consistent with their identities as workers, parents, spouses, and moral citizens. If they (and we) appear to be ignoring gaps between values and behavior, then they (and we) are simply expressing a normal tendency to cope with incongruity by reducing it in the easiest way possible.

The occasional glimpses of self-doubts and questionings may appear to the observer to be refreshing doses of honesty that cast aspersions on the more defensive members of the sample. However, the reflections of these individuals are no more "honest" than those of their assimilative counterparts. The self-doubts and evaluations that make up the identity accommodation process may lead to growth and a "better" adaptation to experiences, but the motivations of those who show identity accommodation are the same as those of the individuals who adapt to their experiences with assimilation. Both processes are methods that individuals use at different times in their adult lives to live at peace with themselves. This sense of peace is what comes from confirmation, however it is achieved, that their identities are being fulfilled in their experiences.

Appendix A
Adult Identity Process Interview*

Part I: Family Identity

1. Please tell me about your family.
   PROBE: What is your family position?
          Who in your family is important to you?
2. What is important to you about your family?
   PROBE: What is important to you about being a _____? (Ask for all questions described in Question 1.)
3. How do you feel about being a _____? (Ask for all positions described in Question 1.)
   PROBE: What do you especially like about being a _____?
          What do you especially dislike about being a _____?
4. How does being a _____ affect the way you feel about yourself as a person? (Ask for all positions described in Question 1.)
   PROBE: What effect does being a _____ have on the way you feel about yourself as a person?
5. How does being a _____ affect the things you do in your everyday life? (Ask for all positions described in Question 1.)
   PROBE: Do you do anything especially because of your being a _____?
6. Are you presently considering any alternatives to your present family involvement as a _____? (Ask for all positions described in Question 1.)
   PROBE: Do you ever think of ways your family situation could be different?
   IF ANSWER TO QUESTION #6 IS "YES" GO TO QUESTIONS 7–10.
   IF ANSWER TO QUESTION #6 IS "NO" GO TO QUESTIONS 11–15.
   ASK ABOUT ALL FAMILY POSITIONS DESCRIBED IN QUESTION 1.
7. What alternatives are you considering?
   PROBE: What other family situation are you thinking about?
8. Why are you considering this alternative? (Ask about all alternatives being considered.)

---

*The structure of the interview is based on Waterman (1980).

PROBE: What is it about your situation that leads you to think about making a change?

9. How seriously are you considering this alternative? (Ask about all alternatives that are being considered.)

    PROBE: How likely is it that you will make this change?

    How ready are you to decide what to do?

    Do you think you will really make this change?

10. How are you trying to work this out for yourself? (Ask about all alternatives that are being considered.)

    PROBE: What are you doing now to help you decide?

    Have you done anything to help you make this decision?

    How are you trying to figure out what to do?

    GO TO WORK SECTION OF THE INTERVIEW

11. Why aren't you considering any alternatives?

    PROBE: Why don't you think you will make any changes?

12. Have you ever thought about any alternatives in the past?

    PROBE: Have you ever thought about having a different family situation than the one you have now?

    How did you reach your present position?

13. Do you think you might consider alternatives in the future?

    PROBE: Do you think it's possible you'll make a change in the future?

    Do you think your family situation will remain the same as it is now?

14. Is there anything that keeps you from considering alternatives now?

    PROBE: Is there any reason why you don't consider alternatives?

    What is it about your present situation that keeps you from wanting to change?

15. Do you have any questions or doubts about your position as a _____? (Ask for all positions described in Question 1.)

    PROBE: Do you ever wonder about your feelings about being a _____?

    IF YES: 15a. What is the nature of your questions/doubts?

    15b. How serious are these questions/doubts?

    15c. What do you question/doubt?

    IF NO: 15d. Why not?

    15e. What would make you question or doubt your feelings about being a _____? (Ask for all positions described in Question 1.)

    GO TO WORK SECTION OF INTERVIEW

Part II: Work Identity

1. What is your current employment status?

    PROBE: What is your current work situation?

    What do you do for a living?

2. What is important to you about your work as a _____?
   PROBE: What is important to you about being a _____?
3. How do you feel about being a _____?
   PROBE: What do you especially like about being a _____?
   What do you especially dislike about being a _____?
4. How does being a _____ affect the way you feel about yourself as a person?
   PROBE: What effect does being a _____ have on the way you feel about yourself as a person?
5. How does being a _____ affect the things you do in your every-day life?
   PROBE: Do you do anything especially because of your being a _____?
6. Are you presently considering any alternatives to your present work as a _____?
   PROBE: Do you ever think of ways your work situation could be different?
   IF ANSWER TO QUESTION #6 IS "YES" GO TO QUESTIONS 7–10.
   IF ANSWER TO QUESTION #6 IS "NO" GO TO QUESTIONS 11–15.
7. What alternatives are you considering?
   PROBE: What other work situation are you thinking about?
8. Why are you considering this alternative? (Ask about all alternatives being considered.)
   PROBE: What is it about your situation that leads you to think about making a change?
9. How seriously are you considering this alternative? (Ask about all alterna-tives that are being considered.)
   PROBE: How likely is it that you will make this change?
   How ready are you to decide what to do?
   Do you think you will really make this change?
10. How are you trying to work this out for yourself? (Ask about all alterna-tives that are being considered.)
    PROBE: What are you doing now to help you decide?
    Have you done anything to help you make this decision?
    How are you trying to figure out what to do?
    GO TO AGE SECTION OF THE INTERVIEW
11. Why aren't you considering any alternatives?
    PROBE: Why don't you think you will make any changes?
12. Have you ever thought about any alternatives in the past?
    PROBE: Have you ever thought about having a different work situation than the one you have now?
    How did you reach your present position?
13. Do you think you might consider alternatives in the future?
    PROBE: Do you think it's possible you'll make a change in the future?
    Do you think your work situation will remain the same as it is now?

14. Is there anything that keeps you from considering alternatives now?
    PROBE: Is there any reason why you don't consider alternatives?
    What is it about your present situation that keeps you from wanting to change?
15. Do you have any questions or doubts about your position as a
    _____?
    PROBE: Do you ever wonder about your feelings about being a
    _____?

    IF YES: 15a. What is the nature of your questions/doubts?
    15b. How serious are these questions/doubts?
    15c. What do you question/doubt?
    IF NO: 15d. Why not?
    15e. What would make you question or doubt your feelings about being a _____?
    GO TO AGE SECTION OF THE INTERVIEW

Part III: Age Identity

1. What is your age?
2. How do you feel about your age?
   PROBE: How do you feel about the fact that you're _____ years old?
3. How important to you is your age?
   PROBE: How important to you is the fact that you're _____ years old?
4. What about your age is important to you?
   PROBE: What things do you think about when you think about age?
   What kinds of things do you focus on when you think about being _____?
   What do you think is important about the fact that you're _____?
   IF AGE NOT IMPORTANT: Why isn't your age important to you?
5. How does being _____ years old make you feel about yourself as a person?
   PROBE: How does the fact that you're _____ years old make you feel about yourself?
   What effect does your age have on the way you view yourself in general?
6. Do you think your views about your age are changing?
   PROBE: Do you have any questions about the way you feel about your age?
   IF ANSWER TO QUESTION #6 IS "YES" GO TO QUESTIONS 7–8.
   IF ANSWER TO QUESTION #6 IS "NO" GO TO QUESTIONS 9–11.
7. How are they changing?/What questions do you have?

PROBE: What is it about your feelings that is changing?

What is is about your feeling that you are questioning?

8. How are you trying to work this out for yourself?

PROBE: What are you trying to do to work this out?

GO TO VALUES SECTION OF THE INTERVIEW

9. Why is this?

PROBE: Why aren't they changing?

Why don't you have any questions?

10. Have your feelings about age ever changed before?

PROBE: Have you ever had any questions about age?

IF YES: 10a. What did you think about then?

PROBE: What changes did you make then?

What did you question?

IF NO: 10b. Why not?

PROBE: Why haven't your feelings ever changed?

Why haven't you had questions?

11. Do you think your feelings about age are likely to change in the future?

PROBE: Do you think you will ever have questions about your age in the future?

IF YES: 11a. What do you think might change?

PROBE: What questions do you think you might have?

IF NO: 11b. Why not?

PROBE: Why don't you think you will change?

GO TO VALUES SECTION OF INTERVIEW

Part IV: Values

1. Please describe for me your major values, the principles you try to live your life for.

PROBE: What is important to you in the way you try to live your life?

2. How strongly do you feel about your values?

PROBE: How important to you is it that you follow this value?

3. What to you is especially important about your values?

PROBE: Why do you think this value is important?

4. How do your values affect the way you feel about yourself as a person?

PROBE: Do you judge yourself by your values? How do you come out on this?

5. What kinds of things do you do especially because of your values?

PROBE: Does belief in this value cause you to do anything you wouldn't otherwise do?

How does belief in your values affect what you do in your everyday life?

6. Do you think your values are changing?

   PROBE: Do you have any questions or doubts about your values?

   IF ANSWER TO QUESTION #6 IS "YES" GO TO QUESTIONS 7-8.

   IF ANSWER TO QUESTION #6 IS "NO" GO TO QUESTIONS 9-11.

7. How are they changing?

   What questions do you have?

   PROBE: What is it about your values that is changing?

   What is it about your values that you are questioning?

8. How are you trying to work this out for yourself?

   PROBE: How seriously are you thinking about changing?

   How serious are these questions for you now?

   END OF THE INTERVIEW

9. Why is this?

   PROBE: Why aren't they changing?

   Why don't you have any questions?

10. Have your values ever changed before?

   PROBE: Have you ever had questions about your values?

   IF YES: 10a. What changed?

   PROBE: What changes did you make then?

   What did you question?

   IF NO: 10b. Why not?

   PROBE: Why haven't your values changed?

   Why haven't you had questions?

11. Do you think your values are likely to change in the future?

   PROBE: Do you think you will ever have questions about your values in the future?

   IF YES: 11a. How do you think they might change?

   PROBE: What questions do you think you might have?

   IF NO: 11b. Why don't you think you will change?

   PROBE: Why don't you think you will have questions?

   END OF THE INTERVIEW

Appendix B
Methodology of the Adult
Identity Process Study

The investigation on which the empirical material on identity was gathered was conducted with the intention of relating autobiographical life histsory material to variables derived from the Adult Identity Interview described in Appendix A.[1] The life history–identity study was to be carried out on a sample stratified according to sex, age, and socioeconomic status, so that the respondents would represent a reasonably wide cross-section of adults living in the community. It was also intended that the sample be large enough to permit reasonable representation across the stratification variables, but of manageable size to make possible relatively intensive interviews with each respondent within a reasonably short time interval given the available funds. As it happened, the respondents represented a diverse group of individuals, but there were also numerous instances of similarity on important characteristics across age, sex, and socioeconomic lines.

Respondents

Sample Selection

The sample was selected from telephone director listings of a moderate-sized city in upstate New York, and its immediate suburbs. Participation of the respondents was solicited through a telephone follow-up to an initial information letter offering $20 for being interviewed for a 2- to 3-hour study of adult life.

Out of the 639 letters mailed, 282 (44.13%) households were reached by telephone. Of those households contacted, 26 persons (9.22%) were not available due to reported illness or hospitalization, because they had moved, or because they were deceased, and another 106 (37.59%) did not meet the sampling criteria of age, sex, or occupational status. A total of 56 (19.86% of the potential participants contacted) refused to participate (their demographic characteristics were not obtained), giving reasons such as not having the time, not being willing to disclose personal history, or presently having "problems." The final sample of 94 therefore represented one-third of the households reached by telephone, and

[1]Supported by the Spencer Foundation and a University of Rochester BRSG-SUB grant, W. Dale Dannefer, Co-Investigator.

TABLE B.1. Sample distribution by age and sex.

Age range	Men	Women
24–32	14	12
33–42	13	12
43–51	10	12
52–61	10	11
Total	47	47

almost two-thirds of the persons contacted who were eligible to participate. The sample selection and interviewing took place over a 9-month period from late in December, 1980 to early September, 1981.

DEMOGRAPHIC CHARACTERISTICS

The respondents' ages ranged from 24 to 61 at the time of testing, with the average age for men equal to 39.68 and 41.70 for women. The distribution of the sample by age group is presented in Table B.1. An attempt had originally been made to obtain an equal number of men and women distributed evenly by age and stratified by social class, but as is apparent from Table B.1, this sampling plan was not strictly followed. The reason for changing the sampling plan was that too many respondents who were willing to participate were being turned down as the cells became filled toward the end of the data collection period, and it was felt that the randomness of the sample was being compromised at that point.

The sample means on relevant demographic variables are shown in Table B.2. Occupational prestige and family socioeconomic status were calculated using Hollingshead's Four Factor Index (1979). As can be seen from Table B.2, men

TABLE B.2. Sample demographic characteristics by sex and age.[a]

Sex	Age	N	Years of education	Occupational prestige	Family SES	Family income	Years married[b]
Male	24–32	14	14.64(1.95)	5.50(2.06)	43.43(10.72)	13–16,999	4.44(2.50)
	33–42	13	14.62(2.31)	5.92(2.43)	44.23(12.86)	20–24,999	7.67(4.35)
	43–51	10	12.80(2.64)	5.50(1.75)	40.10(7.58)	17–19,999	20.88(4.48)
	52–61	10	14.50(3.91)	6.20(2.09)	46.50(11.72)	20–24,999	27.29(9.71)
Total		47					
Female	24–32	12	13.58(2.25)	5.57(2.13)	43.08(11.69)	17–19,999	5.10(2.63)
	33–42	12	14.17(1.68)	5.57(1.18)	43.58(10.77)	20–24,999	13.20(4.79)
	43–51	12	12.92(2.10)	5.75(1.71)	44.08(7.53)	25–34,999	27.88(3.79)
	52–61	11	13.45(2.39)	5.86(1.13)	47.73(10.33)	25–34,999	31.11(3.70)
Total		47					

[a] Data are given as means (standard deviations) except family income which is given as the mean range.
[b] The average number of years married was calculated only for those respondents who were married for the first time at the time of the interview.

TABLE B.3. Distribution of education by sex.

Highest level of Education	Men		Women	
	N	%	N	%
No high school degree	5	10.64	4	8.50
High school degree	11	23.40	18	38.30
Some college	13	27.66	13	27.66
College	10	21.28	8	17.02
Graduate school	8	17.02	4	8.50
Total	47		47	

and women had similar demographic characteristics. With the exception of years married, which showed a linear relationship to age, the four age groups within each sex were very similar on social background variables. Some exceptions to this general observation were the somewhat lower education of 43–51-year-old men compared to other men and the relatively higher education of 33–42-year-old women. The occupational prestige score of the oldest group of men was somewhat higher than that of the rest of the male sample, but the women's was very consistent across the entire age range. The largest gap in total family socio-economic status occurred between the 43–51-year-old and 52–61-year-old men, and among the women the oldest group also had the highest family socioeconomic status. None of these differences, however, were significant.

Education and Occupation

The distribution of highest educational attainment by sex is shown in Table B.3. As can be seen from this table, the sample was spread quite evenly across the middle three educational levels, with the majority having attained a high school degree. While it appears that men were represented more in the college and above

TABLE B.4. Distribution of occupational prestige category by sex.

Occupational prestige category	Men		Women[a]	
	N	%	N	%
Higher executives, major professionals	6	12.77	0	0
Administrators, lesser professionals	6	12.77	2	6.25
Small business owners, minor professionals	7	14.89	10	31.25
Technicians, semiprofessionals	8	17.02	5	15.63
Clerical and sales workers	3	6.38	9	28.13
Skilled workers, craftspersons	9	19.15	3	9.38
Machine operators and semiskilled workers	5	10.64	1	3.13
Unskilled workers	3	6.38	2	6.25
Total	47		32	

[a] For the women, the mean occupational prestige shown on Table B.2 did not include women who were full-time homemakers (whose occupational prestige was rated as 0 because no value for it is given on the Hollingshead Index).

TABLE B.5. Distribution of women's husbands' occupational prestige.

Occupational prestige category	Currently married	
	N	%
Higher executives, major professionals	6	13.04
Administrators, lesser professionals	6	13.04
Small business owners, minor professionals	8	17.39
Technicians, semiprofessionals	11	23.91
Clerical, salesworkers	0	0
Skilled workers, craftspersons	11	23.91
Machine operators, semiskilled workers	3	6.52
Unskilled workers	1	2.17
Total	46	

levels, and women in the high school degree category, the overall sex distribution was similar at all educational levels, $\chi^2(4) = 3.36, p > .05$.

The sample's occupational prestige ratings are shown in Table B.4. The mean occupational prestige score placed the respondents in the range of technicians and semiprofessionals (computer operators, managers, sales managers and representatives, and secretaries). As is apparent from Table B.4, the sample was clustered in the middle four levels of the scale (corresponding to values on Hollingshead's categorical scale of 7 through 4). While there were no overall differences between the two sexes in occupational prestige, it is apparent from Table B.4 that no women were represented in the highest occupational level. Moreover, more men were in the heavier labor categories (skilled and semiskilled workers) compared to women, who were more frequently in the clerical and sales occupations.

Although men and women were found not to differ in total family socioeconomic status, it was considered to be of interest to examine the distribution of occupational prestige categories of the women's husbands to compare to those of the men in the sample. These distributions are shown in Table B.5, which includes women who were presently married and those who were separated, divorced, or widowed. It can be seen from this table that, apart from the fact that

TABLE B.6. Distribution of family socioeconomic status by sex.

Socioeconomic status	Men		Women	
	N	%	N	%
Social Class I	9	19.15	9	19.15
Social Class II	21	44.68	24	51.06
Social Class III	11	23.40	10	21.28
Social Class IV	6	12.77	4	8.51
Total	47		47	

TABLE B.7. Distribution of marital status by sex.

Marital status	Men		Women	
	N	%	N	%
Single	7	14.89	1	2.13
Married	31	65.96	37	78.72
Separated and divorced	3	6.38	4	8.51
Remarried	4	8.51	4	8.51
Widowed	2	4.26	1	2.13
Total	47		47	

no husbands were clerical or sales workers, the distributions of husbands' occupations closely parallels those of the male respondents in the sample.

The socioeconomic status distribution by sex, shown in Table B.6, presents information to substantiate that already given; that is, that the sample was clustered in the middle levels of the occupation and education distributions, and that the sexes were essentially similar in social background factors.

Family Characteristics

The distribution of marital status by sex is shown in Table B.7. From this table, it is apparent that there were no sex differences in marital status. Although the sexes did not differ in marital status or years married (see Table B.2), there were sex differences in family composition. As shown in Table B.8, there were many more women who had large families compared to men, and three times as many men with no children compared to childless women. This difference was significant, $\chi^2(4) = 11.84$, $p < .05$, although the difference in mean number of children (2.64 for women, 1.62 for men) was not ($p > .05$). Although women tended to have a larger spread between the ages of their oldest and youngest children, as can be seen in Table B.9, the difference in these ages was not significant.

The information presented so far regarding the sample characteristics is descriptive of the primary features of age, social class, and family status. Further details regarding the respondents' occupational and family situations appear in the text.

TABLE B.8. Distribution of number of children by sex of respondent.

Number of children	Men		Women	
	N	%	N	%
0	13	27.66	4	8.51
1	10	21.28	8	17.02
2	12	25.53	16	34.04
3	9	19.15	8	17.02
4 or more	3	6.38	11	23.40
Total	47		47	

TABLE B.9. Ages of youngest and oldest children by sex of respondent.

	Men		Women	
	Mean	SD	Mean	SD
Youngest child	13.03	9.64	11.54	8.17
Oldest child	16.35	10.42	17.44	10.40
N	34		43	

Procedure

The first contact that potential respondents had with the study was an introductory letter describing the investigators' affiliation, interest in studying adult development, and a brief description of what the study would involve, should the reader prove to be eligible in terms of sampling criteria and be interested in participating. A remuneration of $20 was offered for participation and the names of the interviewers were given, who, according to the letter, would be calling in the next week or so to inquire further. The next contact was the follow-up telephone call, made by the interviewer. There were one male and one female interviewer. The male was in his early 30s, and the female in her late 30s, so they were both within the age range of the sample. Each was assigned to potential respondents of the same sex. The list of potential names was divided into male- and female-designated households; if a male was not available at a male-designated household, the interviewer went on to the next male-designated household on the list. In the follow-up call, the interviewer ascertained the potential respondent's interest. If the respondent expressed a willingness to participate in the study, his or her demographic characteristics were then obtained. If all characteristics matched those of cells that needed to be filled, an appointment was scheduled either at the respondent's home or at an interview room in the University.

At the outset of the interview session, the Adult Identity Process Interview was administered. The following instructions were read to the respondent:

We are interested in how people feel about various areas of their lives, and about what is important to them. I am going to ask you some questions about your feelings now about the main areas of your life, and about your work, family, values, and attitudes. I would like you to answer these questions as honestly as you can and with a focus on your views and feelings now. Later, I will ask you about your views and feelings about various areas of your life from when you were younger. [This sentence referred to the Life History Interview, which followed the Adult Identity Process Interview.] There are no right or wrong answers to any of the questions I will be asking you; no answer is "better" than the other. I am interested in *your* views and how *you* feel.

The interview will take about one hour or less. I will be tape recording the interview, but I want to assure you that everything you say will be held strictly confidential and heard by our staff only for the purposes of data analysis.

If there are any questions that you do not wish to answer, or if you wish to discontinue the interview at any time, please feel free to do so.

Do you have any questions?

[The consent form, explaining in further detail the interview and data-handling process, was then given to the respondent to sign.]

Fine, let's begin. First I am going to ask you some very general questions about what is important to you in your life now. Here is a drawing of a circle. Please divide this circle into sections as if it were a pie, with one section for each area of your life that is important to you now. Draw the size of the sections according to how important each area is to you. The largest section should be that area which is most important to you, the second largest that which is second most important to you, and so on. If all areas of your life are of equal importance, then make the sections equal in size. Label each section after you draw it in.

After the pie diagram was completed, the interviewer began asking questions about the largest section of the pie to determine why it was important to the respondent and what about the area was of importance. Originally, it had been intended that so-called content-free questions be asked about identity in the largest area of the pie, which we believed would have a structure comparable to that of the Work section of the interview. It was thought that respondents would include as smaller areas of identity such things as leisure or community involvement, and that family would be just one of many such areas mentioned. However, in 84 of the 97 interviews, the largest area in the pie diagram turned out to be family. Since this became apparent early in the study, the "content-free" questions were transformed permanently into questions regarding family, and appear as such in Appendix A. However, the procedure of asking about family only if it was first in importance was retained throughout the course of the study, and so data on family are available only for those 84 persons who regarded it as their major area of identity. Moreover, since there were too few respondents giving "content-free" responses in any one given area, the data from this section of the interview were not analyzed. It is recognized that this procedure resulted in a more limited sample for whom family was the most important area of identity and, for this reason, the results on family identity must be viewed with a certain caution.

Following the Adult Identity Process Interview, there was a short rest period, during which the interviewer and respondent conversed informally, followed by administration of the Life History Interview. At the outset of this interview, the respondent was asked to complete a Life Drawing, which was a simple projective technique comparable to the pie diagram designed to tap the respondent's orientation to his or her past, present, and future life (Whitbourne & Dannefer, 1986). Following this procedure, and on the basis of the drawing the respondent produced, the Life History Interview was administered.

Appendix C
Categories of Interview Statements

TABLE C.1. Categories of family interview statements.

Category	Number of responses		
	Women	Men	Total
Love	8	12	20
Good relationships			
Closeness	3	11	14
Communication	7	20	27
Companionship	10	5	15
Total	20	36	56
Centrality			
Importance	21	11	32
Activities	14	20	34
Total	35	31	66
Generativity	24	25	49
Personal fulfillment			
Personal happiness	43	38	81
Pride	5	7	12
Special qualities	7	6	13
Total	55	51	106
Family tasks and responsibilities			
Household tasks	19	7	26
Money	5	11	16
Caring for children	16	7	23
Responsibility	7	13	20
Total	47	38	85

TABLE C.2. Categories of work interview statements.

	Number of responses			
	Women			
Category	Working women	Home-makers	Men	Total
Intrinsic				
Interest Level	10	4	22	36
Autonomy				
Self-direction	7	3	13	23
Responsibilty	3	0	10	13
Challenge	4	1	10	15
Intellectual nature of work	5	0	16	21
See results	14	12	28	54
People-work	13	7	27	47
Total	56	27	126	209
Extrinsic				
Salary	16	7	26	49
Security	6	6	10	22
Advancement	2	0	11	13
Conditions				
Flexible hours	7	8	12	27
Convenience	2	6	9	17
Physical environment	0	2	9	11
Pressure	13	4	11	28
People				
Co-workers	7	0	6	13
Boss-employee	5	0	8	13
Total	58	33	102	193
Importance	12	15	25	52
The "work" itself	6	8	7	21

TABLE C.3. Categories of values interview statements.

Category	Number of responses		
	Women	Men	Total
Honesty	18	18	36
Interpersonal relationships			
Golden Rule	4	9	13
Love thy Neighbor	7	9	16
Family	16	7	23

References

Aldous, J. (1978). *Family careers: Developmental change in families*. New York: Wiley.

Alpert, J. L., & Richardson, M. S. (1980). Parenting. In L. Poon (Ed.), *Aging in the 1980s: Psychological issues* (pp. 441–454). Washington, DC: American Psychological Association.

Cath, S. H., Gurwitt, A. R., & Ross, J. M. (Eds.). (1982). *Father and child: Developmental and Clinical Perspectives*. Boston: Little Brown.

Chilman, C. S. (1980). Parent satisfactions, concerns, and goals for their children. *Family Relations, 29,* 339–345.

Clausen, J. (1972). The life course of individuals. In M. W. Riley, M. Johnson, & A. Foner (Eds.), *Aging and society* (Vol. III, pp. 457–514). New York: Russell Sage Foundation.

Costa, P. T., Jr., & McCrae, R. R. (1980). Still stable after all these years: Personality as a key to some issues in adulthood and old age. In P. B. Baltes (Ed.), *Life-span development and behavior* (Vol. 3, pp. 65–102). New York: Academic Press.

Cowan, C. P., Cowan, P. A., Coie, L., & Coie, J. D. (1978). Becoming a family: The impact of a child's birth on the couple's relationship. In W. B. Miller & L. F. Newman (Eds.), *The first child and family formation* (pp. 296–324). Chapel Hill, NC: Carolina Population Center.,

DeGrazia, S. (1971). Time and work. In H. M. Yaker, H. Osmond, & F. Cheek (Eds.), *The future of time: Man's temporal environment*. Garden City, NY: Doubleday.

Duvall, E. M. (1977). *Family development* (5th ed.). Philadelphia: Lippincott.

Ebmeyer, J. (1986). *Intimacy and communication in marriage*. Unpublished doctoral dissertation, University of Rochester.

Entwistle, D. R., & Doering, S. G. (1981). *The first birth: A family turning point*. Baltimore, MD: Johns Hopkins Press.

Erikson, E. H. (1963). *Childhood and society* (2nd ed.). New York: Norton.

Erikson, E. H., & Erikson, J. M. (1981). On generativity and identity. *Harvard Educational Review, 51,* 249–269.

Fawcett, J. T. (1978). The value and cost of the first child. In W. B. Miller & L. F. Newman (Eds.), *The first child and family formation* (pp. 244–265). Chapel Hill, NC: Carolina Population Center.

Feldman, H., & Feldman, M. (1975). The family life cycle: Some suggestions for recycling. *Journal of Marriage and the Family, 37,* 277–284.

Ferree, M. M. (1980). Satisfaction with housework: The social context. In S. F. Berk (Ed.), *Women and household labor* (pp. 89–112). Beverly Hills, CA: Sage.

Foote, N. N., & Cottrell, L. S. (1955). *Identity and interpersonal competence*. Chicago: University of Chicago Press.

French, J. R. P., & Kahn, R. L. (1962). A programmatic approach to studying the industrial environment and mental health. *Journal of Social Issues, 18*, 1–47.

Gaesser, D., & Whitbourne, S. K. (1985). Work identity and marital adjustment in blue-collar men. *Journal of Marriage and the Family, 47*, 747–751.

Gilford, R., & Bengston, V. (1979). Measuring marital satisfaction in three generations: Positive and negative dimensions. *Journal of Marriage and the Family, 41*, 387–398.

Gilligan, C. (1982). *In a different voice: Psychological theory and women's development.* Cambridge, MA: Harvard University Press.

Glenn, N. D., & McLanahan, S. (1982). Children and marital happiness: A further specification of the relationship. *Journal of Marriage and the Family, 44*, 63–72.

Greenwald, A. G. (1980). The totalitarian ego: Fabrication and revision of personal history. *American Psychologist, 35*, 603–618.

Hackman, J. R., & Oldham, G. R. (1975). Development of the Job Diagnostic Survey. *Journal of Applied Psychology, 60*, 159–170.

Harry, J. (1976). Evolving sources of happiness for men over the life cycle: A structural analysis. *Journal of Marriage and the Family, 38*, 289–296.

Herzberg, F., Mausner, B., & Snyderman, B. B. (1959). *The motivation to work.* New York: Wiley.

Hill, R., & Mattesich, P. (1979). Family development theory and life-span development. In P. B. Baltes & O. G. Brim, Jr. (Eds.), *Life-span development and behavior* (Vol. 2, pp. 161–204). New York: Academic Press.

Hoffman, L. W., & Manis, J. D. (1978). Influence of children on marital interaction and parental satisfactions and dissatisfactions. In R. M. Lerner & G. B. Spanier (Eds.), *Child influences on marital and family interaction: A life-span perspective* (pp. 165–213). New York: Academic Press.

Holland, J. L. (1973). *Making vocational choices.* Englewood Cliffs, NJ: Prentice-Hall.

Hollingshead, A. B. (1979). *A four-factor index of social status.* Unpublished manuscript, Yale University.

James, W. (1890). *The principles of psychology* (Vol. 1). New York: Holt.

Kagan, J. (1978). The child in the family. In A. S. Rossi, J. Kagan, & T. K. Harevan (Eds.), *The family* (pp. 33–56). New York: W. W. Norton.

Kalleberg, A. (1977). Work values and job rewards: A theory of job satisfaction. *American Sociological Review, 42*, 124–143.

Katz, D., & Kahn, R. L. (1978). *Social psychology of organizations* (2nd Ed.). New York: Wiley.

Kelley, H. H., Berscheid, E., Christiansen, A., Harvey, J. H., Huston, T. L., Levinger, G., McClintock, E., Peplau, L. A., & Peterson, D. R. (1983). Analyzing close relationships. In H. H. Kelley, E. Berscheid, A. Christiansen, J. H. Harvey, T. L. Huston, G. Levinger, E. McClintock, L. A. Peplau, & D. R. Peterson (Eds.), *Close relationships* (pp. 20–67). New York: W. H. Freeman.

Klein, D. C., & Ross, A. (1958). Kindergarten entry: A study of role transition. In M. Krugman (Ed.), *Orthopsychiatry and the school* (pp. 60–69). New York: American Orthopsychiatric Association.

Kohn, M. L., & Schooler, C. (1983). *Work and personality: An inquiry into the impact of social stratification.* Norwood, NJ: Ablex.

Laing, R. (1960). *The divided self.* Chicago: Quadrangle Books.

LaRossa, R., & LaRossa, M. M. (1981). *Transition to parenthood: How infants change families.* Beverly Hills, CA: Sage.

Lawler, E. E., III (1982). Strategies for improving the quality of work life. *American Psychologist, 37,* 486–493.

Levinson, D. J., Darrow, C. N., Klein, E. B., Levinson, M. H., & McKee, B. (1978). *The seasons of a man's life.* New York: Alfred A. Knopf.

Lewis, M., Freneau, P. J., & Roberts, C. L. (1979). Fathers and the postparental transition. *Family Coordinator, 28,* 514–520.

Lodahl, T. M., & Kejner, M. (1965). The definition and measurement of job involvement. *Journal of Applied Psychology, 49,* 24–33.

Marcia, J. E. (1966). Development and validation of ego-identity status. *Journal of Personality and Social Psychology, 3,* 551–558.

Marks, S. R. (1977). Multiple roles and role strain: Some notes on human energy, time, and commitment. *American Sociological Review, 42,* 921–936.

Marks, S. R. (1979). Culture, human energy, and self-actualization: A sociological offering to humanistic psychology. *Journal of Humanistic Psychology, 19,* 27–42.

Maslow, A. H. (1970). *Motivation and personality.* New York: Harper & Row.

McCubbin, H. I., Joy, C. B., Cauble, A. E., Comeau, J. K., Patterson, J. M., & Needle, R. H. (1980). Family stress and coping: A decade review. *Journal of Marriage and the Family, 42,* 855–871.

Mead, G. H. (1934). *Mind, self, and society.* Chicago: University of Chicago Press.

Menaghan, E. (1983). Marital stress and family transitions: A panel analysis. *Journal of Marriage and the Family, 45,* 371–386.

Miller, B. C., & Sollie, D. L. (1980). Normal stresses during the transition to parenthood. *Family Relations, 29,* 459–465.

Mortimer, J., & Lorence, J. T. (1979). Work experience and occupational value socialization: A longitudinal study. *American Journal of Sociology, 84,* 1361–1385.

Neugarten, B. L. (1970). Dynamics of transition of middle age to old age. *Journal of Geriatric Psychiatry, 4,* 71–87.

Oakley, A. (1974). *The sociology of housework.* New York: Pantheon Books.

Oppenheimer, V. K. (1981). The changing nature of life-cycle squeezes: Implications for the socioeconomic position of the elderly. In R. W. Fogel, E. Hatfield, S. B. Kiesler, & E. Shanas (Eds.), *Aging: Stability and Change in the Family* (pp. 47–81). New York: Academic Press.

Parsons, T., & Bales, R. F. (1956). *Family, socialization, and interaction process.* Glencoe, IL: Free Press.

Piaget, J., & Inhelder, B. (1969). *The psychology of the child.* New York: Basic Books.

Porter, B. M. (1954). Measurement of parental acceptance of children. *Journal of Home Economics, 46,* 176–182.

Reinke, B. J., Holmes, D. S., & Harris, R. L. (1985). The timing of psychosocial changes in women's lives: The years 25 to 45. *Journal of Personality and Social Psychology, 48,* 1353–1364.

Renne, K. S. (1970). Correlates of dissatisfaction in marriage. *Journal of Marriage and the Family, 32,* 54–67.

Rogers, C. R. (1951). *Client-centered therapy.* New York: Houghton Mifflin.

Rokeach, M. (1973). *The nature of human values.* New York: Free Press.

Rosenberg, M. (1980). The self-concept: Social product and social force. In M. Rosenberg & R. H. Turner (Eds.), *Social psychology: Sociological perspectives* (pp. 593–624). New York: Basic Books.

Rossi, A. S. (1984). Gender and parenthood. *American Sociological Review, 49,* 1–19.

Rubin, L. B. (1983). *Intimate strangers: Men and women together*. New York: Harper & Row.

Russell, C. S. (1974). Transition to parenthood: Problems and gratifications. *Journal of Marrige and the Family, 36*, 294–302.

Scanzoni, J. (1970). *Opportunity and the family*. New York: The Free Press.

Smelser, N. J., & Erikson, E. H. (Eds.). (1980). *Themes of work and love in adulthood*. Cambridge, MA: Harvard University Press.

Spanier, G. B., Lewis, R. A., & Cole, C. L. (1975). Marital adjustment over the family life cycle: The issue of curvilinearity. *Journal of Marriage and the Family, 37*, 263–275.

Super, D. E. (1969). Vocational development theory: Persons, positions, and processes. *The Counseling Psychologist, 1*, 2–8.

Swidler, A. (1980). Love and adulthood in American culture. In N. J. Smelser & E. H. Erikson (Eds.), *Themes of work and love in adulthood*. Cambridge, MA: Harvard University Press.

Tesser, A., & Campbell, J. (1983). Self-definition and self-evaluation maintenance. In J. Suls & A. G. Greenwald (Eds.), *Psychological perspectives on the self* (Vol. 2, pp. 1–31). Hillsdale, NJ: Erlbaum.

U.S. Department of Labor. (1977). *Dictionary of Occupational Titles*. Washington, DC: Government Printing Office.

Vaillant, G. (1977). *Adaptation to life*. Boston: Little, Brown & Co.

Vaillant, G., & Milofsky, E. (1980). Natural history of male psychological health: IX. Empirical evidence for Erikson's model of the life cycle. *American Journal of Psychiatry, 137*, 1348–1359.

Vanek, J. (1978). Housewives as workers. In A. Stromberg & S. Harkness (Eds.), *Women working* (pp. 392–414). Palo Alto, CA: Mayfield.

Walster, E., Walster, G. W., & Berscheid, E. (1978). *Equity: Theory and research*. Boston: Allyn and Bacon.

Waterman, A. S. (1980). *Ego identity status among married, adult women*. Paper presented at the Eastern Psychological Association Annual Convention, Hartford, Connecticut.

Whitbourne, S. K. (1986). Identity flexibility, openness to experience, and life change in adulthood. *Journal of Personality and Social Psychology, 50*, 163–168.

Whitbourne, S. K., & Dannefer, W. D. (1985-86). The life drawing as a measure of time perspective in adulthood. *International Journal of Aging and Human Development, 22*, 77–85.

Whitbourne, S. K., & Weinstock, C. S. (1986). *Adult development* (2nd ed.). New York: Praeger.

Wood, D. A. (1974). Effect of worker orientation differences on job attitude correlates. *Journal of Applied Psychology, 59*, 54–60.

Wylie, M. L. (1979). The effect of expectations on the transition to parenthood. *Sociological Focus, 12*, 323–329.

Index

Adult Identity Process Interview, 241–246
  method of analysis, 5,14–15,20–22,30,
    43,79
Adult identity processes model, 7,15,
  17,18
Adult identity, definition, 17
Adultery, 68–69
Age differences in personality, 7–12
Aging and identity, 3,9–12,75

Competence, 3,7,9,99–101,108–113,
  116–122,124,126–129,132,135–136,
  137,146,151–152,156,158–162,
  164–168,172–173,176,178–179,187,
  191,196,198–200,205,211,213,
  222–223,228,240

Equilibrium, 18–19,24,29,33–36,47,79,
  114,140,150,173,190,206,223,
  236,239
Equity theory, 48
Erikson's theory, 17,81,86
Extrinsic identity, in work, 100,104,106,
  114–115,123,126,128–160,166–167
  in family, 41,46–60,71–72,78,81–83
  in housework, 173–175,178–181

Family identity, 3–4,6,9–11,14,21–22,
  26–30,32–33,35,37–79,81–97,
  236,255
  centrality of, 63–69,71
  closeness in family relationships,
    39–40,48,60–63
  communication in family relationships,
    40–45,48,60

companionship in close relationships,
  45–48,60
distribution of statements, 255
importance of, 64–69
intergenerational relationships, 40,
  61–63
personal fulfillment, 69–79,236
role obligations in family, 46–60,72,78
Family life cycle, 37,73–74,84–95

Generativity, 81–86,115,240

Homemaker identity,
  23,50,64–65,77,83–84,93–94,123,
  142–143,161–181,203–204

I vs. Me, 4
Identity accommodation, 18–21,26,
  30–36,42,45,56–58,60,71,74,76–77,
  86–97,105,111–113,120,122,124,
  131–132,143,159,164–165,169,173,
  176,192,196–197,200,211,216,220,
  226,230,237
  changes in identity, 120,216
  changes in the family life cycle,
    86–95,169
  favorable changes in identity,
    30–32,42,76–77,111,131–132,159,
    164–165,230
  looking at alternatives, 34–36,45,
    56–58,60,74,105,173,176,192,
    196–197,200,211,226,237
  self-doubts and unfavorable changes in
    identity, 32–33,71,77,112,122,169

unpredictable changes in the family,
    95–97
Identity assimilation, 18–29,36,42–45,
    47,52,54–56,58–59,66–69,72–76,
    85,89,103–105,107–109,111–112,
    117–119,122,125–128,132–138,
    147–155,158–159,164–165,168–174,
    176–178,187,192–193,195–200,208,
    210,215,217–219, 221–222,229–230,
    232–237,230,239–240
  defensive rigidity,
    24–27,29,45,54–55,58,69,72,85,
    104,111–112,118–119,165,168,174,
    176–178,208,210,219,221,234,236,
    237,239
  lack of insight, 27–29,147,221,239
  projection, 22–24,59,68,125–126,159,
    165,168–170,215,229
  self-justification, 21–24,29,42–44,47,
    52,54,56,58–59,66–68,76,89,107,
    109,117–118,122,125–128,135–138,
    148,152–153,158–159,164–165,
    169–174,176,187,192–193,195–200,
    208,215,217–218,222,230,232–234,
    237
Integration of identity areas, 36,183–240
Intrinsic identity,
  in family, 39–48,52,53,55,58,60–63,
    69–79,71–72,78,81
  in housework, 174,176–181
  in work, 99–129,132–135,139,
    142–146,149,151,160,162–173,
    207,256
Intrinsic vs. extrinsic identity, 48–49,51,
    53–55,58,60,78,99–101,104,106,
    115,122,126–129,132–134,151,162,
    175,186,207,230

Mid-life crisis controversy, 7–12

Parenting, 51–61,70,73–76,78,81–97
Personality development in adulthood,
    7–12
Piaget's theory, 17,19
Procedure of study, 13,14,252–253

Retirement, 128
Rogers' theory, 19

Sample description, 3,13,248–251
Schizophrenia, 3
Self-esteem maintenance, 20,36,77
Sex differences in identity, 9,12–13,
    213–214,240
Sex roles, 12,13,47,52,59,61,63,72–74

Transition to parenthood, 11,37,59,75,
    87–89

Values identity, 3,10,24–26,31,34,35,53,
    69,125,137,183,213–240
  distribution of statements, 257
  honesty, 214–227,229
  interpersonal relationships, 225–239

Widowhood, 94
Work and family interactions, 97,99,106,
    126–128,130,135,137,149–152,
    181,183,185–200,203–212
  compatibility model, 185,200–212
  conflict model, 185–200,203,204,
    211–212
Work identity, 3,4,9–11,14,21–22,26–29,
    31,32,34,35,99–181,256
  autonomy, 106–110,113,132,135,139,
    144–146,149,160,207
  conditions of work, 106,123,138–151,
    157
  distribution of statements, 256
  intellectual nature of work, 110–114,
    142–143
  interest value, 99–106,115,123,134
  people factor (extrinsic), 104,142–160
  people-work factor (intrinsic), 122–126,
    151
  salary, 100,126–128,130–140,144–145,
    147,149
  seeing results, 114–122,207
  status, 100,114–115,126,128,132

F

M